kimmel
weygandt
kieso
team for success

FOURTH EDITION

ACCOUNTING

TOOLS FOR BUSINESS DECISION MAKING

ACCOUNTING II/ACC 102

WILEY *Custom*
LEARNING SOLUTIONS

To order books or for customer service, please call 1(800)-CALL-WILEY (225-5945).

Printed in the United States of America.

ISBN 978-1-118-11491-9
Printed and bound by EPAC.

10 9 8 7 6 5 4 3 2 1

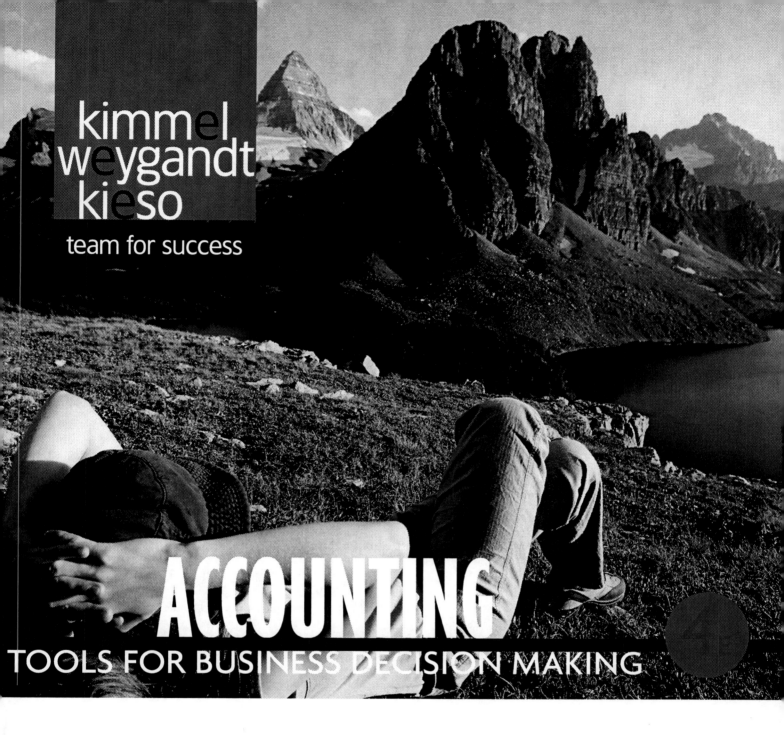

kimmel
weygandt
kieso
team for success

ACCOUNTING
TOOLS FOR BUSINESS DECISION MAKING

Paul D. Kimmel PhD, CPA
University of Wisconsin—Milwaukee
Milwaukee, Wisconsin

Jerry J. Weygandt PhD, CPA
University of Wisconsin—Madison
Madison, Wisconsin

Donald E. Kieso PhD, CPA
Northern Illinois University
DeKalb, Illinois

WILEY

John Wiley & Sons, Inc.

Dedicated to
*the **Wiley sales representatives***
who sell our books and service
our adopters in a professional
and ethical manner and to
Enid, Merlynn, and Donna

Vice President & Publisher	George Hoffman
Associate Publisher	Christopher DeJohn
Project Editor	Ed Brislin
Development Editor	Terry Ann Tatro
Project Manager	Paul Lopez
Production Manager	Dorothy Sinclair
Project Editor	Yana Mermel
Production Editor	Erin Bascom
Senior Production Editor	Trisha McFadden
Associate Director of Marketing	Amy Scholz
Senior Marketing Manager	Ramona Sherman
Executive Media Editor	Allison Morris
Media Editor	Greg Chaput
Creative Director	Harry Nolan
Senior Designer	Madelyn Lesure
Production Management Services	Ingrao Associates
Senior Illustration Editor	Sandra Rigby
Senior Photo Editor	Mary Ann Price
Editorial Assistant	Jacqueline Kepping
Senior Marketing Assistant	Laura Finley
Assistant Marketing Manager	Diane Mars
Cover Design	Maureen Eide
Cover Photo	©Peter McBride/Getty Image, Inc.

This book was set in New Aster by Aptara®, Inc. and printed and bound by RR Donnelley. The cover was printed by RR Donnelley.

To order books or for customer service please, call 1-800-CALL WILEY (225-5945).

Paul D. Kimmel, PhD, CPA; Jerry J. Weygandt, PhD, CPA; and Donald E. Kieso, PhD, CPA
Accounting, Fourth Edition

ISBN-13 978-0-470-53478-6

Printed in the United States of America

10 9 8 7 6 5 4 3 2 1

Contents

chapter 14

MANAGERIAL ACCOUNTING

✔ the navigator

- Scan **Study Objectives** ○
- Read **Feature Story** ○
- Scan **Preview** ○
- Read **Text and Answer** **Do it!**
  p. 753 ○ p. 757 ○ p. 759 ○ p. 767 ○
- Work **Using the Decision Toolkit** ○
- Review **Summary of Study Objectives** ○
- Work **Comprehensive** **Do it!** p. 774 ○
- Answer **Self-Test Questions** ○
- Complete **Assignments** ○
- Go to **WileyPLUS** for practice and tutorials ○

study objectives

After studying this chapter, you should be able to:

1 Explain the distinguishing features of managerial accounting.

2 Identify the three broad functions of management.

3 Define the three classes of manufacturing costs.

4 Distinguish between product and period costs.

5 Explain the difference between a merchandising and a manufacturing income statement.

6 Indicate how cost of goods manufactured is determined.

7 Explain the difference between a merchandising and a manufacturing balance sheet.

8 Identify trends in managerial accounting.

✔ the navigator

The business world changes rapidly. To survive, you must make well-informed, quick decisions. Consider this. In January of 1998, Compaq Computer was the largest seller of personal computers and *Forbes* magazine's "company of the year." During the next two years, it lost $2 billion and its CEO was out of a job.

Compaq fell victim to Dell Computer. Dell pioneered a new way of making and selling computers. It reengineered its supply chain so that it could produce computers with the exact features that customers ordered, ship them within 24 hours of taking the order, and invest almost no money in inventory. Compaq was not able to respond quickly enough. Ultimately, it merged with Hewlett-Packard (HP).

After the merger of HP and Compaq, HP lost significant market share in the PC market to Dell because its cost structure made it hard to compete with Dell on price. To make matters worse for HP, Dell then began selling computer printers, a business that HP had always dominated. Many people predicted that Dell would soon reign supreme over the printer business as well.

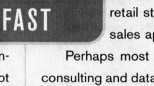

Just when it appeared that Dell could not be beat, HP regained its footing and Dell stumbled. By June 2008, HP had accomplished a remarkable three-year turnaround. With more than $100 billion in sales, HP had become the biggest technology company in the world. How did it do it? HP adopted "lean" manufacturing practices so it could compete with Dell on price. In addition, it developed exciting design innovations that it marketed successfully in retail stores, as compared to Dell's online sales approach.

Perhaps most importantly, HP has expanded its consulting and data storage services. You can only sell a piece of equipment once. But, consulting services provide ongoing, high-margin revenue that frequently results in additional hardware sales. To further expand its service revenue opportunities, in 2008 HP acquired Electronic Data Services (EDS) for $13.9 billion. Although many industry analysts questioned the decision, HP says the move was based on a sound strategy. Now management must prove that it was the correct decision for the future.

This chapter focuses on issues illustrated in the Feature Story about Compaq Computer, Hewlett-Packard, and Dell. These include determining and controlling the costs of material, labor, and overhead and the relationship between costs and profits. In a financial accounting course, you learned about the form and content of **financial statements for external users** of financial information, such as stockholders and creditors. These financial statements represent the principal product of financial accounting. Managerial accounting focuses primarily on the preparation of **reports for internal users** of financial information, such as the managers and officers of a company. In today's rapidly changing global environment, managers often make decisions that determine their company's fate—and their own. Managers are evaluated on the results of their decisions. Managerial accounting provides tools for assisting management in making decisions and for evaluating the effectiveness of those decisions.

The content and organization of this chapter are as follows.

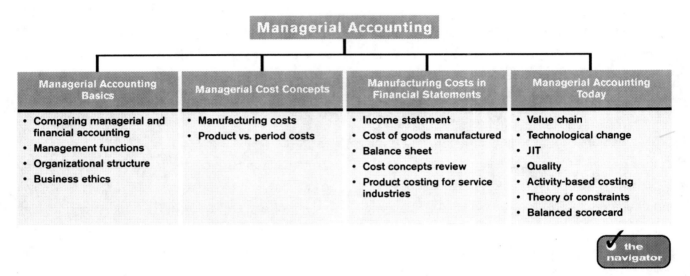

Managerial Accounting Basics

study objective 1**

Explain the distinguishing features of managerial accounting.

Managerial accounting, also called **management accounting**, is a field of accounting that provides economic and financial information for managers and other internal users. The activities that are part of managerial accounting (and the chapters in which they are discussed in this textbook) are as follows.

1. Explaining manufacturing and nonmanufacturing costs and how they are reported in the financial statements (Chapter 14).

2. Computing the cost of providing a service or manufacturing a product (Chapters 15, 16, and 17).

3. Determining the behavior of costs and expenses as activity levels change and analyzing cost–volume–profit relationships within a company (Chapters 18 and 19).

4. Assisting management in profit planning and formalizing these plans in the form of budgets (Chapter 20).

5. Providing a basis for controlling costs and expenses by comparing actual results with planned objectives and standard costs (Chapters 21 and 22).

6. Accumulating and presenting data for management decision making and capital expenditure decisions (Chapter 23).

Managerial accounting applies to all types of businesses—service, merchandising, and manufacturing. It also applies to all forms of business organizations—

proprietorships, partnerships, and corporations. Not-for-profit entities as well as profit-oriented enterprises need managerial accounting.

In the past, managerial accountants were primarily engaged in cost accounting—collecting and reporting costs to management. Recently that role has changed significantly. First, as the business environment has become more automated, methods to determine the amount and type of cost in a product have changed. Second, managerial accountants are now held responsible for strategic cost management; that is, they assist in evaluating how well the company is employing its resources. As a result, managerial accountants now serve as team members alongside personnel from production, marketing, and engineering when the company makes critical strategic decisions.

Opportunities for managerial accountants to advance within the company are considerable. Financial executives must have a background that includes an understanding of managerial accounting concepts. Whatever your position in the company—marketing, sales, or production, knowledge of managerial accounting greatly improves your opportunities for advancement. As the CEO of Microsoft noted: "If you're supposed to be making money in business and supposed to be satisfying customers and building market share, there are numbers that characterize those things. And if somebody can't sort of speak to me quantitatively about it, then I'm nervous."

COMPARING MANAGERIAL AND FINANCIAL ACCOUNTING

There are both similarities and differences between managerial and financial accounting. First, each field of accounting deals with the economic events of a business. Thus, their interests overlap. For example, *determining* the unit cost of manufacturing a product is part of managerial accounting. *Reporting* the total cost of goods manufactured and sold is part of financial accounting. In addition, both managerial and financial accounting require that a company's economic events be quantified and communicated to interested parties.

Illustration 14-1 summarizes the principal differences between financial accounting and managerial accounting. The need for various types of economic data is responsible for many of the differences.

Illustration 14-1
Differences between financial and managerial accounting

Financial Accounting		Managerial Accounting
• External users: stockholders, creditors, and regulators.	**Primary Users of Reports**	• Internal users: officers and managers.
• Financial statements. • Quarterly and annually.	**Types and Frequency of Reports**	• Internal reports. • As frequently as needed.
• General-purpose.	**Purpose of Reports**	• Special-purpose for specific decisions.
• Pertains to business as a whole. • Highly aggregated (condensed). • Limited to double-entry accounting and cost data. • Generally accepted accounting principles.	**Content of Reports**	• Pertains to subunits of the business. • Very detailed. • Extends beyond double-entry accounting to any relevant data. • Standard is relevance to decisions.
• Audited by CPA.	**Verification Process**	• No independent audits.

MANAGEMENT FUNCTIONS

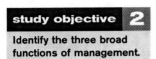

study objective 2

Identify the three broad functions of management.

Managers' activities and responsibilities can be classified into three broad functions:

1. Planning.
2. Directing.
3. Controlling.

In performing these functions, managers make decisions that have a significant impact on the organization.

Planning requires managers to look ahead and to establish objectives. These objectives are often diverse: maximizing short-term profits and market share, maintaining a commitment to environmental protection, and contributing to social programs. For example, Hewlett-Packard, in an attempt to gain a stronger foothold in the computer industry, has greatly reduced its prices to compete with Dell. A key objective of management is to **add value** to the business under its control. Value is usually measured by the trading price of the company's stock and by the potential selling price of the company.

Directing involves coordinating a company's diverse activities and human resources to produce a smooth-running operation. This function relates to implementing planned objectives and providing necessary incentives to motivate employees. For example, manufacturers such as Campbell Soup Company, General Motors, and Dell must coordinate purchasing, manufacturing, warehousing, and selling. Service corporations such as American Airlines, Federal Express, and AT&T must coordinate scheduling, sales, service, and acquisitions of equipment and supplies. Directing also involves selecting executives, appointing managers and supervisors, and hiring and training employees.

The third management function, **controlling**, is the process of keeping the company's activities on track. In controlling operations, managers determine

Management Insight

Even the Best Have to Get Better

Louis Vuitton is a French manufacturer of high-end handbags, wallets, and suitcases. Its reputation for quality and style allows it to charge extremely high prices—for example, $700 for a tote bag. But often in the past, when demand was hot, supply was nonexistent—shelves were empty, and would-be buyers left empty-handed.

Luxury-goods manufacturers used to consider stock-outs to be a good thing, but recently Louis Vuitton changed its attitude. The company adopted "lean" processes used by car manufacturers and electronics companies to speed up production of "hot" products. Work is done by flexible teams, with jobs organized based on how long a task takes. By reducing wasted time and eliminating bottlenecks, what used to take 20 to 30 workers eight days to do now takes 6 to 12 workers one day. Also, production employees who used to specialize on a single task on a single product are now multiskilled. This allows them to quickly switch products to meet demand.

To make sure that the factory is making the right products, within a week of a product launch, Louis Vuitton stores around the world feed sales information to the headquarters in France, and production is adjusted accordingly. Finally, the new production processes have also improved quality. Returns of some products are down by two-thirds, which makes quite a difference to the bottom line when the products are pricey.

Source: Christina Passariello, "Louis Vuitton Tries Modern Methods on Factory Lines," *Wall Street Journal* (October 9, 2006).

? What are some of the steps that this company has taken in order to ensure that production meets demand? (See page 795.)

whether planned goals are being met. When there are deviations from targeted objectives, managers must decide what changes are needed to get back on track. Recent scandals at companies like Enron, Lucent, and Xerox attest to the fact that companies must have adequate controls to ensure that the company develops and distributes accurate information.

How do managers achieve control? A smart manager in a small operation can make personal observations, ask good questions, and know how to evaluate the answers. But using this approach in a large organization would result in chaos. Imagine the president of Dell attempting to determine whether the company is meeting its planned objectives, without some record of what has happened and what is expected to occur. Thus, large businesses typically use a formal system of evaluation. These systems include such features as budgets, responsibility centers, and performance evaluation reports—all of which are features of managerial accounting.

Decision making is not a separate management function. Rather, it is the outcome of the exercise of good judgment in planning, directing, and controlling.

ORGANIZATIONAL STRUCTURE

In order to assist in carrying out management functions, most companies prepare **organization charts** to show the interrelationships of activities and the delegation of authority and responsibility within the company. Illustration 14-2 shows a typical organization chart, which outlines the delegation of responsibility.

Stockholders own the corporation, but they manage it indirectly through a board of directors they elect. Even not-for-profit organizations have boards of directors. The board formulates the operating policies for the company or organization. The board also selects officers, such as a president and one or more vice presidents, to execute policy and to perform daily management functions.

The chief executive officer (CEO) has overall responsibility for managing the business. Obviously, even in a small business, in order to accomplish organizational

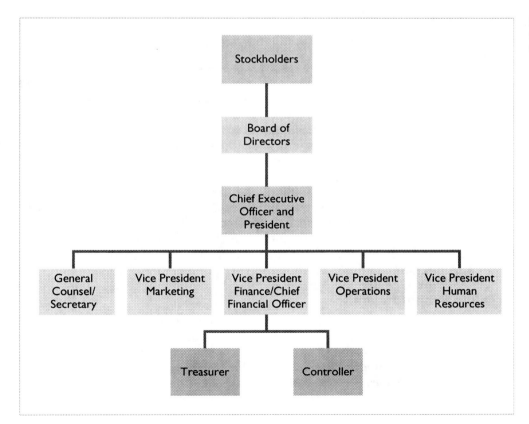

Illustration 14-2
Corporation's organization chart

objectives, the company relies on delegation of responsibilities. As the organization chart on page 751 shows, the CEO delegates responsibilities to other officers. Each member of the organization has a clearly defined role to play.

Responsibilities within the company are frequently classified as either line or staff positions. Employees with line positions are directly involved in the company's primary revenue-generating operating activities. Examples of line positions include the vice president of operations, vice president of marketing, plant managers, supervisors, and production personnel. Employees with staff positions are involved in activities that support the efforts of the line employees. In a firm like General Electric or ExxonMobil, employees in finance, legal, and human resources have staff positions. While activities of staff employees are vital to the company, these employees are nonetheless there to serve the line employees who engage in the company's primary operations.

The chief financial officer (CFO) is responsible for all of the accounting and finance issues the company faces. The CFO is supported by the controller and the treasurer. The controller's responsibilities include (1) maintaining the accounting records, (2) maintaining an adequate system of internal control, and (3) preparing financial statements, tax returns, and internal reports. The treasurer has custody of the corporation's funds and is responsible for maintaining the company's cash position.

Also serving the CFO is the internal audit staff. The staff's responsibilities include reviewing the reliability and integrity of financial information provided by the controller and treasurer. Staff members also ensure that internal control systems are functioning properly to safeguard corporate assets. In addition, they investigate compliance with policies and regulations, and in many companies they determine whether resources are being used in the most economical and efficient fashion.

The vice president of operations oversees employees with line positions. For example, the company might have multiple plant managers, each of whom would report to the vice president of operations. Each plant would also have department managers, such as fabricating, painting, and shipping, each of whom would report to the plant manager.

BUSINESS ETHICS

All employees within an organization are expected to act ethically in their business activities. Given the importance of ethical behavior to corporations and their owners (stockholders), an increasing number of organizations provide codes of business ethics for their employees.

Despite these efforts, recent business scandals resulted in massive investment losses and numerous employee layoffs. A recent survey of fraud by international accounting firm KPMG reported a 13% increase in instances of corporate fraud compared to five years earlier. It noted that while employee fraud (such things as expense-account abuse, payroll fraud, and theft of assets) represented 60% of all instances of fraud, financial reporting fraud (the intentional misstatement of financial reports) was the most costly to companies. That should not be surprising given the long list of companies, such as Enron, Global Crossing, WorldCom, and others, that engaged in massive financial frauds, which led to huge financial losses and thousands of lost jobs.

Creating Proper Incentives

Companies like Motorola, IBM, and Nike use complex systems to control and evaluate the actions of managers. They dedicate substantial resources to monitor and effectively evaluate the actions of employees. Unfortunately, these systems and controls sometimes unwittingly create incentives for managers to take unethical actions. For example, companies prepare budgets to provide direction. Because the budget is also used as an evaluation tool, some managers try to "game" the budgeting process by underestimating their division's predicted performance so that it will be easier to meet their performance targets. On the other hand, if the budget is set at unattainable levels, managers sometimes take unethical actions to meet the targets in order to receive higher compensation or, in some cases, to keep their jobs.

For example, in recent years, airline manufacturer Boeing was plagued by a series of scandals including charges of over-billing, corporate espionage, and illegal conflicts of interest. Some long-time employees of Boeing blame the decline in ethics on a change in the corporate culture that took place after Boeing merged with McDonnell Douglas. They suggest that evaluation systems implemented after the merger to monitor results and evaluate employee performance made employees believe they needed to succeed no matter what actions were required to do so.

As another example, manufacturing companies need to establish production goals for their processes. Again, if controls are not effective and realistic, problems develop. To illustrate, Schering-Plough, a pharmaceutical manufacturer, found that employees were so concerned with meeting production standards that they failed to monitor the quality of the product, and as a result the dosages were often wrong.

Code of Ethical Standards

In response to corporate scandals in 2000 and 2001, the U.S. Congress enacted legislation to help prevent lapses in internal control. This legislation, referred to as the Sarbanes-Oxley Act of 2002 (SOX) has important implications for the financial community. One result of SOX was to clarify top management's responsibility for the company's financial statements. CEOs and CFOs must now certify that financial statements give a fair presentation of the company's operating results and its financial condition. In addition, top managers must certify that the company maintains an adequate system of internal controls to safeguard the company's assets and ensure accurate financial reports.

Another result of SOX is that companies now pay more attention to the composition of the board of directors. In particular, the audit committee of the board of directors must be comprised entirely of independent members (that is, non-employees) and must contain at least one financial expert.

Finally, to increase the likelihood of compliance with the rules that are part of the new legislation, the law substantially increases the penalties for misconduct.

To provide guidance for managerial accountants, the Institute of Management Accountants (IMA) has developed a code of ethical standards, entitled *IMA Statement of Ethical Professional Practice*. Management accountants should not commit acts in violation of these standards. Nor should they condone such acts by others within their organizations. In the remaining chapters, we will address various ethical issues managers face.

before you go on...

Do it!   Indicate whether the following statements are true or false.

MANAGERIAL ACCOUNTING CONCEPTS

1. Managerial accountants have a single role within an organization, collecting and reporting costs to management.

2. Financial accounting reports are general-purpose and intended for external users.

3. Managerial accounting reports are special-purpose and issued as frequently as needed.

4. Managers' activities and responsibilities can be classified into three broad functions: cost accounting, budgeting, and internal control.

5. As a result of the Sarbanes-Oxley Act of 2002, managerial accounting reports must now comply with generally accepted accounting principles (GAAP).

6. Top managers must certify that a company maintains an adequate system of internal controls.

Action Plan

- Understand that managerial accounting is a field of accounting that provides economic and financial information for managers and other internal users.
- Understand that financial accounting provides information for external users.
- Analyze which users require which different types of information.

Solution

1. False. Managerial accountants determine product costs. In addition, managerial accountants are now held responsible for evaluating how well the company is employing its resources. As a result, when the company makes critical strategic decisions, managerial accountants serve as team members alongside personnel from production, marketing, and engineering.
2. True.
3. True.
4. False. Managers' activities are classified into three broad functions: planning, directing, and controlling. Planning requires managers to look ahead to establish objectives. Directing involves coordinating a company's diverse activities and human resources to produce a smooth-running operation. Controlling is keeping the company's activities on track.
5. False. SOX clarifies top management's responsibility for the company's financial statements. In addition, top managers must certify that the company maintains an adequate system of internal control to safeguard the company's assets and ensure accurate financial reports.
6. True.

Related exercise material: **BE14-1, BE14-2, BE14-3, Do it! 14-1,** and **E14-1.**

Managerial Cost Concepts

In order for managers at companies like Dell or Hewlett-Packard to plan, direct, and control operations effectively, they need good information. One very important type of information is related to costs. Managers should ask questions such as the following.

1. What costs are involved in making a product or providing a service?
2. If we decrease production volume, will costs decrease?
3. What impact will automation have on total costs?
4. How can we best control costs?

To answer these questions, managers need reliable and relevant cost information. We now explain and illustrate the various cost categories that companies use.

study objective 3

Define the three classes of manufacturing costs.

Illustration 14-3
Classifications of manufacturing costs

MANUFACTURING COSTS

Manufacturing consists of activities and processes that convert raw materials into finished goods. Contrast this type of operation with merchandising, which sells merchandise in the form in which it is purchased. Manufacturing costs are typically classified as shown in Illustration 14-3.

Manufacturing Costs

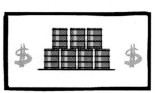

Direct Materials

Direct Labor

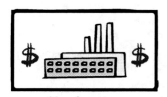

Manufacturing Overhead

Direct Materials

To obtain the materials that will be converted into the finished product, the manufacturer purchases raw materials. **Raw materials** are the basic materials and parts used in the manufacturing process. For example, auto manufacturers such as General Motors, Ford, and Toyota use steel, plastic, and tires as raw materials in making cars.

Direct Materials

Raw materials that can be physically and directly associated with the finished product during the manufacturing process are direct materials. Examples include flour in the baking of bread, syrup in the bottling of soft drinks, and steel in the making of automobiles. Direct materials for Hewlett-Packard and Dell Computer (in the Feature Story) include plastic, glass, hard drives, and processing chips.

Some raw materials cannot be easily associated with the finished product. These are called indirect materials. Indirect materials have one of two characteristics: (1) They do not physically become part of the finished product (such as lubricants and polishing compounds). Or, (2) they cannot be traced because their physical association with the finished product is too small in terms of cost (such as cotter pins and lock washers). Companies account for indirect materials as part of **manufacturing overhead**.

Direct Labor

The work of factory employees that can be physically and directly associated with converting raw materials into finished goods is direct labor. Bottlers at Coca-Cola, bakers at Sara Lee, and typesetters at Aptara Corp. are employees whose activities are usually classified as direct labor. Indirect labor refers to the work of employees that has no physical association with the finished product, or for which it is impractical to trace costs to the goods produced. Examples include wages of maintenance people, time-keepers, and supervisors. Like indirect materials, companies classify indirect labor as **manufacturing overhead**.

Direct Labor

Management Insight

How Many Labor Hours to Build a Car?

Nissan and Toyota were number 1 and 2 in a recent annual study of labor productivity in the auto industry. But U.S. auto manufacturers showed improvements. Labor represents about 15% of the total cost to make a vehicle. Since Nissan required only 28.46 labor hours per vehicle, it saves about $300 to $450 in labor costs to build a car relative to Ford, the least-efficient manufacturer. General Motors (GM) has shown steady improvement over the years. At one point, it needed almost 17 more hours of labor than Toyota to build a car; it now needs only 4 more hours than Toyota. Chrysler says that much of its improvement in labor productivity has come from designing cars that are easier to build.

Source: Rick Popely, "Japanese Automakers Lead Big Three in Productivity Review," *Knight Ridder Tribune News Service* (June 1, 2006), p. 1.

? Why might Nissan production require significantly fewer labor hours? (See page 795.)

Manufacturing Overhead

Manufacturing overhead consists of costs that are indirectly associated with the manufacture of the finished product. These costs may also be manufacturing costs that cannot be classified as direct materials or direct labor. Manufacturing overhead includes indirect materials, indirect labor, depreciation on factory buildings and machines, and insurance, taxes, and maintenance on factory facilities.

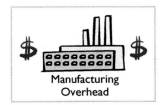

Manufacturing Overhead

One study found the following magnitudes of the three different product costs as a percentage of the total product cost: direct materials 54%, direct labor

13%, and manufacturing overhead 33%. Note that the direct labor component is the smallest. This component of product cost is dropping substantially because of automation. Companies are working hard to increase productivity by decreasing labor. A Nissan Motor plant in Tennessee produces Altima automobiles using only 15.74 labor hours per vehicle, compared to 26 to 28 hours per vehicle at Ford and Daimler plants, for example. In some companies, direct labor has become as little as 5% of the total cost.

Allocating materials and labor costs to specific products is fairly straightforward. Good record keeping can tell a company how much plastic it used in making each type of gear, or how many hours of factory labor it took to assemble a part. But allocating overhead costs to specific products presents problems. How much of the purchasing agent's salary is attributable to the hundreds of different products made in the same plant? What about the grease that keeps the machines humming, or the computers that make sure paychecks come out on time? Boiled down to its simplest form, the question becomes: Which products cause the incurrence of which costs? In subsequent chapters, we show various methods of allocating overhead to products.

PRODUCT VERSUS PERIOD COSTS

study objective **4**

Distinguish between product and period costs.

Alternative Terminology
Product costs are also called *inventoriable costs*.

Each of the manufacturing cost components—direct materials, direct labor, and manufacturing overhead—are product costs. As the term suggests, product costs are costs that are a necessary and integral part of producing the finished product. Companies record product costs, when incurred, as inventory. Under the matching principle, these costs do not become expenses until the company sells the finished goods inventory. At that point, the company records the expense as cost of goods sold.

Period costs are costs that are matched with the revenue of a specific time period rather than included as part of the cost of a salable product. These are nonmanufacturing costs. Period costs include selling and administrative expenses. In order to determine net income, companies deduct these costs from revenues in the period in which they are incurred.

Illustration 14-4 summarizes these relationships and cost terms. Our main concern in this chapter is with product costs.

Illustration 14-4 Product versus period costs

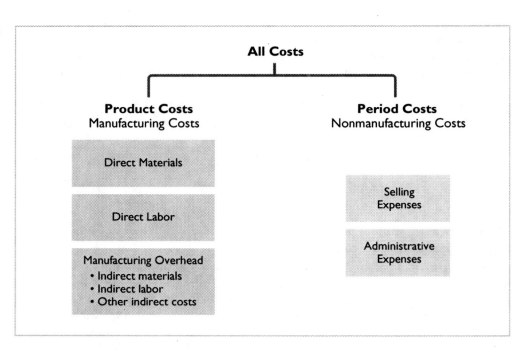

Do it! A bicycle company has these costs: tires, salaries of employees who put tires on the wheels, factory building depreciation, lubricants, spokes, salary of factory manager, handlebars, and salaries of factory maintenance employees. Classify each cost as direct materials, direct labor, or overhead.

MANAGERIAL COST CONCEPTS

Action Plan

- Classify as direct materials any raw materials that can be physically and directly associated with the finished product.

Solution

Tires, spokes, and handlebars are direct materials. Salaries of employees who put tires on the wheels are direct labor. All of the other costs are manufacturing overhead.

- Classify as direct labor the work of factory employees that can be physically and directly associated with the finished product.

Related exercise material: **BE14-4, BE14-5, BE14-6, BE14-7, Do it! 14-2, E14-2, E14-3, E14-4, E14-5, E14-6,** and **E14-7.**

- Classify as manufacturing overhead any costs that are indirectly associated with the finished product.

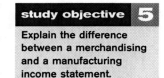

Manufacturing Costs in Financial Statements

The financial statements of a manufacturer are very similar to those of a merchandiser. For example, you will find many of the same sections and same accounts in the financial statements of Procter & Gamble that you find in the financial statements of Dick's Sporting Goods. The principal differences between their financial statements occur in two places: the cost of goods sold section in the income statement and the current assets section in the balance sheet.

INCOME STATEMENT

Under a periodic inventory system, the income statements of a merchandiser and a manufacturer differ in the cost of goods sold section. Merchandisers compute cost of goods sold by adding the beginning merchandise inventory to the **cost of goods purchased** and subtracting the ending merchandise inventory. Manufacturers compute cost of goods sold by adding the beginning finished goods inventory to the **cost of goods manufactured** and subtracting the ending finished goods inventory. Illustration 14-5 shows these different methods.

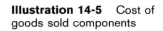

study objective 5

Explain the difference between a merchandising and a manufacturing income statement.

Illustration 14-5 Cost of goods sold components

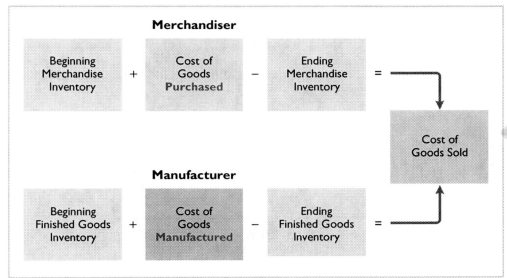

Helpful Hint We assume a periodic inventory system in this illustration.

A number of accounts are involved in determining the cost of goods manufactured. To eliminate excessive detail, income statements typically show only the total cost of goods manufactured. A separate statement, called a Cost of Goods Manufactured Schedule, presents the details. (For more information, see the discussion on page 759 and Illustration 14-8.)

Illustration 14-6 Cost of goods sold sections of merchandising and manufacturing income statements

Illustration 14-6 shows the different presentations of the cost of goods sold sections for merchandising and manufacturing companies. The other sections of an income statement are similar for merchandisers and manufacturers.

MERCHANDISING COMPANY Income Statement (partial) For the Year Ended December 31, 2012		
Cost of goods sold		
Merchandise inventory, January 1		$ 70,000
Cost of goods purchased		650,000
Cost of goods available for sale		720,000
Merchandise inventory, December 31		400,000
Cost of goods sold		$ 320,000

MANUFACTURING COMPANY Income Statement (partial) For the Year Ended December 31, 2012		
Cost of goods sold		
Finished goods inventory, January 1		$ 90,000
Cost of goods manufactured (see Illustration 14-8)		370,000
Cost of goods available for sale		460,000
Finished goods inventory, December 31		80,000
Cost of goods sold		$380,000

Cost of Goods Manufactured

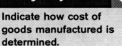

An example may help show how companies determine the cost of goods manufactured. Assume that on January 1, HP has a number of computers in various stages of production. In total, these partially completed units are called **beginning work in process inventory**. The costs the company assigns to beginning work in process inventory are based on the **manufacturing costs incurred in the prior period**.

HP first uses the manufacturing costs incurred in the current year to complete the work that was in process on January 1. It then incurs manufacturing costs for production of new orders. The sum of the direct materials costs, direct labor costs, and manufacturing overhead incurred in the current year is the total manufacturing costs for the current period.

We now have two cost amounts: (1) the cost of the beginning work in process and (2) the total manufacturing costs for the current period. The sum of these costs is the total cost of work in process for the year.

At the end of the year, HP may have some computers that are only partially completed. The costs of these units become the cost of the **ending work in process inventory**. To find the cost of goods manufactured, we subtract this cost from the total cost of work in process. Illustration 14-7 shows the formula for determining the cost of goods manufactured.

Illustration 14-7 Cost of goods manufactured formula

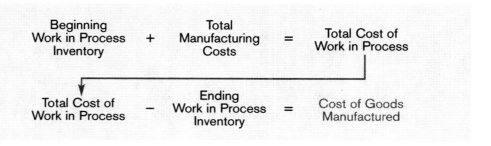

Cost of Goods Manufactured Schedule

The **cost of goods manufactured schedule** reports cost elements used in calculating cost of goods manufactured. Illustration 14-8 shows the schedule for Olsen Manufacturing Company (using assumed data). The schedule presents detailed data for direct materials and for manufacturing overhead.

Review Illustration 14-7 and then examine the cost of goods manufactured schedule in Illustration 14-8. You should be able to distinguish between "Total manufacturing costs" and "Cost of goods manufactured." The difference is the effect of the change in work in process during the period.

Illustration 14-8   Cost of goods manufactured schedule

OLSEN MANUFACTURING COMPANY
Cost of Goods Manufactured Schedule
For the Year Ended December 31, 2012

Work in process, January 1			$ 18,400
Direct materials			
Raw materials inventory, January 1	$ 16,700		
Raw materials purchases	152,500		
Total raw materials available for use	169,200		
Less: Raw materials inventory, December 31	22,800		
Direct materials used		$146,400	
Direct labor		175,600	
Manufacturing overhead			
Indirect labor	14,300		
Factory repairs	12,600		
Factory utilities	10,100		
Factory depreciation	9,440		
Factory insurance	8,360		
Total manufacturing overhead		54,800	
Total manufacturing costs			376,800
Total cost of work in process			395,200
Less: Work in process, December 31			25,200
Cost of goods manufactured			$370,000

DECISION TOOLKIT

DECISION CHECKPOINTS	INFO NEEDED FOR DECISION	TOOL TO USE FOR DECISION	HOW TO EVALUATE RESULTS
Is the company maintaining control over the costs of production?	Cost of material, labor, and overhead	Cost of goods manufactured schedule	Compare the cost of goods manufactured to revenue expected from product sales.

before you go on...

Do it!   The following information is available for Keystone Manufacturing Company.

COST OF GOODS MANUFACTURED

		March 1	March 31
Raw material inventory		$12,000	$10,000
Work in process inventory		2,500	4,000
Materials purchased in March	$ 90,000		
Direct labor in March	75,000		
Manufacturing overhead in March	220,000		

Prepare the cost of goods manufactured schedule for the month of March.

Action Plan

- Start with beginning work in process as the first item in the cost of goods manufactured schedule.
- Sum direct materials used, direct labor, and total manufacturing overhead to determine total manufacturing costs.
- Sum beginning work in process and total manufacturing costs to determine total cost of work in process.
- Cost of goods manufactured is the total cost of work in process less ending work in process.

Solution

KEYSTONE MANUFACTURING COMPANY
Cost of Goods Manufactured Schedule
For the Month Ended March 31

Work in process, March 1			$ 2,500
Direct materials			
Raw materials, March 1	$ 12,000		
Raw material purchases	90,000		
Total raw materials available for use	102,000		
Less: Raw materials, March 31	10,000		
Direct materials used		$ 92,000	
Direct labor		75,000	
Manufacturing overhead		220,000	
Total manufacturing costs			387,000
Total cost of work in process			389,500
Less: Work in process, March 31			4,000
Cost of goods manufactured			$385,500

✓ the navigator

Related exercise material: **BE14-8, BE14-10, BE14-11, Do it! 14-3, E14-8, E14-9, E14-10, E14-11, E14-12, E14-13, E14-14, E14-15, E14-16, and E14-17.**

BALANCE SHEET

study objective **7**

Explain the difference between a merchandising and a manufacturing balance sheet.

The balance sheet for a merchandising company shows just one category of inventory. In contrast, the balance sheet for a manufacturer may have three inventory accounts, as shown in Illustration 14-9.

Illustration 14-9
Inventory accounts for a manufacturer

Raw Materials Inventory
Shows the cost of raw materials on hand.

Work in Process Inventory
Shows the cost applicable to units that have been started into production but are only partially completed.

Finished Goods Inventory
Shows the cost of completed goods on hand.

Finished Goods Inventory is to a manufacturer what Merchandise Inventory is to a merchandiser. Each of these classifications represents the goods that the company has available for sale.

The current assets sections presented in Illustration 14-10 contrast the presentations of inventories for merchandising and manufacturing companies. Manufacturing companies generally list their inventories in the order of their liquidity—the order in which they are expected to be realized in cash. Thus, finished goods inventory comes first. The remainder of the balance sheet is similar for the two types of companies.

MERCHANDISING COMPANY Balance Sheet December 31, 2012			MANUFACTURING COMPANY Balance Sheet December 31, 2012		
Current assets			Current assets		
Cash		$100,000	Cash		$180,000
Receivables (net)		210,000	Receivables (net)		210,000
Merchandise inventory		400,000	Inventories		
Prepaid expenses		22,000	Finished goods	$80,000	
Total current assets		$732,000	Work in process	25,200	
			Raw materials	22,800	128,000
			Prepaid expenses		18,000
			Total current assets		$536,000

Illustration 14-10
Current assets sections of merchandising and manufacturing balance sheets

Each step in the accounting cycle for a merchandiser applies to a manufacturer. For example, prior to preparing financial statements, manufacturers make adjusting entries. The adjusting entries are essentially the same as those of a merchandiser. The closing entries are also similar for manufacturers and merchandisers. *For expanded coverage, see Appendix 14A.*

DECISION TOOLKIT

DECISION CHECKPOINTS	INFO NEEDED FOR DECISION	TOOL TO USE FOR DECISION	HOW TO EVALUATE RESULTS
What is the composition of a manufacturing company's inventory?	Amount of raw materials, work in process, and finished goods inventories	Balance sheet	Determine whether there are sufficient finished goods, raw materials, and work in process inventories to meet forecasted demand.

COST CONCEPTS–A REVIEW

You have learned a number of cost concepts in this chapter. Because many of these concepts are new, we provide here an extended example for review. Suppose you started your own snowboard factory, Terrain Park Boards. Think that's impossible? Burton Snowboards was started by Jake Burton Carpenter, when he was only 23 years old. Jake initially experimented with 100 different prototype designs before settling on a final design. Then Jake, along with two relatives and a friend, started making 50 boards per day in Londonderry, Vermont. Unfortunately, while they made a lot of boards in their first year, they were only able to sell 300 of them. To get by during those early years, Jake taught tennis and tended bar to pay the bills.

Here are some of the costs that your snowboard factory would incur.

1. The materials cost of each snowboard (wood cores, fiberglass, resins, metal screw holes, metal edges, and ink) is $30.

2. The labor costs (for example, to trim and shape each board using jig saws and band saws) are $40.

3. Depreciation on the factory building and equipment (for example, presses, grinding machines, and lacquer machines) used to make the snowboards is $25,000 per year.

4. Property taxes on the factory building (where the snowboards are made) are $6,000 per year.

5. Advertising costs (mostly online and catalogue) are $60,000 per year.

6. Sales commissions related to snowboard sales are $20 per snowboard.

7. Salaries for maintenance employees are $45,000 per year.

8. The salary of the plant manager is $70,000.

9. The cost of shipping is $8 per snowboard.

Illustration 14-11 shows how Terrain Park Boards would assign these manufacturing and selling costs to the various categories.

Illustration 14-11
Assignment of costs to cost categories

| | Product Costs | | | |
Cost Item	Direct Materials	Direct Labor	Manufacturing Overhead	Period Costs
1. Material cost ($30) per board	X			
2. Labor costs ($40) per board		X		
3. Depreciation on factory equipment ($25,000 per year)			X	
4. Property taxes on factory building ($6,000 per year)			X	
5. Advertising costs ($60,000 per year)				X
6. Sales commissions ($20 per board)				X
7. Maintenance salaries (factory facilities) ($45,000 per year)			X	
8. Salary of plant manager ($70,000)			X	
9. Cost of shipping boards ($8 per board)				X

Remember that total manufacturing costs are the sum of the **product costs—** direct materials, direct labor, and manufacturing overhead. If Terrain Park Boards produces 10,000 snowboards the first year, the total manufacturing costs would be $846,000 as shown in Illustration 14-12.

Illustration 14-12
Computation of total manufacturing costs

Cost Number and Item	Manufacturing Cost
1. Material cost ($30 × 10,000)	$300,000
2. Labor cost ($40 × 10,000)	400,000
3. Depreciation on factory equipment	25,000
4. Property taxes on factory building	6,000
7. Maintenance salaries (factory facilities)	45,000
8. Salary of plant manager	70,000
Total manufacturing costs	**$846,000**

Knowing the total manufacturing costs, Terrain Park Boards can compute the manufacturing cost per unit. Assuming 10,000 units, the cost to produce one snowboard is $84.60 ($846,000 ÷ 10,000 units).

In subsequent chapters, we will use extensively the cost concepts discussed in this chapter. Study Illustration 14-11 carefully. If you do not understand any of these classifications, go back and reread the appropriate section in this chapter.

PRODUCT COSTING FOR SERVICE INDUSTRIES

The Feature Story notes HP's belief that its greatest opportunities for growth are in technology services, not hardware. In fact, much of the U.S. economy has shifted toward an emphasis on services. Today, more than 50% of U.S. workers are employed by service companies. Airlines, marketing agencies, cable companies, and governmental agencies are just a few examples of service companies. How do service companies differ from manufacturing companies? One good way to differentiate these two different types of companies is by how quickly the product is used or consumed by the customer—services are consumed immediately. For example, when a restaurant produces a meal, that meal is not put in inventory, but it is instead consumed immediately. An airline uses special equipment to provide its product, but again, the output of that equipment is consumed immediately by the customer in the form of a flight. And a marketing agency performs services for its clients that are immediately consumed by the customer in the form of a marketing plan. For a manufacturing company, like Boeing, it often has a long lead time before its airplane is used or consumed by the customer.

In presenting our initial examples, we used manufacturing companies because accounting for the manufacturing environment requires the use of the broadest range of accounts. That is, the accounts used by service companies represent a subset of those used by manufacturers because service companies are not producing inventory. Neither the restaurant, the airline, or the marketing agency discussed above produces an inventoriable product. However, just like a manufacturer, each needs to keep track of the costs of its services in order to know whether it is generating a profit. A successful restaurateur needs to know the cost of each offering on the menu, an airline needs to know the cost of flight service to each destination, and a marketing agency needs to know the cost to develop a marketing plan. Thus, the techniques shown in this chapter, to accumulate manufacturing costs to determine manufacturing inventory, are equally useful for determining the costs of providing services.

For example, let's consider the costs that HP might incur on a consulting engagement. A significant portion of its costs would be salaries of consulting personnel. It might also incur travel costs, materials, software costs, and depreciation charges on equipment used by the employees to provide the consulting service. In the same way that it needs to keep track of the cost of manufacturing its computers and printers, HP needs to know what its costs are on each consulting job. It could prepare a cost of services provided schedule similar to the cost of goods manufactured schedule in Illustration 14-8 (page 759). The structure would be essentially the same as the cost of goods manufactured schedule, but section headings would be reflective of the costs of the particular service organization.

Managers of service companies look to managerial accounting to answer many questions. In some instances, the managerial accountant may need to develop new systems for measuring the cost of serving individual customers. In others, companies may need new operating controls to improve the quality and efficiency of specific services. Many of the examples we present in subsequent chapters will be based on service companies. To highlight the relevance of the techniques used in this course for service companies, we have placed a service

Ethics Note Do telecommunications companies have an obligation to provide service to remote or low-user areas for a fee that may be less than the cost of the service?

company icon next to those items in the text and end-of-chapter materials that relate to nonmanufacturing companies.

 **Service Company Insight**

Low Fares but Decent Profits

During 2008, when other airlines were cutting flight service due to the recession, Allegiant Airlines increased capacity by 21%. Sounds crazy, doesn't it? But it must know something, because while the other airlines were losing money, it was generating profits. Consider also that its average one-way fare is only $83. So how does it make money? As a low-budget airline, it focuses on controlling costs. It purchases used planes for $4 million each rather than new planes for $40 million. It flies out of small towns, so wages are low and competition is nonexistent. It only flies a route if its 150-passenger planes are nearly full (it averages about 90% of capacity). If a route isn't filling up, it quits flying it as often or cancels it altogether. It adjusts its prices weekly. The bottom line is that it knows its costs to the penny. Knowing what your costs are might not be glamorous, but it sure beats losing money.

Source: Susan Carey, "For Allegiant, Getaways Mean Profits," *Wall Street Journal Online* (February 18, 2009).

? What are some of the line items that would appear in the cost of services provided schedule of an airline? (See page 795.)

Managerial Accounting Today

study objective 8

Identify trends in managerial accounting.

In recent years, the competitive environment for U.S. business has changed significantly. For example, the airline, financial services, and telecommunications industries have been deregulated. Global competition has intensified. The world economy now has the European Union, NAFTA, and ASEAN. Countries like China and India are becoming economic powerhouses. As indicated earlier, managerial accountants must be forward-looking, acting as advisors and information providers to different members of the organization. Some of the issues they face are discussed below.

THE VALUE CHAIN

The value chain refers to all activities associated with providing a product or service. For a manufacturer these include research and development, product design, acquisition of raw materials, production, sales and marketing, delivery, customer relations, and subsequent service. Illustration 14-13 depicts the value chain for a manufacturer. In recent years, companies have made huge strides in analyzing all stages of the value chain in an effort to improve productivity and eliminate waste. Japanese automobile manufacturer Toyota pioneered many of these innovations.

Illustration 14-13 A manufacturer's value chain

| Research & development and product design | Acquisition of raw materials | Production | Sales & marketing | Delivery | Customer relations and subsequent services |

In the 1980s, many companies purchased giant machines to replace humans in the manufacturing process. These machines were designed to produce large batches of products. In recent years these large-batch manufacturing processes have been recognized as very wasteful. They require vast amounts of inventory storage capacity and considerable movement of materials. Consequently, many companies have reengineered their manufacturing processes. As one example, the manufacturing company Pratt and Whitney replaced many large machines with smaller, more flexible ones and reorganized its plants for more efficient flow of goods. Pratt and Whitney reduced the time that its turbine engine blades spend in the grinding section of its factory from 10 days down to 2 hours. It cut the total amount of time spent making a blade from 22 days to 7 days. Analysis of the value chain has made companies far more responsive to customer needs and has improved profitability.

TECHNOLOGICAL CHANGE

Technology has played a large role in the value chain. Computerization and automation have permitted companies to be more effective in streamlining production and thus enhancing the value chain. For example, many companies now employ enterprise resource planning (ERP) software systems to manage their value chain. ERP systems provide a comprehensive, centralized, integrated source of information that companies can use to manage all major business processes, from purchasing to manufacturing to human resources.

In large companies, an ERP system might replace as many as 200 individual software packages. For example, an ERP system can eliminate the need for individual software packages for personnel, inventory management, receivables, and payroll. Because the value chain extends beyond the walls of the company, ERP systems enable a two-way flow of information between a company and its major suppliers, customers, and business partners. Such systems both collect and disperse information throughout the value chain. The largest ERP provider, German corporation SAP AG, has more than 36,000 customers worldwide.

Another example of technological change is **computer-integrated manufacturing (CIM)**. Using CIM, many companies can now manufacture products that are untouched by human hands. An example is the use of robotic equipment in the steel and automobile industries. Workers monitor the manufacturing process by watching instrument panels. Automation significantly reduces direct labor costs in many cases.

Also, the widespread use of computers has greatly reduced the cost of accumulating, storing, and reporting managerial accounting information. Computers now make it possible to do more detailed costing of products, processes, and services than was possible under manual processing.

Technology is also affecting the value chain through business-to-business (B2B) e-commerce on the Internet. The Internet has dramatically changed the way corporations do business with one another. Interorganizational information systems connected over the Internet enable suppliers to share information nearly instantaneously. The Internet has also changed the marketplace, often cutting out intermediaries. Industries such as the automobile, airline, hotel, and electronics industries have made commitments to purchase some or all of their supplies and raw materials in the huge B2B electronic marketplaces. For example, Hilton Hotels recently agreed to purchase as much as $1.5 billion of bed sheets, pest control services, and other items from an online supplier, PurchasePro.com.

JUST-IN-TIME INVENTORY METHODS

Many companies have significantly lowered inventory levels and costs using just-in-time (JIT) inventory methods. Under a just-in-time method, goods are manufactured or purchased just in time for sale. As noted in the Feature Story, Dell

Ethics Note Does just-in-time inventory justify "just-in-time" employees obtained through temporary employment services?

is famous for having developed a system for making computers in response to individual customer requests. Even though each computer is custom-made to meet each customer's particular specifications, it takes Dell less than 48 hours to assemble the computer and put it on a truck. By integrating its information systems with those of its suppliers, Dell reduced its inventories to nearly zero. This is a huge advantage in an industry where products become obsolete nearly overnight.

QUALITY

JIT inventory systems require an increased emphasis on product quality. If products are produced only as they are needed, it is very costly for the company to stop production because of defects or machine breakdowns. Many companies have installed total quality management (TQM) systems to reduce defects in finished products. The goal is to achieve zero defects. These systems require timely data on defective products, rework costs, and the cost of honoring warranty contracts. Often, companies use this information to help redesign the product in a way that makes it less prone to defects. Or they may use the information to reengineer the production process to reduce setup time and decrease the potential for error. TQM systems also provide information on nonfinancial measures such as customer satisfaction, number of service calls, and time to generate reports. Attention to these measures, which employees can control, leads to increased profitability.

ACTIVITY-BASED COSTING

As discussed earlier, overhead costs have become an increasingly large component of product and service costs. By definition, overhead costs cannot be directly traced to individual products. But to determine each product's cost, overhead must be **allocated** to the various products. In order to obtain more accurate product costs, many companies now allocate overhead using activity-based costing (ABC). Under ABC, companies allocate overhead based on each product's use of activities in making the product. For example, companies can keep track of their cost of setting up machines for each batch of a production process. Then companies can allocate part of the total set-up cost to a particular product based on the number of set-ups that product required.

Activity-based costing is beneficial because it results in more accurate product costing and in more careful scrutiny of all activities in the value chain. For example, if a product's cost is high because it requires a high number of set-ups, management will be motivated to determine how to produce the product using the optimal number of machine set-ups. Both manufacturing and service companies now widely use ABC. Allied Signal and Coca-Cola have both enjoyed improved results from ABC. Fidelity Investments uses ABC to identify which customers cost the most to serve.

THEORY OF CONSTRAINTS

All companies have certain aspects of their business that create "bottlenecks"—constraints that limit the company's potential profitability. An important aspect of managing the value chain is identifying these constraints. The theory of constraints is a specific approach used to identify and manage constraints in order to achieve the company's goals. Automobile manufacturer General Motors has implemented the theory of constraints in all of its North American plants. GM has found that it is most profitable when it focuses on fixing bottlenecks, rather than worrying about whether all aspects of the company are functioning at full capacity. It has greatly improved the company's ability to effectively use overtime labor while meeting customer demand. Chapter 19 discusses an application of the theory of constraints.

BALANCED SCORECARD

As companies implement various business practice innovations, managers sometimes focus too enthusiastically on the latest innovation, to the detriment of other areas of the business. For example, in focusing on improving quality, companies sometimes have lost sight of cost/benefit considerations. Similarly, in focusing on reducing inventory levels through just-in-time, companies sometimes have lost sales due to inventory shortages. The balanced scorecard is a performance-measurement approach that uses both financial and nonfinancial measures to evaluate all aspects of a company's operations in an **integrated** fashion. The performance measures are linked in a cause-and-effect fashion to ensure that they all tie to the company's overall objectives.

For example, the company may desire to increase its return on assets, a common financial performance measure (calculated as net income divided by average total assets). It will then identify a series of linked goals. If the company accomplishes each goal, the ultimate result will be an increase in return on assets. For example, in order to increase return on assets, sales must increase. In order to increase sales, customer satisfaction must be increased. In order to increase customer satisfaction, product defects must be reduced. In order to reduce product defects, employee training must be increased. Note the linkage, which starts with employee training and ends with return on assets. Each objective will have associated performance measures.

The use of the balanced scorecard is widespread among well-known and respected companies. For example, Hilton Hotels Corporation uses the balanced scorecard to evaluate the performance of employees at all of its hotel chains. Wal-Mart employs the balanced scorecard, and actually extends its use to evaluation of its suppliers. For example, Wal-Mart recently awarded Welch Company the "Dry Grocery Division Supplier of the Year Award" for its balanced scorecard results. We discuss the balanced scorecard further in Chapter 22.

before you go on...

Do it!

Match the descriptions that follow with the corresponding terms.

Descriptions:

1. _____ All activities associated with providing a product or service.

2. _____ A method of allocating overhead based on each product's use of activities in making the product.

3. _____ Systems implemented to reduce defects in finished products with the goal of achieving zero defects.

4. _____ A performance-measurement approach that uses both financial and nonfinancial measures, tied to company objectives, to evaluate a company's operations in an integrated fashion.

5. _____ Inventory system in which goods are manufactured or purchased just as they are needed for use.

Terms:

a. Activity-based costing

b. Balanced scorecard

c. Just-in-time (JIT) inventory

d. Total quality management (TQM)

e. Value chain

TRENDS IN MANAGERIAL ACCOUNTING

Action Plan

• Develop a forward-looking view, in order to advise and provide information to various members of the organization.

• Understand current business trends and issues.

Solution

1. e	2. a	3. d	4. b	5. c

Related exercise material: **Do it!** 14-4 and E14-18.

USING THE DECISION TOOLKIT

Giant Manufacturing Co. Ltd. specializes in manufacturing many different models of bicycles. Assume that the market has responded enthusiastically to a new model, the Jaguar. As a result, the company has established a separate manufacturing facility to produce these bicycles. The company produces 1,000 bicycles per month. Giant's monthly manufacturing cost and other expenses data related to these bicycles are as follows.

1. Rent on manufacturing equipment (lease cost) $2,000/month
2. Insurance on manufacturing building $750/month
3. Raw materials (frames, tires, etc.) $80/bicycle
4. Utility costs for manufacturing facility $1,000/month
5. Supplies for administrative office $800/month
6. Wages for assembly line workers in manufacturing facility $30/bicycle
7. Depreciation on office equipment $650/month

8. Miscellaneous manufacturing materials (lubricants, solders, etc.) $1.20/bicycle
9. Property taxes on manufacturing building $2,400/year
10. Manufacturing supervisor's salary $3,000/month
11. Advertising for bicycles $30,000/year
12. Sales commissions $10/bicycle
13. Depreciation on manufacturing building $1,500/month

Instructions

(a) Prepare an answer sheet with the following column headings.

Cost Item	Product Costs			Period Costs
	Direct Materials	Direct Labor	Manufacturing Overhead	

Enter each cost item on your answer sheet, placing an "X" mark under the appropriate headings.

(b) Compute total manufacturing costs for the month.

Solution

(a)

Cost Item	Product Costs			Period Costs
	Direct Materials	Direct Labor	Manufacturing Overhead	
1. Rent on manufacturing equipment ($2,000/month)			X	
2. Insurance on manufacturing building ($750/month)			X	
3. Raw materials ($80/bicycle)	X			
4. Manufacturing utilities ($1,000/month)			X	
5. Office supplies ($800/month)				X

Cost Item	Product Costs			Period Costs
	Direct Materials	Direct Labor	Manufacturing Overhead	
6. Wages for workers ($30/bicycle)		X		
7. Depreciation on office equipment ($650/month)				X
8. Miscellaneous manufacturing materials ($1.20/bicycle)			X	
9. Property taxes on manufacturing building ($2,400/year)			X	
10. Manufacturing supervisor's salary ($3,000/month)			X	
11. Advertising cost ($30,000/year)				X
12. Sales commissions ($10/bicycle)				X
13. Depreciation on manufacturing building ($1,500/month)			X	

(b)

Cost Item	Manufacturing Cost
Rent on manufacturing equipment	$ 2,000
Insurance on manufacturing building	750
Raw materials ($80 × 1,000)	80,000
Manufacturing utilities	1,000
Labor ($30 × 1,000)	30,000
Miscellaneous materials ($1.20 × 1,000)	1,200
Property taxes on manufacturing building ($2,400 ÷ 12)	200
Manufacturing supervisor's salary	3,000
Depreciation on manufacturing building	1,500
Total manufacturing costs	$119,650

Summary of Study Objectives

1 **Explain the distinguishing features of managerial accounting.** The *primary users* of managerial accounting reports are internal users, who are officers, department heads, managers, and supervisors in the company. Managerial accounting issues internal reports as frequently as the need arises. The purpose of these reports is to provide special-purpose information for a particular user for a specific decision. The content of managerial accounting reports pertains to subunits of the business, may be very detailed, and may extend beyond the double-entry accounting system. The reporting standard is relevance to the decision being made. No independent audits are required in managerial accounting.

2 **Identify the three broad functions of management.** The three functions are planning, directing, and controlling. Planning requires management to look ahead and to establish objectives. Directing involves coordinating the diverse activities and human resources of a company to produce a smooth-running operation. Controlling is the process of keeping the activities on track.

3 **Define the three classes of manufacturing costs.** Manufacturing costs are typically classified as either (1) direct materials, (2) direct labor, or (3) manufacturing overhead. Raw materials that can be physically and directly associated with the finished product during the manufacturing process are called direct materials. The work of factory employees that can be physically and directly associated with converting raw materials into finished goods is considered direct labor. Manufacturing overhead consists of costs that are indirectly associated with the manufacture of the finished product.

4 **Distinguish between product and period costs.** Product costs are costs that are a necessary and integral part of producing the finished product. Product costs are also called inventoriable costs. Under the matching principle, these costs do not become expenses until the company sells the finished goods inventory. Period costs are costs that are identified with a specific time period rather than with a salable product. These costs relate to nonmanufacturing costs and therefore are not inventoriable costs.

5 **Explain the difference between a merchandising and a manufacturing income statement.** The difference between a merchandising and a manufacturing income statement is in the cost of goods sold section. A manufacturing cost of goods sold section shows beginning and ending finished goods inventories and the cost of goods manufactured.

6 **Indicate how cost of goods manufactured is determined.** Companies add the cost of the beginning work in process to the total manufacturing costs for the current year to arrive at the total cost of work in process for the year. They then subtract the ending

work in process from the total cost of work in process to arrive at the cost of goods manufactured.

7 **Explain the difference between a merchandising and a manufacturing balance sheet.** The difference between a merchandising and a manufacturing balance sheet is in the current assets section. The current assets section of a manufacturing company's balance sheet presents three inventory accounts: finished goods inventory, work in process inventory, and raw materials inventory.

8 **Identify trends in managerial accounting.** Managerial accounting has experienced many changes in recent years. Among these are a shift toward addressing the needs of service companies and improving practices to better meet the needs of managers. Improved practices include a focus on managing the value chain through techniques such as just-in-time inventory and technological applications such as enterprise resource management, computer-integrated manufacturing, and B2B e-commerce. In addition, techniques such as just-in-time inventory, total quality management, activity-based costing, and theory of constraints are improving decision making. Finally, the balanced scorecard is now used by many companies in order to attain a more comprehensive view of the company's operations.

DECISION TOOLKIT   A SUMMARY

DECISION CHECKPOINTS	INFO NEEDED FOR DECISION	TOOL TO USE FOR DECISION	HOW TO EVALUATE RESULTS
Is the company maintaining control over the costs of production?	Cost of material, labor, and overhead	Cost of goods manufactured schedule	Compare the cost of goods manufactured to revenue expected from product sales.
What is the composition of a manufacturing company's inventory?	Amount of raw materials, work in process, and finished goods inventories	Balance sheet	Determine whether there are sufficient finished goods, raw materials, and work in process inventories to meet forecasted demand.

appendix 14A

Accounting Cycle for a Manufacturing Company

study objective 9

Prepare a worksheet and closing entries for a manufacturing company.

The accounting cycle for a manufacturing company is the same as for a merchandising company when companies use a periodic inventory system. The journalizing and posting of transactions is the same, except for the additional manufacturing inventories and manufacturing cost accounts. Similarly, the preparation of a trial balance and the journalizing and posting of adjusting entries are the same. Some changes, however, occur in using a worksheet and in preparing closing entries.

To illustrate the changes in the worksheet, we will use the cost of goods manufactured schedule for Olsen Manufacturing presented in Illustration 14-8 (page 759), along with other assumed data. For convenience, we reproduce the cost of goods manufactured schedule in Illustration 14A-1.

Illustration 14A-1 Cost of goods manufactured schedule

OLSEN MANUFACTURING COMPANY
Cost of Goods Manufactured Schedule
For the Year Ended December 31, 2012

Work in process, January 1			$ 18,400
Direct materials			
Raw materials inventory, January 1	$ 16,700		
Raw materials purchases	152,500		
Total raw materials available for use	169,200		
Less: Raw materials inventory, December 31	22,800		
Direct materials used		$146,400	
Direct labor		175,600	
Manufacturing overhead			
Indirect labor	14,300		
Factory repairs	12,600		
Factory utilities	10,100		
Factory depreciation	9,440		
Factory insurance	8,360		
Total manufacturing overhead		54,800	
Total manufacturing costs			376,800
Total cost of work in process			395,200
Less: Work in process, December 31			25,200
Cost of goods manufactured			$370,000

WORKSHEET

When a company uses a worksheet in preparing financial statements, it needs two additional columns for the cost of goods manufactured schedule. As illustrated in the worksheet in Illustration 14A-2 (page 772), we insert debit and credit columns for this schedule before the income statement columns.

In completing the cost of goods manufactured columns, you would enter the beginning inventories of raw materials and work in process as debits. In addition, you would enter all of the manufacturing costs as debits. The reason is that each of these amounts increases cost of goods manufactured. In contrast, you would enter ending inventories for raw materials and work in process as credits in the cost of goods manufactured columns because they have the opposite effect—they decrease cost of goods manufactured. The balancing amount for these columns is the cost of goods manufactured. Note that the amount ($370,000) agrees with the amount reported for cost of goods manufactured in Illustration 14A-1. This amount is also entered in the income statement debit column.

The income statement and balance sheet columns for a manufacturing company are basically the same as for a merchandising company. For example, the treatment of the finished goods inventories is identical with the treatment of merchandise inventory: The beginning inventory appears in the debit column of the income statement, and the ending finished goods inventory appears in the income statement credit column as well as in the balance sheet debit column.

OLSEN MANUFACTURING COMPANY
Worksheet (Partial)
For the Year Ended December 31, 2012

	A	B	C	D	E	F	G	H	I
		Adjusted Trial Balance		Cost of Goods Manufactured		Income Statement		Balance Sheet	
		Dr.	Cr.	Dr.	Cr.	Dr.	Cr.	Dr.	Cr.
6	Cash	42,500						42,500	
7	Accounts Receivable (Net)	71,900						71,900	
8	Finished Goods Inventory	24,600				24,600	19,500	19,500	
9	Work in Process Inventory	18,400		18,400	25,200			25,200	
10	Raw Material Inventory	16,700		16,700	22,800			22,800	
11	Plant Assets	724,000						724,000	
12	Accumulated Depreciation		278,400						278,400
13	Notes Payable		100,000						100,000
14	Accounts Payable		40,000						40,000
15	Income Taxes Payable		5,000						5,000
16	Common Stock		200,000						200,000
17	Retained Earnings		205,100						205,100
18	Sales		680,000				680,000		
19	Raw Materials Purchases	152,500		152,500					
20	Direct Labor	175,600		175,600					
21	Indirect Labor	14,300		14,300					
22	Factory Repairs	12,600		12,600					
23	Factory Utilities	10,100		10,100					
24	Factory Depreciation	9,440		9,440					
25	Factory Insurance	8,360		8,360					
26	Selling Expenses	114,900				114,900			
27	Administrative Expenses	92,600				92,600			
28	Income Tax Expense	20,000				20,000			
29	Totals	1,508,500	1,508,500	418,000	48,000				
30	Cost of Goods Manufactured				370,000	370,000			
31	Totals			418,000	418,000	622,100	699,500	905,900	828,500
32	Net Income					77,400			77,400
33	Totals					699,500	699,500	905,900	905,900

Illustration 14A-2 Partial worksheet

As in the case of a merchandising company, manufacturing companies can prepare financial statements from the statement columns of the worksheet. They also can prepare the cost of goods manufactured schedule directly from the worksheet.

CLOSING ENTRIES

The closing entries are different for manufacturing and merchandising companies. Manufacturing companies use a Manufacturing Summary account to close all accounts that appear in the cost of goods manufactured schedule. The balance of the Manufacturing Summary account is the Cost of Goods Manufactured for the period. Manufacturing Summary is then closed to Income Summary.

Companies can prepare the closing entries from the worksheet. As illustrated below, they first prepare the closing entries for the manufacturing accounts. The closing entries for Olsen Manufacturing are as follows.

Dec. 31	Work in Process Inventory (Dec. 31)	25,200	
	Raw Materials Inventory (Dec. 31)	22,800	
	Manufacturing Summary		48,000
	(To record ending raw materials and		
	work in process inventories)		

Dec. 31	Manufacturing Summary	418,000	
	Work in Process Inventory (Jan. 1)		18,400
	Raw Materials Inventory (Jan. 1)		16,700
	Raw Materials Purchases		152,500
	Direct Labor		175,600
	Indirect Labor		14,300
	Factory Repairs		12,600
	Factory Utilities		10,100
	Factory Depreciation		9,440
	Factory Insurance		8,360
	(To close beginning raw materials and work in process inventories and manufacturing cost accounts)		
31	Finished Goods Inventory (Dec. 31)	19,500	
	Sales	680,000	
	Income Summary		699,500
	(To record ending finished goods inventory and close sales account)		
31	Income Summary	622,100	
	Finished Goods Inventory (Jan. 1)		24,600
	Manufacturing Summary		370,000
	Selling Expenses		114,900
	Administrative Expenses		92,600
	Income Tax Expense		20,000
	(To close beginning finished goods inventory, manufacturing summary, and expense accounts)		
31	Income Summary	77,400	
	Retained Earnings		77,400
	(To close net income to retained earnings)		

After posting, the summary accounts will show the following.

Manufacturing Summary

| Dec. 31 | Close | 418,000 | Dec. 31 | Close | 48,000 |
| | | | 31 | Close | 370,000 |

Income Summary

| Dec. 31 | Close | 622,100 | Dec. 31 | Close | 699,500 |
| 31 | Close | 77,400 | | | |

Illustration 14A-3
Summary accounts for a manufacturing company, after posting

Summary of Study Objective for Appendix 14A

9 Prepare a worksheet and closing entries for a manufacturing company. The worksheet for the cost of goods manufactured needs two additional columns. In these columns, manufacturing companies enter the beginning inventories of raw materials and work in process as debits, and the ending inventories as credits. All manufacturing costs are entered as debits. To close all of the accounts that appear in the cost of goods manufactured schedule, manufacturers use a Manufacturing Summary account.

Glossary

Activity-based costing (ABC) *(p. 766)* A method of allocating overhead based on each product's use of activities in making the product.

Balanced scorecard *(p. 767)* A performance-measurement approach that uses both financial and nonfinancial measures, tied to company objectives, to evaluate a company's operations in an integrated fashion.

Board of directors *(p. 751)* The group of officials elected by the stockholders of a corporation to formulate operating policies, select officers, and otherwise manage the company.

Chief executive officer (CEO) *(p. 751)* Corporate officer who has overall responsibility for managing the business and delegates responsibilities to other corporate officers.

Chief financial officer (CFO) *(p. 752)* Corporate officer who is responsible for all of the accounting and finance issues of the company.

Controller *(p. 752)* Financial officer responsible for a company's accounting records, system of internal control, and preparation of financial statements, tax returns, and internal reports.

Cost of goods manufactured *(p. 758)* Total cost of work in process less the cost of the ending work in process inventory.

Direct labor *(p. 755)* The work of factory employees that can be physically and directly associated with converting raw materials into finished goods.

Direct materials *(p. 755)* Raw materials that can be physically and directly associated with manufacturing the finished product.

Enterprise resource planning (ERP) system *(p. 765)* Software that provides a comprehensive, centralized, integrated source of information used to manage all major business processes.

Indirect labor *(p. 755)* Work of factory employees that has no physical association with the finished product, or for which it is impractical to trace the costs to the goods produced.

Indirect materials *(p. 755)* Raw materials that do not physically become part of the finished product or cannot be traced because their physical association with the finished product is too small.

Just-in-time (JIT) inventory *(p. 765)* Inventory system in which goods are manufactured or purchased just in time for sale.

Line positions *(p. 752)* Jobs that are directly involved in a company's primary revenue-generating operating activities.

Managerial accounting *(p. 748)* A field of accounting that provides economic and financial information for managers and other internal users.

Manufacturing overhead *(p. 755)* Manufacturing costs that are indirectly associated with the manufacture of the finished product.

Period costs *(p. 756)* Costs that are matched with the revenue of a specific time period and charged to expense as incurred.

Product costs *(p. 756)* Costs that are a necessary and integral part of producing the finished product.

Sarbanes-Oxley Act of 2002 (SOX) *(p. 753)* Law passed by Congress in 2002 intended to reduce unethical corporate behavior.

Staff positions *(p. 752)* Jobs that support the efforts of line employees.

Theory of constraints *(p. 766)* A specific approach used to identify and manage constraints in order to achieve the company's goals.

Total cost of work in process *(p. 758)* Cost of the beginning work in process plus total manufacturing costs for the current period.

Total manufacturing costs *(p. 758)* The sum of direct materials, direct labor, and manufacturing overhead incurred in the current period.

Total quality management (TQM) *(p. 766)* Systems implemented to reduce defects in finished products with the goal of achieving zero defects.

Treasurer *(p. 752)* Financial officer responsible for custody of a company's funds and for maintaining its cash position.

Value chain *(p. 764)* All activities associated with providing a product or service.

Comprehensive

Superior Manufacturing Company has the following cost and expense data for the year ending December 31, 2012.

Raw materials, 1/1/12	$ 30,000	Insurance, factory	$ 14,000
Raw materials, 12/31/12	20,000	Property taxes, factory building	6,000
Raw materials purchases	205,000	Sales (net)	1,500,000
Indirect materials	15,000	Delivery expenses	100,000
Work in process, 1/1/12	80,000	Sales commissions	150,000
Work in process, 12/31/12	50,000	Indirect labor	90,000
Finished goods, 1/1/12	110,000	Factory machinery rent	40,000
Finished goods, 12/31/12	120,000	Factory utilities	65,000
Direct labor	350,000	Depreciation, factory building	24,000
Factory manager's salary	35,000	Administrative expenses	300,000

Instructions

(a) Prepare a cost of goods manufactured schedule for Superior Company for 2012.

(b) Prepare an income statement for Superior Company for 2012.

(c) Assume that Superior Company's accounting records show the balances of the following current asset accounts: Cash $17,000, Accounts Receivable (net) $120,000, Prepaid Expenses $13,000, and Short-term Investments $26,000. Prepare the current assets section of the balance sheet for Superior Company as of December 31, 2012.

Solution to Comprehensive **Do it!**

(a)

SUPERIOR MANUFACTURING COMPANY
Cost of Goods Manufactured Schedule
For the Year Ended December 31, 2012

Work in process, 1/1			$ 80,000
Direct materials			
Raw materials inventory, 1/1	$ 30,000		
Raw materials purchases	205,000		
Total raw materials available for use	235,000		
Less: Raw materials inventory, 12/31	20,000		
Direct materials used		$215,000	
Direct labor		350,000	
Manufacturing overhead			
Indirect labor	90,000		
Factory utilities	65,000		
Factory machinery rent	40,000		
Factory manager's salary	35,000		
Depreciation, factory building	24,000		
Indirect materials	15,000		
Insurance, factory	14,000		
Property taxes, factory building	6,000		
Total manufacturing overhead		289,000	
Total manufacturing costs			854,000
Total cost of work in process			934,000
Less: Work in process, 12/31			50,000
Cost of goods manufactured			$ 884,000

(b)

SUPERIOR MANUFACTURING COMPANY
Income Statement
For the Year Ended December 31, 2012

Sales (net)		$1,500,000
Cost of goods sold		
Finished goods inventory, January 1	$110,000	
Cost of goods manufactured	884,000	
Cost of goods available for sale	994,000	
Less: Finished goods inventory, December 31	120,000	
Cost of goods sold		874,000
Gross profit		626,000
Operating expenses		
Administrative expenses	300,000	
Sales commissions	150,000	
Delivery expenses	100,000	
Total operating expenses		550,000
Net income		$ 76,000

Action Plan

• Start with beginning work in process as the first item in the cost of goods manufactured schedule.

• Sum direct materials used, direct labor, and total manufacturing overhead to determine total manufacturing costs.

• Sum beginning work in process and total manufacturing costs to determine total cost of work in process.

• Cost of goods manufactured is the total cost of work in process less ending work in process.

• In the cost of goods sold section of the income statement, show beginning and ending finished goods inventory and cost of goods manufactured.

• In the balance sheet, list manufacturing inventories in the order of their expected realization in cash, with finished goods first.

(c)

SUPERIOR MANUFACTURING COMPANY
Balance Sheet (partial)
December 31, 2012

Current assets		
Cash		$ 17,000
Short-term investments		26,000
Accounts receivable (net)		120,000
Inventories		
Finished goods	$120,000	
Work in process	50,000	
Raw materials	20,000	190,000
Prepaid expenses		13,000
Total current assets		$366,000

PLUS Self-Test, Brief Exercises, Exercises, Problem Set A, and many more resources are available for practice in WileyPLUS

Note: All asterisked Questions, Exercises, and Problems relate to material in the appendix to the chapter.

Self-Test Questions

Answers are on page 795.

(SO 1) **1.** Managerial accounting:
(a) is governed by generally accepted accounting principles.
(b) places emphasis on special-purpose information.
(c) pertains to the entity as a whole and is highly aggregated.
(d) is limited to cost data.

(SO 2) **2.** The management of an organization performs several broad functions. They are:
(a) planning, directing, and selling.
(b) planning, directing, and controlling.
(c) planning, manufacturing, and controlling.
(d) directing, manufacturing, and controlling.

(SO 2) **3.** After passage of the Sarbanes-Oxley Act of 2002:
(a) reports prepared by managerial accountants must by audited by CPAs.
(b) CEOs and CFOs must certify that financial statements give a fair presentation of the company's operating results.
(c) the audit committee, rather than top management, is responsible for the company's financial statements.
(d) reports prepared by managerial accountants must comply with generally accepted accounting principles (GAAP).

(SO 3) **4.** Direct materials are a:

	Product Cost	Manufacturing Overhead	Period Cost
(a)	Yes	Yes	No
(b)	Yes	No	No
(c)	Yes	Yes	Yes
(d)	No	No	No

5. Which of the following costs would a computer manufacturer include in manufacturing overhead? (SO 3)
(a) The cost of the disk drives.
(b) The wages earned by computer assemblers.
(c) The cost of the memory chips.
(d) Depreciation on testing equipment.

6. Which of the following is *not* an element of manufacturing overhead? (SO 3)
(a) Sales manager's salary.
(b) Plant manager's salary.
(c) Factory repairman's wages.
(d) Product inspector's salary.

7. Indirect labor is a: (SO 4)
(a) nonmanufacturing cost.
(b) raw material cost.
(c) product cost.
(d) period cost.

8. Which of the following costs are classified as a period cost? (SO 4)
(a) Wages paid to a factory custodian.
(b) Wages paid to a production department supervisor.
(c) Wages paid to a cost accounting department supervisor.
(d) Wages paid to an assembly worker.

9. For the year, Redder Company has cost of goods manufactured of $600,000, beginning finished goods inventory of $200,000, and ending finished goods inventory of $250,000. The cost of goods sold is: (SO 5)
(a) $450,000.
(b) $500,000.
(c) $550,000.
(d) $600,000.

(SO 5) **10.** Cost of goods available for sale is a step in the calculation of cost of goods sold of:
  (a) a merchandising company but not a manufacturing company.
  (b) a manufacturing company but not a merchandising company.
  (c) a merchandising company and a manufacturing company.
  (d) neither a manufacturing company nor a merchandising company.

(SO 6) **11.** A cost of goods manufactured schedule shows beginning and ending inventories for:
  (a) raw materials and work in process only.
  (b) work in process only.
  (c) raw materials only.
  (d) raw materials, work in process, and finished goods.

(SO 6) **12.** The formula to determine the cost of goods manufactured is:
  (a) Beginning raw materials inventory + Total manufacturing costs − Ending work in process inventory.
  (b) Beginning work in process inventory + Total manufacturing costs − Ending finished goods inventory.
  (c) Beginning finished good inventory + Total manufacturing costs − Ending finished goods inventory.
  (d) Beginning work in process inventory + Total manufacturing costs − Ending work in process inventory.

(SO 7) **13.** A manufacturer may report three inventories on its balance sheet: (1) raw materials, (2) work in process, and (3) finished goods. Indicate in what sequence these inventories generally appear on a balance sheet.
  (a) (1), (2), (3)
  (b) (2), (3), (1)
  (c) (3), (1), (2)
  (d) (3), (2), (1)

14. Which of the following managerial accounting techniques attempts to allocate manufacturing overhead in a more meaningful fashion? (SO 8)
  (a) Just-in-time inventory.
  (b) Total-quality management.
  (c) Balanced scorecard.
  (d) Activity-based costing.

15. Examples of recent trends in the economic environment of U.S. businesses are: (SO 8)
  (a) increasing deregulation, decreasing global competition, and a shift toward providing services rather than goods.
  (b) increasing deregulation, increasing global competition, and a shift toward providing goods rather than services.
  (c) decreasing deregulation, decreasing global competition, and a shift toward providing services rather than goods.
  (d) increasing deregulation, increasing global competition, and a shift toward providing services rather than goods.

Go to the book's companion website, **www.wiley.com/college/kimmel**, for additional Self-Test Questions.

Questions

1. (a) "Managerial accounting is a field of accounting that provides economic information for all interested parties." Do you agree? Explain.
  (b) Joe Delong believes that managerial accounting serves only manufacturing firms. Is Joe correct? Explain.

2. Distinguish between managerial and financial accounting as to (a) primary users of reports, (b) types and frequency of reports, and (c) purpose of reports.

3. How does the content of reports and the verification of reports differ between managerial and financial accounting?

4. In what ways can the budgeting process create incentives for unethical behavior?

5. Linda Olsen is studying for the next accounting midterm examination. Summarize for Linda what she should know about management functions.

6. "Decision making is management's most important function." Do you agree? Why or why not?

7. Explain the primary difference between line positions and staff positions, and give examples of each.

8. What new rules were enacted under the Sarbanes-Oxley Act to address unethical accounting practices?

9. Tony Andres is studying for his next accounting examination. Explain to Tony what he should know about the differences between the income statements for a manufacturing and for a merchandising company.

10. Jerry Lang is unclear as to the difference between the balance sheets of a merchandising company and a manufacturing company. Explain the difference to Jerry.

11. How are manufacturing costs classified?

12. Mel Finney claims that the distinction between direct and indirect materials is based entirely on physical association with the product. Is Mel correct? Why?

13. Tina Burke is confused about the differences between a product cost and a period cost. Explain the differences to Tina.

14. Identify the differences in the cost of goods sold section of an income statement between a merchandising company and a manufacturing company.

15. The determination of the cost of goods manufactured involves the following factors: (A) beginning work in process inventory, (B) total manufacturing costs, and (C) ending work in process inventory. Identify the meaning of x in the following formulas:
  (a) A + B = x
  (b) A + B − C = x

16. Sealy Manufacturing has beginning raw materials inventory $12,000, ending raw materials inventory $15,000, and raw materials purchases $170,000. What is the cost of direct materials used?

17. Tate Manufacturing Inc. has beginning work in process $26,000, direct materials used $240,000, direct labor $220,000, total manufacturing overhead $180,000, and ending work in process $32,000. What are the total manufacturing costs?

18. Using the data in Question 17, what are (a) the total cost of work in process and (b) the cost of goods manufactured?

19. In what order should manufacturing inventories be listed in a balance sheet?

20. How does the output of manufacturing operations differ from that of service operations?

21. Discuss whether the product costing techniques discussed in this chapter apply equally well to manufacturers and service companies.

22. What is the value chain? Describe, in sequence, the main components of a manufacturer's value chain.

23. What is an enterprise resource planning (ERP) system? What are its primary benefits?

24. Why is product quality important for companies that implement a just-in-time inventory system?

25. Explain what is meant by "balanced" in the balanced scorecard approach.

26. What is activity-based costing, and what are its potential benefits?

*27. How, if at all, does the accounting cycle differ between a manufacturing company and a merchandising company?

*28. What typical account balances are carried into the cost of goods manufactured columns of the manufacturing worksheet?

*29. Prepare the closing entries for (a) ending work in process and raw materials inventories and (b) manufacturing summary. Use XXXs for amounts.

Brief Exercises

Distinguish between managerial and financial accounting.

(SO 1), C

BE14-1 Complete the following comparison table between managerial and financial accounting.

	Financial Accounting	Managerial Accounting
Primary users of reports		
Types of reports		
Frequency of reports		
Purpose of reports		
Content of reports		
Verification process		

Identify important regulatory changes.

(SO 2), C

BE14-2 The Sarbanes-Oxley Act of 2002 (SOX) has important implications for the financial community. Explain two implications of SOX.

Identify the three management functions.

(SO 2), C

BE14-3 Listed below are the three functions of the management of an organization.

1. Planning   2. Directing   3. Controlling

Identify which of the following statements best describes each of the above functions.

(a) ____ requires management to look ahead and to establish objectives. A key objective of management is to add value to the business.

(b) ____ involves coordinating the diverse activities and human resources of a company to produce a smooth-running operation. This function relates to the implementation of planned objectives.

(c) ____ is the process of keeping the activities on track. Management must determine whether goals are being met and what changes are necessary when there are deviations.

Classify manufacturing costs.

(SO 3), C

BE14-4 Determine whether each of the following costs should be classified as direct materials (DM), direct labor (DL), or manufacturing overhead (MO).

(a) ____Frames and tires used in manufacturing bicycles.

(b) ____Wages paid to production workers.

(c) ____Insurance on factory equipment and machinery.

(d) ____Depreciation on factory equipment.

Classify manufacturing costs.

(SO 3), C

BE14-5 Indicate whether each of the following costs of an automobile manufacturer would be classified as direct materials, direct labor, or manufacturing overhead.

(a) ____Windshield.

(b) ____Engine.

(c) ____Wages of assembly line worker.

(d) ____Depreciation of factory machinery.

(e) ____Factory machinery lubricants.

(f) ____Tires.

(g) ____Steering wheel.

(h) ____Salary of painting supervisor.

BE14-6 Identify whether each of the following costs should be classified as product costs or period costs.

(a) ____Manufacturing overhead.
(b) ____Selling expenses.
(c) ____Administrative expenses.
(d) ____Advertising expenses.
(e) ____Direct labor.
(f) ____Direct material.

Identify product and period costs.
(SO 4), C

BE14-7 Presented below are Dieker Company's monthly manufacturing cost data related to its personal computer products.

(a) Utilities for manufacturing equipment $116,000
(b) Raw material (CPU, chips, etc.) $ 85,000
(c) Depreciation on manufacturing building $880,000
(d) Wages for production workers $191,000

Classify manufacturing costs.
(SO 3), C

Enter each cost item in the following table, placing an "X" under the appropriate headings.

| | **Product Costs** | | |
	Direct Materials	Direct Labor	Factory Overhead
(a)			
(b)			
(c)			
(d)			

BE14-8 Francum Manufacturing Company has the following data: direct labor $209,000, direct materials used $180,000, total manufacturing overhead $208,000, and beginning work in process $25,000. Compute (a) total manufacturing costs and (b) total cost of work in process.

Compute total manufacturing costs and total cost of work in process.
(SO 6), AP

BE14-9 In alphabetical order below are current asset items for Ruiz Company's balance sheet at December 31, 2012. Prepare the current assets section (including a complete heading).

Accounts receivable	$200,000
Cash	62,000
Finished goods	91,000
Prepaid expenses	38,000
Raw materials	73,000
Work in process	87,000

Prepare current assets section.
(SO 7), AP

BE14-10 Presented below are incomplete manufacturing cost data. Determine the missing amounts for three different situations.

	Direct Materials Used	Direct Labor Used	Factory Overhead	Total Manufacturing Costs
(1)	$40,000	$61,000	$ 50,000	?
(2)	?	$75,000	$140,000	$296,000
(3)	$55,000	?	$111,000	$310,000

Determine missing amounts in computing total manufacturing costs.
(SO 6), AP

BE14-11 Use the same data from BE14–10 above and the data below. Determine the missing amounts.

	Total Manufacturing Costs	Work in Process (1/1)	Work in Process (12/31)	Cost of Goods Manufactured
(1)	?	$120,000	$82,000	?
(2)	$296,000	?	$98,000	$321,000
(3)	$410,000	$463,000	?	$715,000

Determine missing amounts in computing cost of goods manufactured.
(SO 6), AP

*****BE14-12** Kline Manufacturing Company uses a worksheet in preparing financial statements. The following accounts are included in the adjusted trial balance: Finished Goods Inventory $28,000, Work in Process Inventory $21,600, Raw Materials Purchases $175,000, and Direct Labor $140,000. Indicate the worksheet column(s) to which each account should be extended.

Identify worksheet columns for selected accounts.
(SO 9), C

Do it! Review

Identify managerial accounting concepts.

(SO 1, 2), C

Do it! 14-1 Indicate whether the following statements are true or false.

1. Managerial accountants explain and report manufacturing and nonmanufacturing costs, determine cost behaviors, and perform cost-volume-profit analysis, but are not involved in the budget process.
2. Financial accounting reports pertain to subunits of the business and are very detailed.
3. Managerial accounting reports must follow GAAP and are audited by CPAs.
4. Managers' activities and responsibilities can be classified into three broad functions: planning, directing, and controlling.
5. As a result of the Sarbanes-Oxley Act of 2002 (SOX), top managers must certify that the company maintains an adequate system of internal control.
6. Management accountants follow a code of ethics developed by the Institute of Management Accountants.

Identify managerial cost concepts.

(SO 3, 4), C

Do it! 14-2 A music company has these costs:

Advertising	Paper inserts for CD cases
Blank CDs	CD plastic cases
Depreciation of CD image burner	Salaries of sales representatives
	Salaries of factory maintenance employees
Salary of factory manager	Salaries of employees who burn music onto CDs
Factory supplies used	

Classify each cost as a period or a product cost. Within the product cost category, indicate if the cost is part of direct materials (DM), direct labor (DL), or manufacturing overhead (MO).

Prepare cost of goods manufactured schedule.

(SO 6), AP

Do it! 14-3 The following information is available for Fishel Manufacturing Company.

	April 1	April 30
Raw material inventory	$10,000	$14,000
Work in process inventory	5,000	3,500

Materials purchased in April	$98,000
Direct labor in April	80,000
Manufacturing overhead in April	180,000

Prepare the cost of goods manufactured schedule for the month of April.

Identify trends in managerial accounting.

(SO 8), C

Do it! 14-4 Match the descriptions that follow with the corresponding terms.

Descriptions:

1. _____ Inventory system in which goods are manufactured or purchased just as they are needed for sale.
2. _____ A method of allocating overhead based on each product's use of activities in making the product.
3. _____ Systems that are especially important to firms adopting just-in-time inventory methods.
4. _____ One part of the value chain for a manufacturing company.
5. _____ The U.S. economy is trending toward this.
6. _____ A performance-measurement approach that uses both financial and nonfinancial measures, tied to company objectives, to evaluate a company's operations in an integrated fashion.

Terms:

(a) Activity-based costing
(b) Balanced scorecard
(c) Total quality management (TQM)
(d) Research and development, and product design
(e) Service industries
(f) Just-in-time (JIT) inventory

Exercises

E14-1 Richard Larkin has prepared the following list of statements about managerial accounting and financial accounting.

1. Financial accounting focuses on providing information to internal users.
2. Analyzing cost-volume-profit relationships is part of managerial accounting.
3. Preparation of budgets is part of financial accounting.
4. Managerial accounting applies only to merchandising and manufacturing companies.
5. Both managerial accounting and financial accounting deal with many of the same economic events.
6. Managerial accounting reports are prepared only quarterly and annually.
7. Financial accounting reports are general-purpose reports.
8. Managerial accounting reports pertain to subunits of the business.
9. Managerial accounting reports must comply with generally accepted accounting principles.
10. Although managerial accountants are expected to behave ethically, there is no code of ethical standards for managerial accountants.

Identify distinguishing features of managerial accounting.
(SO 1), C

Instructions
Identify each statement as true or false. If false, indicate how to correct the statement.

E14-2 Presented below is a list of costs and expenses usually incurred by Barnum Corporation, a manufacturer of furniture, in its factory.
1. Salaries for assembly line inspectors.
2. Insurance on factory machines.
3. Property taxes on the factory building.
4. Factory repairs.
5. Upholstery used in manufacturing furniture.
6. Wages paid to assembly line workers.
7. Factory machinery depreciation.
8. Glue, nails, paint, and other small parts used in production.
9. Factory supervisors' salaries.
10. Wood used in manufacturing furniture.

Classify costs into three classes of manufacturing costs.
(SO 3), C

Instructions
Classify the above items into the following categories: (a) direct materials, (b) direct labor, and (c) manufacturing overhead.

E14-3 Ryan Corporation incurred the following costs while manufacturing its product.

Identify types of cost and explain their accounting.
(SO 3, 4), C

Materials used in product	$100,000	Advertising expense	$45,000
Depreciation on plant	60,000	Property taxes on plant	14,000
Property taxes on store	7,500	Delivery expense	21,000
Labor costs of assembly-line workers	110,000	Sales commissions	35,000
Factory supplies used	13,000	Salaries paid to sales clerks	50,000

Instructions
(a) Identify each of the above costs as direct materials, direct labor, manufacturing overhead, or period costs.
(b) Explain the basic difference in accounting for product costs and period costs.

E14-4 Knight Company reports the following costs and expenses in May.

Determine the total amount of various types of costs.
(SO 3, 4), AP

Factory utilities	$ 15,500	Direct labor	$69,100
Depreciation on factory equipment	12,650	Sales salaries	46,400
Depreciation on delivery trucks	3,800	Property taxes on factory building	2,500
Indirect factory labor	48,900	Repairs to office equipment	1,300
Indirect materials	80,800	Factory repairs	2,000
Direct materials used	137,600	Advertising	15,000
Factory manager's salary	8,000	Office supplies used	2,640

Instructions

From the information, determine the total amount of:
(a) Manufacturing overhead.
(b) Product costs.
(c) Period costs.

Classify various costs into different cost categories.

(SO 3, 4), C

E14-5 Ikerd Company is a manufacturer of personal computers. Various costs and expenses associated with its operations are as follows.
1. Property taxes on the factory building.
2. Production superintendents' salaries.
3. Memory boards and chips used in assembling computers.
4. Depreciation on the factory equipment.
5. Salaries for assembly line quality control inspectors.
6. Sales commissions paid to sell personal computers.
7. Electrical components used in assembling computers.
8. Wages of workers assembling personal computers.
9. Soldering materials used on factory assembly lines.
10. Salaries for the night security guards for the factory building.

The company intends to classify these costs and expenses into the following categories: (a) direct materials, (b) direct labor, (c) manufacturing overhead, and (d) period costs.

Instructions

List the items (1) through (10). For each item, indicate the cost category to which it belongs.

Classify various costs into different cost categories.

(SO 3), C

E14-6 The administrators of Crawford County's Memorial Hospital are interested in identifying the various costs and expenses that are incurred in producing a patient's X-ray. A list of such costs and expenses is presented below.
1. Salaries for the X-ray machine technicians.
2. Wages for the hospital janitorial personnel.
3. Film costs for the X-ray machines.
4. Property taxes on the hospital building.
5. Salary of the X-ray technicians' supervisor.
6. Electricity costs for the X-ray department.
7. Maintenance and repairs on the X-ray machines.
8. X-ray department supplies.
9. Depreciation on the X-ray department equipment.
10. Depreciation on the hospital building.

Homework materials related to service companies are indicated by this icon.

The administrators want these costs and expenses classified as: (a) direct materials, (b) direct labor, or (c) service overhead.

Instructions

List the items (1) through (10). For each item, indicate the cost category to which the item belongs.

Classify various costs into different cost categories.

(SO 4), AP

E14-7 Kwik Delivery Service reports the following costs and expenses in June 2012.

Indirect materials	$ 5,400	Drivers' salaries	$16,000
Depreciation on delivery equipment	11,200	Advertising	3,600
Dispatcher's salary	5,000	Delivery equipment repairs	300
Property taxes on office building	870	Office supplies	650
CEO's salary	12,000	Office utilities	990
Gas and oil for delivery trucks	2,200	Repairs on office equipment	180

Instructions

Determine the total amount of (a) delivery service (product) costs and (b) period costs.

Compute cost of goods manufactured and sold.

(SO 5, 6), AP

E14-8 Lopez Corporation incurred the following costs while manufacturing its product.

Materials used in product	$120,000	Advertising expense	$45,000
Depreciation on plant	60,000	Property taxes on plant	14,000
Property taxes on store	7,500	Delivery expense	21,000
Labor costs of assembly-line		Sales commissions	35,000
workers	110,000	Salaries paid to sales	
Factory supplies used	23,000	clerks	50,000

Work in process inventory was $12,000 at January 1 and $15,500 at December 31. Finished goods inventory was $60,000 at January 1 and $45,600 at December 31.

Instructions
(a) Compute cost of goods manufactured.
(b) Compute cost of goods sold.

E14-9 An incomplete cost of goods manufactured schedule is presented below.

Determine missing amounts in cost of goods manufactured schedule.

(SO 6), AP

MOLINA MANUFACTURING COMPANY
Cost of Goods Manufactured Schedule
For the Year Ended December 31, 2012

Work in process (1/1)			$210,000
Direct materials			
Raw materials inventory (1/1)	$?		
Add: Raw materials purchases	158,000		
Total raw materials available for use	?		
Less: Raw materials inventory (12/31)	22,500		
Direct materials used		$190,000	
Direct labor		?	
Manufacturing overhead			
Indirect labor	18,000		
Factory depreciation	36,000		
Factory utilities	68,000		
Total overhead		122,000	
Total manufacturing costs			?
Total cost of work in process			?
Less: Work in process (12/31)			81,000
Cost of goods manufactured			$530,000

Instructions
Complete the cost of goods manufactured schedule for Molina Manufacturing Company.

E14-10 Manufacturing cost data for Copa Company are presented below.

Determine the missing amount of different cost items.

(SO 6), AN

	Case A	Case B	Case C
Direct materials used	(a)	$68,400	$130,000
Direct labor	$ 57,000	86,000	(g)
Manufacturing overhead	46,500	81,600	102,000
Total manufacturing costs	195,650	(d)	253,700
Work in process 1/1/12	(b)	16,500	(h)
Total cost of work in process	221,500	(e)	337,000
Work in process 12/31/12	(c)	11,000	70,000
Cost of goods manufactured	185,275	(f)	(i)

Instructions
Indicate the missing amount for each letter (a) through (i).

E14-11 Incomplete manufacturing cost data for Colaw Company for 2012 are presented as follows for four different situations.

Determine the missing amount of different cost items, and prepare a condensed cost of goods manufactured schedule.

(SO 6), AN

	Direct Materials Used	Direct Labor Used	Manufac- turing Overhead	Total Manufac- turing Costs	Work in Process 1/1	Work in Process 12/31	Cost of Goods Manufac- tured
(1)	$127,000	$140,000	$ 87,000	(a)	$33,000	(b)	$360,000
(2)	(c)	200,000	132,000	$450,000	(d)	$40,000	470,000
(3)	80,000	100,000	(e)	255,000	60,000	80,000	(f)
(4)	70,000	(g)	75,000	288,000	45,000	(h)	270,000

Instructions
(a) Indicate the missing amount for each letter.
(b) Prepare a condensed cost of goods manufactured schedule for situation (1) for the year ended December 31, 2012.

Prepare a cost of goods manufactured schedule and a partial income statement.
(SO 5, 6), AP

E14-12 Cepeda Corporation has the following cost records for June 2012.

Indirect factory labor	$ 4,500	Factory utilities	$ 400
Direct materials used	20,000	Depreciation, factory equipment	1,400
Work in process, 6/1/12	3,000	Direct labor	40,000
Work in process, 6/30/12	3,800	Maintenance, factory equipment	1,800
Finished goods, 6/1/12	5,000	Indirect materials	2,200
Finished goods, 6/30/12	7,500	Factory manager's salary	3,000

Instructions
(a) Prepare a cost of goods manufactured schedule for June 2012.
(b) Prepare an income statement through gross profit for June 2012 assuming net sales are $92,100.

Classify various costs into different categories and prepare cost of services provided schedule.
(SO 4, 5, 6), AN

E14-13 Joyce Tombert, the bookkeeper for Marks Consulting, a political consulting firm, has recently completed a managerial accounting course at her local college. One of the topics covered in the course was the cost of goods manufactured schedule. Joyce wondered if such a schedule could be prepared for her firm. She realized that, as a service-oriented company, it would have no Work in Process inventory to consider.

Listed below are the costs her firm incurred for the month ended August 31, 2012.

Supplies used on consulting contracts	$ 1,200
Supplies used in the administrative offices	1,500
Depreciation on equipment used for contract work	900
Depreciation used on administrative office equipment	1,050
Salaries of professionals working on contracts	15,600
Salaries of administrative office personnel	7,700
Janitorial services for professional offices	400
Janitorial services for administrative offices	500
Insurance on contract operations	800
Insurance on administrative operations	900
Utilities for contract operations	1,400
Utilities for administrative offices	1,300

Instructions
(a) Prepare a schedule of cost of contract services provided (similar to a cost of goods manufactured schedule) for the month.
(b) For those costs not included in (a), explain how they would be classified and reported in the financial statements.

Prepare a cost of goods manufactured schedule and a partial income statement.
(SO 5, 6, 7), AP

E14-14 The following information is available for Aikman Company.

	January 1, 2012	2012	December 31, 2012
Raw materials inventory	$21,000		$30,000
Work in process inventory	13,500		17,200
Finished goods inventory	27,000		21,000
Materials purchased		$150,000	
Direct labor		220,000	
Manufacturing overhead		180,000	
Sales		910,000	

Instructions
(a) Compute cost of goods manufactured.
(b) Prepare an income statement through gross profit.
(c) Show the presentation of the ending inventories on the December 31, 2012, balance sheet.
(d) How would the income statement and balance sheet of a merchandising company be different from Aikman's financial statements?

Indicate in which schedule or financial statement(s) different cost items will appear. (SO 5, 6, 7), C

E14-15 Chambers Manufacturing Company produces blankets. From its accounting records, it prepares the following schedule and financial statements on a yearly basis.
(a) Cost of goods manufactured schedule.

(b) Income statement.
(c) Balance sheet.

The following items are found in its ledger and accompanying data.

1. Direct labor
2. Raw materials inventory, 1/1
3. Work in process inventory, 12/31
4. Finished goods inventory, 1/1
5. Indirect labor
6. Depreciation on factory machinery
7. Work in process, 1/1
8. Finished goods inventory, 12/31
9. Factory maintenance salaries
10. Cost of goods manufactured
11. Depreciation on delivery equipment
12. Cost of goods available for sale
13. Direct materials used
14. Heat and electricity for factory
15. Repairs to roof of factory building
16. Cost of raw materials purchases

Instructions
List the items (1)–(16). For each item, indicate by using the appropriate letter or letters, the schedule and/or financial statement(s) in which the item will appear.

E14-16 An analysis of the accounts of Roberts Manufacturing reveals the following manufacturing cost data for the month ended June 30, 2012.

Prepare a cost of goods manufactured schedule, and present the ending inventories on the balance sheet.
(SO 6, 7), AP

Inventories	Beginning	Ending
Raw materials	$9,000	$13,100
Work in process	5,000	7,000
Finished goods	9,000	8,000

Costs incurred: Raw materials purchases $54,000, direct labor $47,000, manufacturing overhead $19,900. The specific overhead costs were: indirect labor $5,500, factory insurance $4,000, machinery depreciation $4,000, machinery repairs $1,800, factory utilities $3,100, miscellaneous factory costs $1,500. Assume that all raw materials used were direct materials.

Instructions
(a) Prepare the cost of goods manufactured schedule for the month ended June 30, 2012.
(b) Show the presentation of the ending inventories on the June 30, 2012, balance sheet.

E14-17 Buhler Motor Company manufactures automobiles. During September 2012, the company purchased 5,000 head lamps at a cost of $10 per lamp. Buhler withdrew 4,650 lamps from the warehouse during the month. Fifty of these lamps were used to replace the head lamps in autos used by traveling sales staff. The remaining 4,600 lamps were put in autos manufactured during the month.

Of the autos put into production during September 2012, 90% were completed and transferred to the company's storage lot. Of the cars completed during the month, 70% were sold by September 30.

Determine the amount of cost to appear in various accounts, and indicate in which financial statements these accounts would appear.
(SO 5, 6, 7), AP

Instructions
(a) Determine the cost of head lamps that would appear in each of the following accounts at September 30, 2012: Raw Materials, Work in Process, Finished Goods, Cost of Goods Sold, and Selling Expenses.
(b) ▒▒▒▒▶ Write a short memo to the chief accountant, indicating whether and where each of the accounts in (a) would appear on the income statement or on the balance sheet at September 30, 2012.

E14-18 The following is a list of terms related to managerial accounting practices.
1. Activity-based costing.
2. Just-in-time inventory.
3. Balanced scorecard.
4. Value chain.

Identify various managerial accounting practices.
(SO 8), C

Instructions
Match each of the terms with the statement below that best describes the term.
(a) ____ A performance-measurement technique that attempts to consider and evaluate all aspects of performance using financial and nonfinancial measures in an integrated fashion.
(b) ____ The group of activities associated with providing a product or service.

(c) ____ An approach used to reduce the cost associated with handling and holding inventory by reducing the amount of inventory on hand.

(d) ____ A method used to allocate overhead to products based on each product's use of the activities that cause the incurrence of the overhead cost.

Prepare a partial worksheet for a manufacturing firm.
(SO 9), AP

*E14-19 Data for Roberts Manufacturing are presented in E14-16.

Instructions
Beginning with the adjusted trial balance, prepare a partial worksheet for Roberts Manufacturing using the format shown in Illustration 14A-2.

Exercises: Set B and Challenge Exercises

Visit the book's companion website, at **www.wiley.com/college/kimmel**, and choose the Student Companion site to access Exercise Set B and Challenge Exercises.

Problems: Set A

Classify manufacturing costs into different categories and compute the unit cost.
(SO 3, 4), AP

P14-1A Lott Company specializes in manufacturing a unique model of bicycle helmet. The model is well accepted by consumers, and the company has enough orders to keep the factory production at 10,000 helmets per month (80% of its full capacity). Lott's monthly manufacturing cost and other expense data are as follows.

Rent on factory equipment	$ 9,000
Insurance on factory building	1,500
Raw materials (plastics, polystyrene, etc.)	75,000
Utility costs for factory	900
Supplies for general office	300
Wages for assembly line workers	53,000
Depreciation on office equipment	800
Miscellaneous materials (glue, thread, etc.)	1,100
Factory manager's salary	5,700
Property taxes on factory building	400
Advertising for helmets	14,000
Sales commissions	10,000
Depreciation on factory building	1,500

Instructions

(a) DM $75,000
    DL $53,000
    MO $20,100
    PC $25,100

(a) Prepare an answer sheet with the following column headings.

	Product Costs			
Cost Item	**Direct Materials**	**Direct Labor**	**Manufacturing Overhead**	**Period Costs**

Enter each cost item on your answer sheet, placing the dollar amount under the appropriate headings. Total the dollar amounts in each of the columns.

(b) Compute the cost to produce one helmet.

Classify manufacturing costs into different categories and compute the unit cost.
(SO 3, 4), AP

P14-2A Bell Company, a manufacturer of audio systems, started its production in October 2012. For the preceding 3 years, Bell had been a retailer of audio systems. After a thorough survey of audio system markets, Bell decided to turn its retail store into an audio equipment factory.

Raw materials cost for an audio system will total $74 per unit. Workers on the production lines are on average paid $12 per hour. An audio system usually takes 5 hours to complete. In addition, the rent on the equipment used to assemble audio systems amounts to $4,900 per month. Indirect materials cost $5 per system. A supervisor was hired to oversee production; her monthly salary is $3,000.

Factory janitorial costs are $1,300 monthly. Advertising costs for the audio system will be $9,500 per month. The factory building depreciation expense is $7,800 per year. Property taxes on the factory building will be $9,000 per year.

Instructions

(a) Prepare an answer sheet with the following column headings.

Cost Item	Product Costs			Period Costs
	Direct Materials	Direct Labor	Manufacturing Overhead	

Assuming that Bell manufactures, on average, 1,500 audio systems per month, enter each cost item on your answer sheet, placing the dollar amount per month under the appropriate headings. Total the dollar amounts in each of the columns.

(b) Compute the cost to produce one audio system.

P14-3A Incomplete manufacturing costs, expenses, and selling data for two different cases are as follows.

Indicate the missing amount of different cost items, and prepare a condensed cost of goods manufactured schedule, an income statement, and a partial balance sheet.

(SO 5, 6, 7), AN

	Case	
	1	2
Direct materials used	$ 9,600	$ (g)
Direct labor	5,000	8,000
Manufacturing overhead	8,000	4,000
Total manufacturing costs	(a)	16,000
Beginning work in process inventory	1,000	(h)
Ending work in process inventory	(b)	3,000
Sales	24,500	(i)
Sales discounts	2,500	1,400
Cost of goods manufactured	17,000	22,000
Beginning finished goods inventory	(c)	3,300
Goods available for sale	20,000	(j)
Cost of goods sold	(d)	(k)
Ending finished goods inventory	3,400	2,500
Gross profit	(e)	7,000
Operating expenses	2,500	(l)
Net income	(f)	5,000

Instructions

(a) Indicate the missing amount for each letter.

(b) Prepare a condensed cost of goods manufactured schedule for Case 1.

(c) Prepare an income statement and the current assets section of the balance sheet for Case 1. Assume that in Case 1 the other items in the current assets section are as follows: Cash $4,000, Receivables (net) $15,000, Raw Materials $600, and Prepaid Expenses $400.

P14-4A The following data were taken from the records of Clarkson Manufacturing Company for the fiscal year ended June 30, 2012.

Prepare a cost of goods manufactured schedule, a partial income statement, and a partial balance sheet.

(SO 5, 6, 7), AP

Raw Materials		Factory Insurance	$ 4,600	
Inventory 7/1/11	$ 48,000	Factory Machinery		
Raw Materials		Depreciation	16,000	
Inventory 6/30/12	39,600	Factory Utilities	27,600	
Finished Goods		Office Utilities Expense	8,650	
Inventory 7/1/11	96,000	Sales	534,000	
Finished Goods		Sales Discounts	4,200	
Inventory 6/30/12	75,900	Plant Manager's Salary	58,000	
Work in Process		Factory Property Taxes	9,600	
Inventory 7/1/11	19,800	Factory Repairs	1,400	
Work in Process		Raw Materials Purchases	96,400	
Inventory 6/30/12	18,600	Cash	32,000	
Direct Labor	139,250			
Indirect Labor	24,460			
Accounts Receivable	27,000			

Instructions

(a) Prepare a cost of goods manufactured schedule. (Assume all raw materials used were direct materials.)

(b) Prepare an income statement through gross profit.

(c) Prepare the current assets section of the balance sheet at June 30, 2012.

Prepare a cost of goods manufactured schedule and a correct income statement.

(SO 5, 6), AN

P14-5A Phillips Company is a manufacturer of computers. Its controller resigned in October 2012. An inexperienced assistant accountant has prepared the following income statement for the month of October 2012.

PHILLIPS COMPANY
Income Statement
For the Month Ended October 31, 2012

Sales (net)		$780,000
Less: Operating expenses		
Raw materials purchases	$264,000	
Direct labor cost	190,000	
Advertising expense	90,000	
Selling and administrative salaries	75,000	
Rent on factory facilities	60,000	
Depreciation on sales equipment	45,000	
Depreciation on factory equipment	31,000	
Indirect labor cost	28,000	
Utilities expense	12,000	
Insurance expense	8,000	803,000
Net loss		$(23,000)

Prior to October 2012, the company had been profitable every month. The company's president is concerned about the accuracy of the income statement. As her friend, you have been asked to review the income statement and make necessary corrections. After examining other manufacturing cost data, you have acquired additional information as follows.

1. Inventory balances at the beginning and end of October were:

	October 1	October 31
Raw materials	$18,000	$29,000
Work in process	16,000	14,000
Finished goods	30,000	45,000

2. Only 75% of the utilities expense and 60% of the insurance expense apply to factory operations. The remaining amounts should be charged to selling and administrative activities.

Instructions

(a) CGM $577,800
(b) NI $ 1,000

(a) Prepare a schedule of cost of goods manufactured for October 2012.
(b) Prepare a correct income statement for October 2012.

Complete a worksheet; prepare a cost of goods manufactured schedule, an income statement, and a balance sheet; journalize and post the closing entries.

(SO 9), AP

*P14-6A Garrett Manufacturing Company uses a simple manufacturing accounting system. At the end of its fiscal year on August 31, 2012, the adjusted trial balance contains the following accounts.

Debits		Credits	
Cash	$ 16,700	Accumulated Depreciation	$ 353,000
Accounts Receivable (net)	62,900	Notes Payable	45,000
Finished Goods Inventory	56,000	Accounts Payable	36,200
Work in Process Inventory	27,800	Income Taxes Payable	9,000
Raw Materials Inventory	37,200	Common Stock	352,000
Plant Assets	870,000	Retained Earnings	215,300
Raw Materials Purchases	236,500	Sales	988,000
Direct Labor	283,900		$1,998,500
Indirect Labor	27,400		
Factory Repairs	17,200		
Factory Depreciation	16,000		
Factory Manager's Salary	60,000		
Factory Insurance	11,000		
Factory Property Taxes	14,900		
Factory Utilities	13,300		
Selling Expenses	96,500		
Administrative Expenses	115,200		
Income Tax Expense	36,000		
	$1,998,500		

Physical inventory accounts on August 31, 2012, show the following inventory amounts: Finished Goods $50,600, Work in Process $23,400, and Raw Materials $44,500.

Instructions
(a) Enter the adjusted trial balance data on a worksheet in financial statement order and complete the worksheet.
(b) Prepare a cost of goods manufactured schedule for the year.
(c) Prepare an income statement for the year and a balance sheet at August 31, 2012.
(d) Journalize the closing entries.
(e) Post the closing entries to Manufacturing Summary and to Income Summary.

(b) CGM $677,300
(c) NI $ 57,600

Problems: Set B

P14-1B   Agler Company specializes in manufacturing motorcycle helmets. The company has enough orders to keep the factory production at 1,000 motorcycle helmets per month. Agler's monthly manufacturing cost and other expense data are as follows.

Classify manufacturing costs into different categories and compute the unit cost.
(SO 3, 4), AP

Maintenance costs on factory building	$ 1,500
Factory manager's salary	5,500
Advertising for helmets	8,000
Sales commissions	4,000
Depreciation on factory building	700
Rent on factory equipment	6,000
Insurance on factory building	3,000
Raw materials (plastic, polystyrene, etc.)	25,000
Utility costs for factory	800
Supplies for general office	200
Wages for assembly line workers	54,000
Depreciation on office equipment	500
Miscellaneous materials (glue, thread, etc.)	2,000

Instructions
(a) Prepare an answer sheet with the following column headings.

(a) DM $25,000
DL $54,000
MO $19,500
PC $12,700

	Product Costs			
Cost Item	Direct Materials	Direct Labor	Manufacturing Overhead	Period Costs

Enter each cost item on your answer sheet, placing the dollar amount under the appropriate headings. Total the dollar amounts in each of the columns.
(b) Compute the cost to produce one motorcycle helmet.

P14-2B   Elliott Company, a manufacturer of tennis rackets, started production in November 2011. For the preceding 5 years, Elliott had been a retailer of sports equipment. After a thorough survey of tennis racket markets, Elliott decided to turn its retail store into a tennis racket factory.

Classify manufacturing costs into different categories and compute the unit cost.
(SO 3, 4), AP

Raw materials cost for a tennis racket will total $23 per racket. Workers on the production lines are paid on average $15 per hour. A racket usually takes 2 hours to complete. In addition, the rent on the equipment used to produce rackets amounts to $1,300 per month. Indirect materials cost $3 per racket. A supervisor was hired to oversee production; her monthly salary is $3,500.

Janitorial costs are $1,400 monthly. Advertising costs for the rackets will be $8,000 per month. The factory building depreciation expense is $8,400 per year. Property taxes on the factory building will be $9,600 per year.

Instructions
(a) Prepare an answer sheet with the following column headings.

(a) DM $57,500
DL $75,000
MO $15,200
PC $ 8,000

	Product Costs			
Cost Item	Direct Materials	Direct Labor	Manufacturing Overhead	Period Costs

Assuming that Elliott manufactures, on average, 2,500 tennis rackets per month, enter each cost item on your answer sheet, placing the dollar amount per month under the appropriate headings. Total the dollar amounts in each of the columns.
(b) Compute the cost to produce one racket.

Indicate the missing amount of different cost items, and prepare a condensed cost of goods manufactured schedule, an income statement, and a partial balance sheet.

(SO 5, 6, 7), AN

P14-3B Incomplete manufacturing costs, expenses, and selling data for two different cases are as follows.

	Case A	Case B
Direct materials used	$ 6,300	$ (g)
Direct labor	3,000	4,000
Manufacturing overhead	6,000	5,000
Total manufacturing costs	(a)	16,000
Beginning work in process inventory	1,000	(h)
Ending work in process inventory	(b)	2,000
Sales	22,500	(i)
Sales discounts	1,500	1,200
Cost of goods manufactured	15,800	20,000
Beginning finished goods inventory	(c)	5,000
Goods available for sale	18,300	(j)
Cost of goods sold	(d)	(k)
Ending finished goods inventory	1,200	2,500
Gross profit	(e)	6,000
Operating expenses	2,700	(l)
Net income	(f)	2,200

Instructions
(a) Indicate the missing amount for each letter.
(b) Prepare a condensed cost of goods manufactured schedule for Case A.

(c) Current assets $15,600

(c) Prepare an income statement and the current assets section of the balance sheet for Case A. Assume that in Case A the other items in the current assets section are as follows: Cash $3,000, Receivables (net) $10,000, Raw Materials $700, and Prepaid Expenses $200.

Prepare a cost of goods manufactured schedule, a partial income statement, and a partial balance sheet.

(SO 5, 6, 7), AP

P14-4B The following data were taken from the records of Moxie Manufacturing Company for the year ended December 31, 2012.

Raw Materials		Factory Insurance	$ 7,400
Inventory 1/1/12	$ 47,000	Factory Machinery	
Raw Materials		Depreciation	7,700
Inventory 12/31/12	44,200	Factory Utilities	12,900
Finished Goods		Office Utilities Expense	8,600
Inventory 1/1/12	85,000	Sales	465,000
Finished Goods		Sales Discounts	2,500
Inventory 12/31/12	57,800	Plant Manager's Salary	60,000
Work in Process		Factory Property Taxes	6,100
Inventory 1/1/12	9,500	Factory Repairs	800
Work in Process		Raw Materials Purchases	62,500
Inventory 12/31/12	8,000	Cash	18,000
Direct Labor	145,100		
Indirect Labor	18,100		
Accounts Receivable	27,000		

Instructions

(a) CGM $324,900

(a) Prepare a cost of goods manufactured schedule. (Assume all raw materials used were direct materials.)

(b) Gross profit $110,400
(c) Current assets $155,000

(b) Prepare an income statement through gross profit.
(c) Prepare the current assets section of the balance sheet at December 31.

P14-5B Ortiz Company is a manufacturer of toys. Its controller resigned in August 2012. An inexperienced assistant accountant has prepared the following income statement for the month of August 2012.

Prepare a cost of goods manufactured schedule and a correct income statement.

(SO 5, 6), AN

ORTIZ COMPANY
Income Statement
For the Month Ended August 31, 2012

Sales (net)		$675,000
Less: Operating expenses		
Raw materials purchases	$220,000	
Direct labor cost	160,000	
Advertising expense	75,000	
Selling and administrative salaries	70,000	
Rent on factory facilities	60,000	
Depreciation on sales equipment	50,000	
Depreciation on factory equipment	35,000	
Indirect labor cost	20,000	
Utilities expense	10,000	
Insurance expense	5,000	705,000
Net loss		$ (30,000)

Prior to August 2012, the company had been profitable every month. The company's president is concerned about the accuracy of the income statement. As her friend, you have been asked to review the income statement and make necessary corrections. After examining other manufacturing cost data, you have acquired additional information as follows.

1. Inventory balances at the beginning and end of August were:

	August 1	August 31
Raw materials	$19,500	$35,000
Work in process	25,000	21,000
Finished goods	40,000	52,000

2. Only 60% of the utilities expense and 70% of the insurance expense apply to factory operations; the remaining amounts should be charged to selling and administrative activities.

Instructions
(a) Prepare a cost of goods manufactured schedule for August 2012.
(b) Prepare a correct income statement for August 2012.

(a) CGM $493,000
(b) NL $ (6,500)

Problems: Set C

Visit the book's companion website, at **www.wiley.com/college/kimmel**, and choose the Student Companion site to access Problem Set C.

Waterways Continuing Problem

(*Note:* The Waterways Problem begins in Chapter 14 and continues in the remaining chapters. You can also find this problem at the book's Student Companion site.)

WCP14 Waterways Corporation is a private corporation formed for the purpose of providing the products and the services needed to irrigate farms, parks, commercial projects, and private lawns. It has a centrally located factory in a U.S. city that manufactures the products it markets to retail outlets across the nation. It also maintains a division that provides installation and warranty servicing in six metropolitan areas.

The mission of Waterways is to manufacture quality parts that can be used for effective irrigation projects that also conserve water. By that effort, the company hopes to satisfy its customers, provide rapid and responsible service, and serve the community and the employees who represent them in each community.

The company has been growing rapidly, so management is considering new ideas to help the company continue its growth and maintain the high quality of its products.

Waterways was founded by Will Winkman, who is the company president and chief executive officer (CEO). Working with him from the company's inception was Will's brother, Ben, whose sprinkler designs and ideas about the installation of proper systems have been a major basis of the company's success. Ben is the vice president who oversees all aspects of design and production in the company.

The factory itself is managed by Todd Senter who hires his line managers to supervise the factory employees. The factory makes all of the parts for the irrigation systems. The purchasing department is managed by Hector Hines.

The installation and training division is overseen by vice president Henry Writer, who supervises the managers of the six local installation operations. Each of these local managers hires his or her own local service people. These service employees are trained by the home office under Henry Writer's direction because of the uniqueness of the company's products.

There is a small human resources department under the direction of Sally Fenton, a vice president who handles the employee paperwork, though hiring is actually performed by the separate departments. Sam Totter is the vice president who heads the sales and marketing area; he oversees 10 well-trained salespeople.

The accounting and finance division of the company is headed by Abe Headman, who is the chief financial officer (CFO) and a company vice president; he is a member of the Institute of Management Accountants and holds a certificate in management accounting. He has a small staff of Certified Public Accountants, including a controller and a treasurer, and a staff of accounting input operators who maintain the financial records.

A partial list of Waterway's accounts and their balances for the month of November follows.

Accounts Receivable	$275,000
Advertising Expenses	54,000
Cash	260,000
Depreciation—Factory Equipment	16,800
Depreciation—Office Equipment	2,400
Direct Labor	42,000
Factory Supplies Used	16,800
Factory Utilities	10,200
Finished Goods Inventory, November 30	68,800
Finished Goods Inventory, October 31	72,550
Indirect Labor	48,000
Office Supplies Expense	1,600
Other Administrative Expenses	72,000
Prepaid Expenses	41,250
Raw Materials Inventory, November 30	52,700
Raw Materials Inventory, October 31	38,000
Raw Materials Purchases	184,500
Rent—Factory Equipment	47,000
Repairs—Factory Equipment	4,500
Salaries	325,000
Sales	1,350,000
Sales Commissions	40,500
Work in Process Inventory, October 31	52,700
Work in Process Inventory, November 30	42,000

Instructions

(a) Based on the information given, construct an organizational chart of Waterways Corporation.

(b) A list of accounts and their values are given above. From this information, prepare a cost of goods manufactured schedule, an income statement, and a partial balance sheet for Waterways Corporation for the month of November.

broadening your perspective

DECISION MAKING ACROSS THE ORGANIZATION

BYP14-1 Wendall Manufacturing Company specializes in producing fashion outfits. On July 31, 2012, a tornado touched down at its factory and general office. The inventories in the warehouse and the factory were completely destroyed as was the general office nearby. Next morning, through a careful search of the disaster site, however, Bill Francis, the company's controller, and Elizabeth Walton, the cost accountant, were able to recover a small part of manufacturing cost data for the current month.

"What a horrible experience," sighed Bill "And the worst part is that we may not have enough records to use in filing an insurance claim."

"It was terrible," replied Elizabeth. "However, I managed to recover some of the manufacturing cost data that I was working on yesterday afternoon. The data indicate that our direct labor cost in July totaled $250,000 and that we had purchased $365,000 of raw materials. Also, I recall that the amount of raw materials used for July was $350,000. But I'm not sure this information will help. The rest of our records are blown away."

"Well, not exactly," said Bill. "I was working on the year-to-date income statement when the tornado warning was announced. My recollection is that our sales in July were $1,240,000 and our gross profit ratio has been 40% of sales. Also, I can remember that our cost of goods available for sale was $770,000 for July."

"Maybe we can work something out from this information!" exclaimed Elizabeth. "My experience tells me that our manufacturing overhead is usually 60% of direct labor."

"Hey, look what I just found," cried Elizabeth. "It's a copy of this June's balance sheet, and it shows that our inventories as of June 30 are Finished goods $38,000, Work in process $25,000, and Raw materials $19,000."

"Super," yelled Bill. "Let's go work something out."

In order to file an insurance claim, Wendall Company must determine the amount of its inventories as of July 31, 2012, the date of the tornado touchdown.

Instructions
With the class divided into groups, determine the amount of cost in the Raw Materials, Work in Process, and Finished Goods inventory accounts as of the date of the tornado touchdown.

MANAGERIAL ANALYSIS

BYP14-2 Tenrack is a fairly large manufacturing company located in the southern United States. The company manufactures tennis rackets, tennis balls, tennis clothing, and tennis shoes, all bearing the company's distinctive logo, a large green question mark on a white flocked tennis ball. The company's sales have been increasing over the past 10 years.

The tennis racket division has recently implemented several advanced manufacturing techniques. Robot arms hold the tennis rackets in place while glue dries, and machine vision systems check for defects. The engineering and design team uses computerized drafting and testing of new products. The following managers work in the tennis racket division.

Jason Dennis, sales manager (supervises all sales representatives).
Peggy Groneman, technical specialist (supervises computer programmers).
Dave Marley, cost accounting manager (supervises cost accountants).
Kevin Carson, production supervisor (supervises all manufacturing employees).
Sally Renner, engineer (supervises all new-product design teams).

Instructions
(a) What are the primary information needs of each manager?
(b) Which, if any, financial accounting report(s) is each likely to use?
(c) Name one special-purpose management accounting report that could be designed for each manager. Include the name of the report, the information it would contain, and how frequently it should be issued.

REAL-WORLD FOCUS

BYP14-3 Anchor Glass Container Corporation, the third largest manufacturer of glass containers in the United States, supplies beverage and food producers and consumer products manufacturers nationwide. Parent company Consumers Packaging Inc. (*Toronto Stock Exchange:* CGC) is a leading international designer and manufacturer of glass containers.

The following management discussion appeared in a recent annual report of Anchor Glass.

ANCHOR GLASS CONTAINER CORPORATION
Management Discussion

Cost of Products Sold Cost of products sold as a percentage of net sales was 89.3% in the current year compared to 87.6% in the prior year. The increase in cost of products sold as a percentage of net sales principally reflected the impact of operational problems during the second quarter of the current year at a major furnace at one of the Company's plants, higher downtime, and costs and expenses associated with an increased number of scheduled capital improvement projects, increases in labor, and certain other manufacturing costs (with no corresponding selling price increases in the current year). Reduced fixed costs from the closing of the Streator, Illinois, plant in June of the current year and productivity and efficiency gains partially offset these cost increases.

Instructions
What factors affect the costs of products sold at Anchor Glass Container Corporation?

MANAGERIAL ACCOUNTING ON THE WEB

BYP14-4 The Institute of Management Accountants (IMA) is an organization dedicated to excellence in the practice of management accounting and financial management.

Address: **www.imanet.org,** or go to **www.wiley.com/college/kimmel**

Instructions
At the IMA's home page, locate the answers to the following questions.
(a) How many members does the IMA have, and what are their job titles?
(b) What are some of the benefits of joining the IMA as a student?
(c) Use the chapter locator function to locate the IMA chapter nearest you, and find the name of the chapter president.

COMMUNICATION ACTIVITY

BYP14-5 Refer to Problem 14–5A and add the following requirement.
Prepare a letter to the president of the company, Shelly Phillips, describing the changes you made. Explain clearly why net income is different after the changes. Keep the following points in mind as you compose your letter.

1. This is a letter to the president of a company, who is your friend. The style should be generally formal, but you may relax some requirements. For example, you may call the president by her first name.

2. Executives are very busy. Your letter should tell the president your main results first (for example, the amount of net income).

3. You should include brief explanations so that the president can understand the changes you made in the calculations.

ETHICS CASE

BYP14-6 Steve Morgan, controller for Newton Industries, was reviewing production cost reports for the year. One amount in these reports continued to bother him—advertising. During the year, the company had instituted an expensive advertising campaign to sell some of its slower-moving products. It was still too early to tell whether the advertising campaign was successful.

There had been much internal debate as how to report advertising cost. The vice president of finance argued that advertising costs should be reported as a cost of production, just like direct materials and direct labor. He therefore recommended that this cost be identified as manufacturing overhead and reported as part of inventory costs until sold. Others disagreed. Morgan believed that this cost should be reported as an expense of the current period, based on the conservatism principle. Others argued that it should be reported as Prepaid Advertising and reported as a current asset.

The president finally had to decide the issue. He argued that these costs should be reported as inventory. His arguments were practical ones. He noted that the company was experiencing financial difficulty and expensing this amount in the current period might jeopardize a planned bond offering. Also, by reporting the advertising costs as inventory rather than as prepaid advertising, less attention would be directed to it by the financial community.

Instructions
(a) Who are the stakeholders in this situation?
(b) What are the ethical issues involved in this situation?
(c) What would you do if you were Steve Morgan?

"ALL ABOUT YOU" ACTIVITY

BYP14-7   The primary purpose of managerial accounting is to provide information useful for management decisions. Many of the managerial accounting techniques that you learn in this course will be useful for decisions you make in your everyday life.

Instructions
For each of the following managerial accounting techniques, read the definition provided and then provide an example of a personal situation that would benefit from use of this technique.
(a) Break-even point (page 951).
(b) Budget (page 1032).
(c) Balanced scorecard (page 1153).
(d) Capital budgeting (page 1198).

Answers to Insight and Accounting Across the Organization Questions

p. 750 Even the Best Have to Get Better Q: What are some of the steps that this company has taken in order to ensure that production meets demand? **A:** The company has organized flexible teams, with jobs arranged by the amount of time a task takes. Employees now are multiskilled, so they can switch between tasks and products. Also, the stores now provide sales data more quickly to the manufacturing facility, so that production levels can be changed more quickly to respond to demand.

p. 755 How Many Labor Hours to Build a Car? Q: Why might Nissan production require significantly fewer labor hours? **A:** Nissan's U.S. factories are probably newer than those of Daimler-Chrysler and Ford. Newer factories tend to be more highly automated, with less reliance on production-line employees.

p. 764 Low Fares but Decent Profits Q: What are some of the cost items that would appear in the cost of services provided schedule of an airline? **A:** Some of the cost items that would appear in the cost of services provided schedule of an airline would be fuel, flight crew salaries, maintenance wages, depreciation on equipment, airport gate fees, and food-service costs.

Answers to Self-Test Questions

1. b **2.** b **3.** b **4.** b **5.** d **6.** a **7.** c **8.** c **9.** c ($200,000 + $600,000 − $250,000) **10.** c **11.** a **12.** d **13.** d **14.** d **15.** d

✔ **Remember to go back to the navigator box on the chapter opening page and check off your completed work.**

JOB ORDER COSTING

study objectives

After studying this chapter, you should be able to:

1 Explain the characteristics and purposes of cost accounting.

2 Describe the flow of costs in a job order costing system.

3 Explain the nature and importance of a job cost sheet.

4 Indicate how the predetermined overhead rate is determined and used.

5 Prepare entries for jobs completed and sold.

6 Distinguish between under- and overapplied manufacturing overhead.

✔ the navigator

Western States Fire Apparatus, Inc., of Cornelius, Oregon, is one of the few U.S. companies that makes fire trucks. The company builds about 25 trucks per year. Founded in 1941, the company is run by the children and grandchildren of the original founder.

"We buy the chassis, which is the cab and the frame," says Susan Scott, the company's bookkeeper. "In our computer, we set up an account into which all of the direct material that is purchased for that particular job is charged." Other direct materials include the water pump—which can cost $10,000—the lights, the siren, ladders, and hoses.

As for direct labor, the production workers fill out time tickets that tell what jobs they worked on. Usually, the company is building four trucks at any one time. On payday, the controller allocates the payroll

"... AND WE'D LIKE IT IN RED"

to the appropriate job record. The company allocates indirect materials, such as nuts and bolts, wiring, lubricants, and abrasives, to each job in proportion to direct material dollars. It allocates other costs, such as insurance and supervisors' salaries, based on direct labor hours. "We need to allocate overhead in order to know what kind of price we have to charge when we submit our bids," she says.

Western gets orders through a "blind-bidding" process. That is, Western submits its bid without knowing the bid prices made by its competitors. "If we bid too low, we won't make a profit. If we bid too high, we don't get the job."

Regardless of the final price for the truck, the quality had better be first-rate. "The fire departments let you know if they don't like what you did, and you usually end up fixing it."

✔ **the navigator**

INSIDE CHAPTER 15 . . .

The Feature Story about Western States Fire Apparatus describes the manufacturing costs used in making a fire truck. It demonstrates that accurate costing is critical to the company's success. For example, in order to submit accurate bids on new jobs and to know whether it profited from past jobs, the company needs a good costing system. This chapter illustrates how these manufacturing costs are assigned to specific jobs, such as the manufacture of individual fire trucks. We begin the discussion in this chapter with an overview of the flow of costs in a job order cost accounting system. We then use a case study to explain and illustrate the documents, entries, and accounts in this type of cost accounting system.

The content and organization of Chapter 15 are as follows.

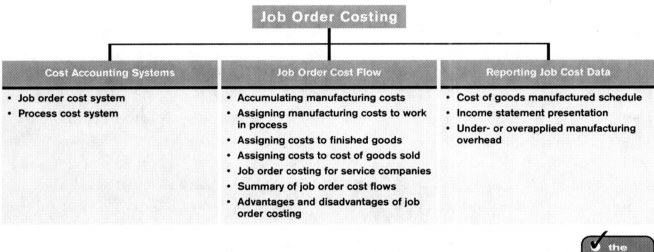

Cost Accounting Systems

study objective 1

Explain the characteristics and purposes of cost accounting.

Cost accounting involves the measuring, recording, and reporting of product costs. From the data accumulated, companies determine both the total cost and the unit cost of each product. The accuracy of the product cost information produced by the cost accounting system is critical to the success of the company. Companies use this information to determine which products to produce, what price to charge, and the amounts to produce. Accurate product cost information is also vital for effective evaluation of employee performance.

A cost accounting system consists of accounts for the various manufacturing costs. These accounts are fully integrated into the general ledger of a company. An important feature of a cost accounting system is the use of **a perpetual inventory system**. Such a system **provides immediate, up-to-date information on the cost of a product**.

There are two basic types of cost accounting systems: (1) a job order cost system and (2) a process cost system. Although cost accounting systems differ widely from company to company, most involve one of these two traditional product costing systems.

JOB ORDER COST SYSTEM

Under a job order cost system, the company assigns costs to each **job** or to each **batch** of goods. An example of a job is the manufacture of a mainframe computer by IBM, the production of a movie by Disney, or the making of a fire truck by Western States. An example of a batch is the printing of 225 wedding invitations by a local print shop, or the printing of a weekly issue of *Fortune* magazine by a high-tech printer such as Quad Graphics. Companies may complete jobs or batches to fill a specific customer order or to replenish inventory.

An important feature of job order costing is that each job or batch has its own distinguishing characteristics. For example, each house is custom built, each consulting engagement by a CPA firm is unique, and each printing job is different. **The objective is to compute the cost per job.** At each point in manufacturing a product or providing a service, the company can identify the job and its associated costs. A job order cost system measures costs for each completed job, rather than for set time periods. Illustration 15-1 shows the recording of costs in a job order cost system.

Illustration 15-1 Job order cost system

Job Order Cost System
Two jobs: Wedding Invitations and Menus

Black ink $ →
Typesetting $ →
225 Invitations $ →
225 Envelopes $
Vellum stock, pure white $
Job # 9501

Typesetting $ → MENU
Lamination $ →
→ Colored ink $
→ Yellow stock $
→ 50 Copies $
Job # 9502

Each job has distinguishing characteristics and related costs.

PROCESS COST SYSTEM

A company uses a process cost system when it manufactures a large volume of similar products. Production is continuous. Examples of a process cost system are the manufacture of cereal by Kellogg, the refining of petroleum by ExxonMobil, and the production of automobiles by General Motors. Process costing accumulates product-related costs **for a period of time** (such as a week or a month) instead of assigning costs to specific products or job orders. In process costing, companies assign the costs to departments or processes for the specified period of time. Illustration 15-2 shows examples of the use of a process cost system. We will discuss the process cost system further in Chapter 16.

Illustration 15-2 Process cost system

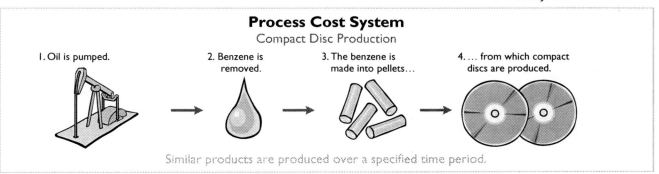

Process Cost System
Compact Disc Production

1. Oil is pumped. → 2. Benzene is removed. → 3. The benzene is made into pellets... → 4. ... from which compact discs are produced.

Similar products are produced over a specified time period.

Can a company use both types of cost systems? Yes. For example, General Motors uses process cost accounting for its standard model cars, such as Saturns and Corvettes, and job order cost accounting for a custom-made limousine for the President of the United States.

The objective of both cost accounting systems is to provide unit cost information for product pricing, cost control, inventory valuation, and financial statement presentation.

Management Insight

Jobs Won, Money Lost

Many companies suffer from poor cost accounting. As a result, they sometimes make products they should not be selling at all, or they buy other products that they could more profitably make themselves. Also, inaccurate cost data leads companies to misallocate capital and frustrates efforts by plant managers to improve efficiency.

For example, consider the case of a diversified company in the business of rebuilding diesel locomotives. The managers thought they were making money, but a consulting firm found that the company had seriously underestimated costs. The company bailed out of the business, and not a moment too soon. Says the consultant who advised the company, "The more contracts it won, the more money it lost." Given that situation, a company cannot stay in business very long!

 What type of costs do you think the company had been underestimating? (See page 837.)

Job Order Cost Flow

study objective 2

Describe the flow of costs in a job order costing system.

The flow of costs (direct materials, direct labor, and manufacturing overhead) in job order cost accounting parallels the physical flow of the materials as they are converted into finished goods. As shown in Illustration 15-3, companies assign manufacturing costs to the Work in Process Inventory account. When a job is completed, the company transfers the cost of the job to Finished Goods Inventory. Later when the goods are sold, the company transfers their cost to Cost of Goods Sold.

Illustration 15-3 Flow of costs in job order costing

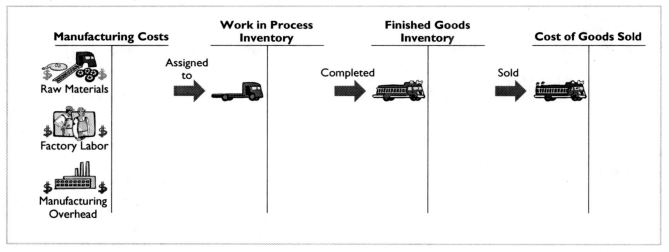

Illustration 15-3 provides a basic overview of the flow of costs in a manufacturing setting. A more detailed presentation of the flow of costs is shown in Illustration 15-4. The box in its lower-right corner indicates two major steps in the flow of costs: (1) *accumulating* the manufacturing costs incurred, and (2) *assigning* the accumulated costs to the work done. As shown, the company accumulates manufacturing costs incurred in entries 1–3 by debits to Raw Materials Inventory, Factory Labor, and Manufacturing Overhead. When the company incurs these costs, it does not attempt to associate the costs with specific jobs. The remaining entries (entries 4–8) assign manufacturing costs incurred. In the remainder of this chapter, we will use a case study to explain how a job order cost system operates.

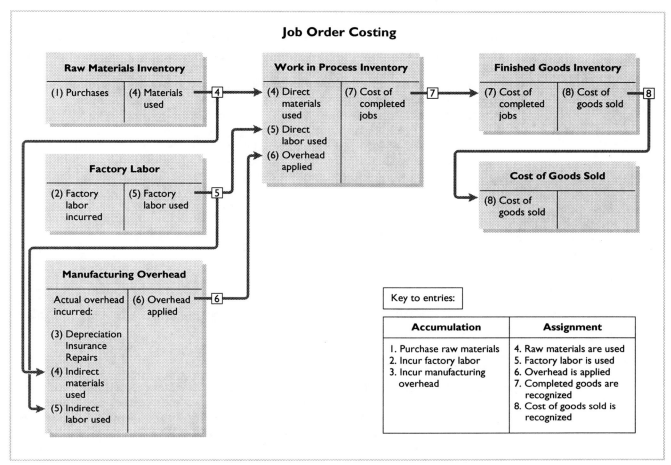

Illustration 15-4   Job
order costing system

ACCUMULATING MANUFACTURING COSTS

To illustrate a job order cost system, we will use the January transactions of Wallace Manufacturing Company, which makes machine tools.

Raw Materials Costs

When Wallace receives the raw materials it has purchased, **it debits the cost of the materials to Raw Materials Inventory**. The company would debit this account for the invoice cost of the raw materials and freight costs chargeable to the purchaser. It would credit the account for purchase discounts taken and purchase returns and allowances. Wallace makes **no effort at this point to associate the cost of materials with specific jobs or orders**.

To illustrate, assume that Wallace Manufacturing purchases 2,000 handles (Stock No. AA2746) at $5 per unit ($10,000) and 800 modules (Stock No. AA2850) at $40 per unit ($32,000) for a total cost of $42,000 ($10,000 + $32,000). The entry to record this purchase on January 4 is:

	(1)		
Jan. 4	Raw Materials Inventory	42,000	
	Accounts Payable		42,000
	(Purchase of raw materials on account)		

As we will explain later in the chapter, the company subsequently assigns raw materials inventory to work in process and manufacturing overhead.

Factory Labor Costs

In a manufacturing company, the cost of factory labor consists of three costs: (1) gross earnings of factory workers, (2) employer payroll taxes on these earnings, and (3) fringe benefits (such as sick pay, pensions, and vacation pay) incurred by the employer. **Companies debit labor costs to Factory Labor as they incur those costs.**

To illustrate, assume that Wallace Manufacturing incurs $32,000 of factory labor costs. Of that amount, $27,000 relates to wages payable and $5,000 relates to payroll taxes payable in February. The entry to record factory labor for the month is:

	(2)		
Jan. 31	Factory Labor	32,000	
	Factory Wages Payable		27,000
	Employer Payroll Taxes Payable		5,000
	(To record factory labor costs)		

The company subsequently assigns factory labor to work in process and manufacturing overhead.

Manufacturing Overhead Costs

A company has many types of overhead costs. It may recognize these costs **daily**, as in the case of machinery repairs and the use of indirect materials and indirect labor. Or, it may record overhead costs **periodically** through adjusting entries. Companies record property taxes, depreciation, and insurance periodically, for example. This is done using a summary entry, which summarizes the totals from multiple transactions.

Using assumed data, the summary entry for manufacturing overhead in Wallace Manufacturing Company is:

	(3)		
Jan. 31	Manufacturing Overhead	13,800	
	Utilities Payable		4,800
	Prepaid Insurance		2,000
	Accounts Payable (for repairs)		2,600
	Accumulated Depreciation		3,000
	Property Taxes Payable		1,400
	(To record overhead costs)		

The company subsequently assigns manufacturing overhead to work in process.

before you go on...

MANUFACTURING COSTS

Do it! During the current month, Ringling Company incurs the following manufacturing costs:

(a) Raw material purchases of $4,200 on account.
(b) Incurs factory labor of $18,000. Of that amount, $15,000 relates to wages payable and $3,000 relates to payroll taxes payable.
(c) Factory utilities of $2,200 are payable, prepaid factory insurance of $1,800 has expired, and depreciation on the factory building is $3,500.

Prepare journal entries for each type of manufacturing cost.

Solution

(a)	Raw Materials Inventory	4,200	
	Accounts Payable		4,200
	(Purchases of raw materials on account)		
(b)	Factory Labor	18,000	
	Factory Wages Payable		15,000
	Employer Payroll Taxes Payable		3,000
	(To record factory labor costs)		
(c)	Manufacturing Overhead	7,500	
	Utilities Payable		2,200
	Prepaid Insurance		1,800
	Accumulated Depreciation		3,500
	(To record overhead costs)		

Action Plan

- In accumulating manufacturing costs, debit at least one of three accounts: Raw Materials Inventory, Factory Labor, and Manufacturing Overhead.
- Manufacturing overhead costs may be recognized daily. Or manufacturing overhead may be recorded periodically through a summary entry.

Related exercise material: **BE15-1, BE15-2, Do it! 15-1, E15-1, E15-7, E15-8, and E15-11.**

ASSIGNING MANUFACTURING COSTS TO WORK IN PROCESS

As Illustration 15-4 (page 801) shows, assigning manufacturing costs to work in process results in the following entries:

1. **Debits** made to Work in Process Inventory.
2. **Credits** made to Raw Materials Inventory, Factory Labor, and Manufacturing Overhead.

An essential accounting record in assigning costs to jobs is a **job cost sheet**, as shown in Illustration 15-5. A job cost sheet is a form used to record the costs chargeable to a specific job and to determine the total and unit costs of the completed job.

study objective 3
Explain the nature and importance of a job cost sheet.

Illustration 15-5 Job cost sheet

Helpful Hint In today's electronic environment, companies typically maintain job cost sheets as computer files.

Job Cost Sheet

Job No. _____ Quantity _____
Item _____ Date Requested _____
For _____ Date Completed _____

Date	Direct Materials	Direct Labor	Manufacturing Overhead

Cost of completed job
Direct materials $ _____
Direct labor _____
Manufacturing overhead _____
Total cost $ _____
Unit cost (total dollars ÷ quantity) $ _____

Companies keep a separate job cost sheet for each job. The job cost sheets constitute the subsidiary ledger for the Work in Process Inventory account. A **subsidiary ledger** consists of individual records for each individual item—in this case, each job. The Work in Process account is referred to as a **control account** because it summarizes the detailed data regarding specific jobs contained in the job cost sheets. **Each entry to Work in Process Inventory must be accompanied by a corresponding posting to one or more job cost sheets.**

Raw Materials Costs

Helpful Hint Approvals are an important part of a materials requisition slip because they help to establish individual accountability over inventory.

Companies assign raw materials costs when their materials storeroom issues the materials. Requests for issuing raw materials are made on a prenumbered materials requisition slip. The materials issued may be used directly on a job, or they may be considered indirect materials. As Illustration 15-6 shows, the requisition should indicate the quantity and type of materials withdrawn and the account to be charged. The company will charge direct materials to Work in Process Inventory, and indirect materials to Manufacturing Overhead.

Illustration 15-6
Materials requisition slip

| Wallace Manufacturing Company |
| **Materials Requisition Slip** |

Deliver to: Assembly Department   Req. No. R247
Charge to: Work in Process—Job No. 101   Date: 1/6/12

Quantity	Description	Stock No.	Cost per Unit	Total
200	Handles	AA2746	$5.00	$1,000

Requested by *Bruce Howart*   Received by *Herb Crowley*
Approved by *Kap Shin*   Costed by *Heather Remmers*

Ethics Note The internal control principle of documentation includes prenumbering to enhance accountability.

The company may use any of the inventory costing methods (FIFO, LIFO, or average-cost) in costing the requisitions **to the individual job cost sheets.**

Periodically, the company journalizes the requisitions. For example, if Wallace Manufacturing uses $24,000 of direct materials and $6,000 of indirect materials in January, the entry is:

	(4)		
Jan. 31	Work in Process Inventory	24,000	
	Manufacturing Overhead	6,000	
	Raw Materials Inventory		30,000
	(To assign materials to jobs and overhead)		

Illustration 15-7 shows the posting of requisition slip R247 to Job No. 101 and other assumed postings to the job cost sheets for materials. The requisition slips provide the basis for total direct materials costs of $12,000 for Job No. 101, $7,000 for Job No. 102, and $5,000 for Job No. 103. After the company has completed all postings, the sum of the direct materials columns of the job cost sheets (the subsidiary accounts) should equal the direct materials debited to Work in Process Inventory (the control account).

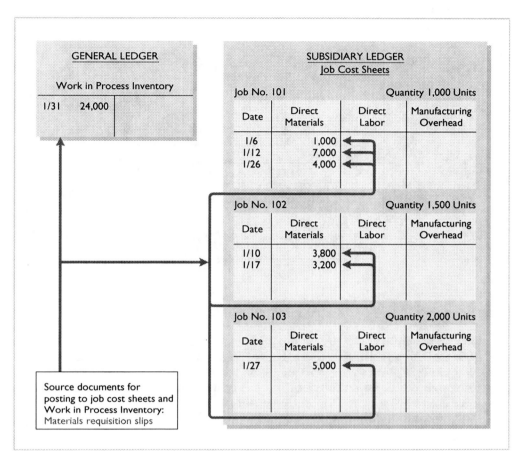

Illustration 15-7 Job cost sheets—direct materials

Helpful Hint Companies post to control accounts monthly, and post to job cost sheets daily.

Factory Labor Costs

Companies assign factory labor costs to jobs on the basis of time tickets prepared when the work is performed. The time ticket indicates the employee, the hours worked, the account and job to be charged, and the total labor cost. Many companies accumulate these data through the use of bar coding and scanning devices. When they start and end work, employees scan bar codes on their identification badges and bar codes associated with each job they work on. When direct labor is involved, the time ticket must indicate the job number, as shown in Illustration 15-8 (page 806). The employee's supervisor should approve all time tickets.

The time tickets are later sent to the payroll department, which applies the employee's hourly wage rate and computes the total labor cost. Finally, the company journalizes the time tickets. It debits the account Work in Process Inventory for direct labor and debits Manufacturing Overhead for indirect labor. For example, if the $32,000 total factory labor cost consists of $28,000 of direct labor and $4,000 of indirect labor, the entry is:

	(5)		
Jan. 31	Work in Process Inventory	28,000	
	Manufacturing Overhead	4,000	
	Factory Labor		32,000
	(To assign labor to jobs and overhead)		

As a result of this entry, Factory Labor has a zero balance, and gross earnings are assigned to the appropriate manufacturing accounts.

Illustration 15-8
Time ticket

Wallace Manufacturing Company
Time Ticket

Date: 1/6/12

| Employee | John Nash | Employee No. | 124 |
| Charge to: | Work in Process | Job No. | 101 |

Time			Hourly Rate	Total Cost
Start	Stop	Total Hours		
0800	1200	4	10.00	40.00

Approved by *Bob Kadler*   Costed by *M Cher*

Let's assume that the labor costs chargeable to Wallace's three jobs are $15,000, $9,000, and $4,000. Illustration 15-9 shows the Work in Process Inventory and job cost sheets after posting. As in the case of direct materials, the postings to the direct labor columns of the job cost sheets should equal the posting of direct labor to Work in Process Inventory.

Illustration 15-9 Job cost sheets—direct labor

Helpful Hint Prove the $28,000 direct labor charge to Work in Process Inventory by totaling the charges by jobs:

101	$15,000
102	9,000
103	4,000
	$28,000

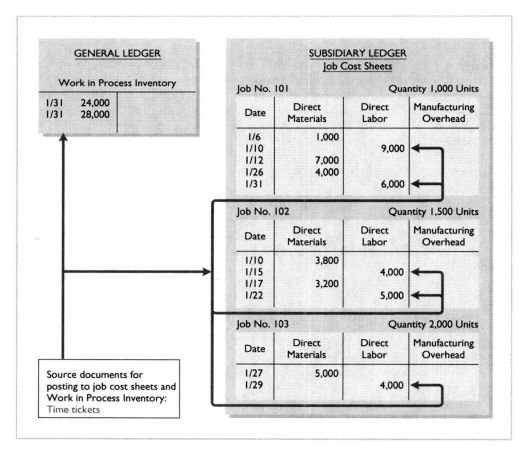

GENERAL LEDGER

Work in Process Inventory

1/31	24,000
1/31	28,000

SUBSIDIARY LEDGER
Job Cost Sheets

Job No. 101   Quantity 1,000 Units

Date	Direct Materials	Direct Labor	Manufacturing Overhead
1/6	1,000		
1/10		9,000	
1/12	7,000		
1/26	4,000		
1/31		6,000	

Job No. 102   Quantity 1,500 Units

Date	Direct Materials	Direct Labor	Manufacturing Overhead
1/10	3,800		
1/15		4,000	
1/17	3,200		
1/22		5,000	

Job No. 103   Quantity 2,000 Units

Date	Direct Materials	Direct Labor	Manufacturing Overhead
1/27	5,000		
1/29		4,000	

Source documents for posting to job cost sheets and Work in Process Inventory: Time tickets

Manufacturing Overhead Costs

Companies charge the actual costs of direct materials and direct labor to specific jobs. In contrast, manufacturing **overhead** relates to production operations **as a whole**. As a result, overhead costs cannot be assigned to specific jobs on the basis of actual costs incurred. Instead, companies assign manufacturing overhead to work in process and to specific jobs **on an estimated basis through the use of a predetermined overhead rate**.

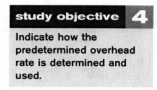

study objective **4**

Indicate how the predetermined overhead rate is determined and used.

The predetermined overhead rate is based on the relationship between estimated annual overhead costs and expected annual operating activity, expressed in terms of a common **activity base**. The company may state the activity in terms of direct labor costs, direct labor hours, machine hours, or any other measure that will provide an equitable basis for applying overhead costs to jobs. Companies establish the predetermined overhead rate at the beginning of the year. Small companies often use a single, company-wide predetermined overhead rate. Large companies often use rates that vary from department to department. The formula for a predetermined overhead rate is as follows.

$$\text{Estimated Annual Overhead Costs} \div \text{Expected Annual Operating Activity} = \text{Predetermined Overhead Rate}$$

Illustration 15-10
Formula for predetermined overhead rate

Overhead relates to production operations as a whole. To know what "the whole" is, the logical thing is to wait until the end of the year's operations. At that time the company knows all of its costs for the period. As a practical matter, though, managers cannot wait until the end of the year. To price products accurately, they need information about product costs of specific jobs completed during the year. Using a predetermined overhead rate enables a cost to be determined for the job immediately. Illustration 15-11 indicates how manufacturing overhead is assigned to work in process.

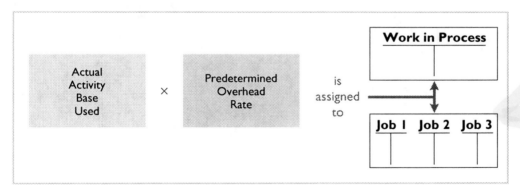

Illustration 15-11   Using predetermined overhead rates

Wallace Manufacturing uses direct labor cost as the activity base. Assuming that the company expects annual overhead costs to be $280,000 and direct labor costs for the year to be $350,000, the overhead rate is 80%, computed as follows.

$$\$280,000 \div \$350,000 = 80\%$$

This means that for every dollar of direct labor, Wallace will assign 80 cents of manufacturing overhead to a job. The use of a predetermined overhead rate enables the company to determine the approximate total cost of each job **when it completes the job.**

Historically, companies used direct labor costs or direct labor hours as the activity base. The reason was the relatively high correlation between direct labor and manufacturing overhead. Today, more companies are using **machine hours as the activity base, due to increased reliance on automation in manufacturing operations**. Or, as mentioned in Chapter 14 (and discussed more fully in Chapter 17), many companies now use activity-based costing to more accurately allocate overhead costs based on the activities that give rise to the costs.

A company may use more than one activity base. For example, if a job is manufactured in more than one factory department, each department may have its own overhead rate. In the Feature Story about fire trucks, Western States Fire Apparatus uses two bases in assigning overhead to jobs: direct materials dollars for indirect materials, and direct labor hours for such costs as insurance and supervisors' salaries.

Wallace Manufacturing applies manufacturing overhead to work in process when it assigns direct labor costs. It also applies manufacturing overhead to specific jobs at the same time. For January, Wallace applied overhead of $22,400 (direct labor cost of $28,000 × 80%). The following entry records this application.

	(6)		
Jan. 31	Work in Process Inventory	22,400	
	Manufacturing Overhead		22,400
	(To assign overhead to jobs)		

The overhead that Wallace applies to each job will be 80% of the direct labor cost of the job for the month. Illustration 15-12 shows the Work in Process Inventory account and the job cost sheets after posting. Note that the debit of $22,400 to Work in Process Inventory equals the sum of the overhead applied to jobs: Job 101 $12,000 + Job 102 $7,200 + Job 103 $3,200.

Illustration 15-12
Job cost sheets—manufacturing overhead applied

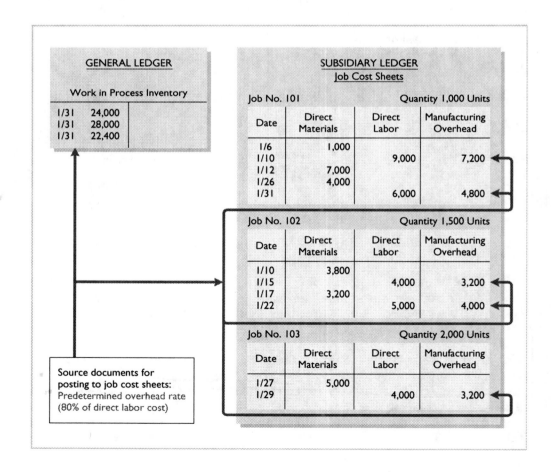

At the end of each month, **the balance in Work in Process Inventory should equal the sum of the costs shown on the job cost sheets of unfinished jobs.** Illustration 15-13 presents proof of the agreement of the control and subsidiary accounts in Wallace Manufacturing. (It assumes that all jobs are still in process.)

Work in Process Inventory		Job Cost Sheets	
Jan. 31	24,000	No. 101	$ 39,000
31	28,000	102	23,200
31	22,400	103	12,200
	74,400		$74,400

Illustration 15-13   Proof of job cost sheets to work in process inventory

DECISION TOOLKIT

DECISION CHECKPOINTS	INFO NEEDED FOR DECISION	TOOL TO USE FOR DECISION	HOW TO EVALUATE RESULTS
What is the cost of a job?	Cost of material, labor, and overhead assigned to a specific job	Job cost sheet	Compare costs to those of previous periods and to those of competitors to ensure that costs are in line. Compare costs to expected selling price or service fees charged to determine overall profitability.

before you go on...

Do it!

Danielle Company is working on two job orders. The job cost sheets show the following:

    Direct materials—Job 120 $6,000; Job 121 $3,600
    Direct labor—Job 120 $4,000; Job 121 $2,000
    Manufacturing overhead—Job 120 $5,000; Job 121 $2,500

Prepare the three summary entries to record the assignment of costs to Work in Process from the data on the job cost sheets.

Work in Process

Solution

The three summary entries are:

Work in Process Inventory ($6,000 + $3,600)	9,600	
Raw Materials Inventory		9,600
(To assign materials to jobs)		
Work in Process Inventory ($4,000 + $2,000)	6,000	
Factory Labor		6,000
(To assign labor to jobs)		
Work in Process Inventory ($5,000 + $2,500)	7,500	
Manufacturing Overhead		7,500
(To assign overhead to jobs)		

Action Plan

- Recognize that Work in Process Inventory is the control account for all unfinished job cost sheets.
- Debit Work in Process Inventory for the materials, labor, and overhead charged to the job cost sheets.
- Credit the accounts that were debited when the manufacturing costs were accumulated.

Related exercise material: **BE15-3, BE15-4, BE15-7, Do it! 15-2, E15-2, E15-7,** and **E15-8.**

ASSIGNING COSTS TO FINISHED GOODS

When a job is completed, Wallace summarizes the costs and completes the lower portion of the applicable job cost sheet. For example, if we assume that Wallace completes Job No. 101 on January 31, the job cost sheet appears as shown in Illustration 15-14 (page 810).

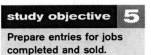

study objective 5

Prepare entries for jobs completed and sold.

Illustration 15-14
Completed job cost sheet

Job Cost Sheet

Job No.	101	Quantity	1,000
Item	Magnetic Sensors	Date Requested	February 5
For	Tanner Company	Date Completed	January 31

Date	Direct Materials	Direct Labor	Manufacturing Overhead
1/6	$ 1,000		
1/10		$ 9,000	$ 7,200
1/12	7,000		
1/26	4,000		
1/31		6,000	4,800
	$12,000	$15,000	$12,000

Cost of completed job
Direct materials	$	12,000
Direct labor		15,000
Manufacturing overhead		12,000
Total cost	$	39,000
Unit cost ($39,000 ÷ 1,000)	$	39.00

When a job is finished, Wallace makes an entry to transfer its total cost to finished goods inventory. The entry is as follows.

```
                              (7)
Jan. 31 │ Finished Goods Inventory              39,000
        │     Work in Process Inventory                  39,000
        │     (To record completion of Job No. 101)
```

Finished Goods Inventory is a control account. It controls individual finished goods records in a finished goods subsidiary ledger. The company posts directly from completed job cost sheets to the receipts columns. Illustration 15-15 shows the finished goods inventory record for Job No. 101.

ASSIGNING COSTS TO COST OF GOODS SOLD

Companies recognize cost of goods sold when each sale occurs. To illustrate the entries a company makes when it sells a completed job, assume that on January 31 Wallace Manufacturing sells on account Job 101. The job cost $39,000, and it sold for $50,000. The entries to record the sale and recognize cost of goods sold are:

```
                              (8)
Jan. 31 │ Accounts Receivable                   50,000
        │     Sales                                      50,000
        │     (To record sale of Job No. 101)
     31 │ Cost of Goods Sold                     39,000
        │     Finished Goods Inventory                   39,000
        │     (To record cost of Job No. 101)
```

As Illustration 15-15 shows, Wallace records, in the issues section of the finished goods record, the units sold, the cost per unit, and the total cost of goods sold for each job sold.

JOB ORDER COSTING FOR SERVICE COMPANIES

Our extended job order costing example focuses on a manufacturer so that you see the flow of costs through the inventory accounts. It is important to understand,

Illustration 15-15
Finished goods record

Finished Goods.xls

File Edit View Insert Format Tools Data Window Help

	A	B	C	D	E	F	G	H	I	J
1	Item: Magnetic Sensors								Job No: 101	
2										
3			Receipts			Issues			Balance	
4	Date	Units	Cost	Total	Units	Cost	Total	Units	Cost	Total
5	1/31	1,000	$39	$39,000				1,000	$39	$39,000
6	1/31				1,000	$39	$39,000			– 0 –
7										

however, that job order costing is also commonly used by service companies. While service companies do not have inventory, the techniques of job order costing are still quite useful in many service-industry environments. Consider, for example, the Mayo Clinic (health care), PriceWaterhouseCoopers (accounting firm), and Goldman Sachs (financial services firm). These companies need to keep track of the cost of jobs performed for specific customers to evaluate the profitability of medical treatments, audits, or consulting engagements.

Many service organizations bill their customers using cost-plus contracts. Cost-plus contracts mean that the customer's bill is the sum of the costs incurred on the job, plus a profit amount that is calculated as a percentage of the costs incurred. In order to minimize conflict with customers and reduce potential contract disputes, service companies that use cost-plus contracts must maintain accurate and up-to-date costing records. Up-to-date cost records enable a service company to immediately notify a customer of cost overruns due to customer requests for changes to the original plan or unexpected complications. Timely recordkeeping allows the contractor and customer to consider alternatives before it is too late.

A service company that uses a job order costing system does not have inventory accounts. It does, however, use an account (often called Service Contracts in Process) to record job costs prior to completion. Job cost sheets for a service company keep track of the materials, labor, and overhead used on a particular job similar to a manufacturer. A number of the exercises at the end of this chapter apply job order costing to service companies.

Service Company Insight

Sales Are Nice, but Service Revenue Pays the Bills

Jet engines are one of the many products made by the industrial operations division of General Electric (GE). At prices as high as $30 million per engine, you can bet that GE does its best to keep track of costs. It might surprise you that GE doesn't make much profit on the sale of each engine. So why does it bother making them? Service revenue — during one recent year, about 75% of the division's revenues came from servicing its own products. One estimate is that the $13 billion in aircraft engines sold during a recent three-year period will generate about $90 billion in service revenue over the 30-year life of the engines. Because of the high product costs, both the engines themselves and the subsequent service are most likely accounted for using job order costing. Accurate service cost records are important because GE needs to generate high profit margins on its service jobs to make up for the low margins on the original sale. It also needs good cost records for its service jobs in order to control its costs. Otherwise, a competitor, such as Pratt and Whitney, might submit lower bids for service contracts and take lucrative service jobs away from GE.

Source: Paul Glader, "GE's Focus on Services Faces Test," *Wall Street Journal Online* (March 3, 2009).

? Explain why GE would use job order costing to keep track of the cost of repairing a malfunctioning engine for a major airline. (See page 837.)

SUMMARY OF JOB ORDER COST FLOWS

Illustration 15-16 (below) shows a completed flowchart for a job order cost accounting system. All postings are keyed to entries 1–8 in Wallace Manufacturing's accounts presented in the cost flow graphic in Illustration 15-4 (page 801).

The cost flows in the diagram can be categorized as one of four types:

- **Accumulation:** The company first accumulates costs by (1) purchasing raw materials, (2) incurring labor costs, and (3) incurring manufacturing overhead costs.

- **Assignment to Jobs:** Once the company has incurred manufacturing costs, it must assign them to specific jobs. For example, as it uses raw materials on specific jobs (4), it assigns them to work in process, or treats them as manufacturing overhead if the raw materials cannot be associated with a specific job. Similarly, it either assigns factory labor (5) to work in process, or treats it as manufacturing overhead if the factory labor cannot be associated with a specific job. Finally it assigns manufacturing overhead (6) to work in process using a *predetermined overhead rate*. This deserves emphasis: **Do not assign overhead using actual overhead costs, but instead use a predetermined rate.**

- **Completed Jobs:** As jobs are completed (7), the company transfers the cost of the completed job out of work in process inventory into finished goods inventory.

- **When Goods Are Sold:** As specific items are sold (8), the company transfers their cost out of finished goods inventory into cost of goods sold.

Illustration 15-17 (next page) summarizes the flow of documents in a job order cost system.

Illustration 15-16
Flow of costs in a job order cost system

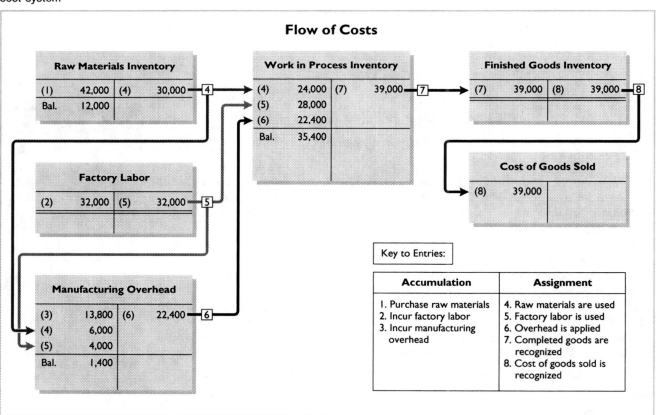

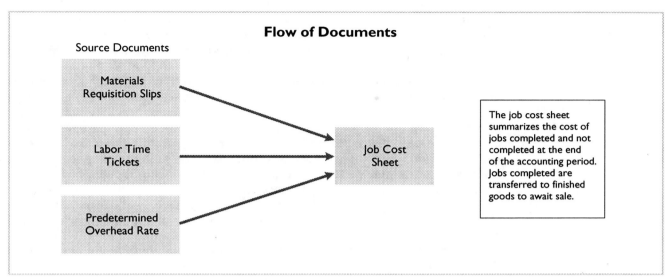

Flow of Documents

Source Documents

Materials Requisition Slips

Labor Time Tickets

Predetermined Overhead Rate

Job Cost Sheet

The job cost sheet summarizes the cost of jobs completed and not completed at the end of the accounting period. Jobs completed are transferred to finished goods to await sale.

Illustration 15-17 Flow of documents in a job order cost system

before you go on...

Do it! During the current month, Onyx Corporation completed Job 109 and Job 112. Job 109 cost $19,000 and Job 112 cost $27,000. Job 112 was sold on account for $42,000. Journalize the entries for the completion of the two jobs and the sale of Job 112.

COMPLETION AND SALE OF JOBS

Action Plan

• Debit Finished Goods for the cost of completed jobs.

• Debit Cost of Goods Sold for the cost of jobs sold.

Solution

Finished Goods Inventory	46,000	
Work in Process Inventory		46,000
(To record completion of Job 109, costing $19,000 and Job 112, costing $27,000)		
Accounts Receivable	42,000	
Sales		42,000
(To record sale of Job 112)		
Cost of Goods Sold	27,000	
Finished Goods Inventory		27,000
(To record cost of goods sold for Job 112)		

Related exercise material: **BE15-8, Do it! 15-3, E15-2, E15-3, E15-4, E15-6, E15-7,** and **E15-10.**

ADVANTAGES AND DISADVANTAGES OF JOB ORDER COSTING

An advantage of job order costing is it is more precise in assignment of costs to projects than process costing. For example, assume that Juan Company (home manufacturer) builds 10 custom homes a year at a total cost of $2,000,000. One way to determine the cost of the homes is to divide the total construction cost incurred during the year by the number of homes produced during the year. For Juan Company, an average cost of $200,000 ($2,000,000 ÷ 10) is computed. If the homes are identical, then this approach is adequate for purposes of determining profit per home. But if the homes vary in terms of size, style, and material types, using the average cost of $200,000 to determine profit per home is inappropriate. Instead, Juan Company should use a job order costing system to determine the specific cost incurred to build each home and the amount of profit made on each. Thus, job order costing provides more useful information for determining the profitability of particular projects and for estimating costs when preparing bids on future jobs.

One disadvantage of job order costing is that it requires a significant amount of data entry. For Juan Company, it is much easier to simply keep track of total costs incurred during the year than it is to keep track of the costs incurred on each job (home built). Recording this information is time-consuming, and if the data is not entered accurately, then the product costs are not accurate. In recent years, technological advances, such as bar-coding devices for both labor costs and materials, have increased the accuracy and reduced the effort needed to record costs on specific jobs. These innovations expand the opportunities to apply job order costing in a wider variety of business settings, thus improving management's ability to control costs and make better informed decisions.

A common problem of all costing systems is how to allocate overhead to the finished product. Overhead often represents more than 50 percent of a product's cost, and this cost is often difficult to allocate meaningfully to the product. How, for example, is the salary of Juan Company's president allocated to the various homes that may differ in size, style, and materials used? The accuracy of the job order costing system is largely dependent on the accuracy of the overhead allocation process. Even if the company does a good job of keeping track of the specific amounts of materials and labor used on each job, if the overhead costs are not allocated to individual jobs in a meaningful way, the product costing information is not useful. This issue will be addressed in more detail in Chapter 17.

Reporting Job Cost Data

At the end of a period, companies prepare financial statements that present aggregate data on all jobs manufactured and sold. The cost of goods manufactured schedule in job order costing is the same as in Chapter 14 with one exception: **The schedule shows manufacturing overhead applied, rather than actual overhead costs. The company adds this amount to direct materials and direct labor to determine total manufacturing costs.**

Companies prepare the cost of goods manufactured schedule directly from the Work in Process Inventory account. Illustration 15-18 shows a condensed schedule for Wallace Manufacturing Company for January.

Helpful Hint Companies usually prepare monthly financial statements for management use only.

Illustration 15-18
Cost of goods manufactured schedule

WALLACE MANUFACTURING COMPANY		
Cost of Goods Manufactured Schedule		
For the Month Ending January 31, 2012		
Work in process, January 1		$ −0−
Direct materials used	$24,000	
Direct labor	28,000	
Manufacturing overhead applied	22,400	
Total manufacturing costs		74,400
Total cost of work in process		74,400
Less: Work in process, January 31		35,400
Cost of goods manufactured		$39,000

Note that the cost of goods manufactured ($39,000) agrees with the amount transferred from Work in Process Inventory to Finished Goods Inventory in journal entry No. 7 in Illustration 15-16 (page 812).

The income statement and balance sheet are the same as those illustrated in Chapter 14. For example, Illustration 15-19 shows the partial income statement for Wallace Manufacturing for the month of January.

Illustration 15-19 Partial income statement

WALLACE MANUFACTURING COMPANY		
Income Statement (partial)		
For the Month Ending January 31, 2012		
Sales		$50,000
Cost of goods sold		
Finished goods inventory, January 1	$ –0–	
Cost of goods manufactured (see Illustration 15-18)	39,000	
Cost of goods available for sale	39,000	
Less: Finished goods inventory, January 31	–0–	
Cost of goods sold		39,000
Gross profit		$11,000

UNDER- OR OVERAPPLIED MANUFACTURING OVERHEAD

When Manufacturing Overhead has a **debit balance**, overhead is said to be underapplied. Underapplied overhead means that the overhead assigned to work in process is less than the overhead incurred. Conversely, when manufacturing overhead has a **credit balance**, overhead is overapplied. Overapplied overhead means that the overhead assigned to work in process is greater than the overhead incurred. Illustration 15-20 shows these concepts.

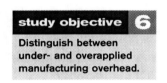

study objective 6

Distinguish between under- and overapplied manufacturing overhead.

Illustration 15-20
Under- and overapplied overhead

Manufacturing Overhead

Actual	Applied
(Costs incurred)	(Costs assigned)

Manufacturing Overhead

If actual is *greater* than applied, manufacturing overhead is underapplied.

If actual is *less* than applied, manufacturing overhead is overapplied.

Year-End Balance

At the end of the year, all manufacturing overhead transactions are complete. There is no further opportunity for offsetting events to occur. At this point, Wallace eliminates any balance in Manufacturing Overhead by an adjusting entry. It considers under- or overapplied overhead to be an **adjustment to cost of goods sold**. Thus, Wallace **debits underapplied overhead to Cost of Goods Sold**. It **credits overapplied overhead to Cost of Goods Sold**.

To illustrate, assume that Wallace Manufacturing has a $2,500 credit balance in Manufacturing Overhead at December 31. The adjusting entry for the overapplied overhead is:

Dec. 31	Manufacturing Overhead	2,500	
	Cost of Goods Sold		2,500
	(To transfer overapplied overhead to		
	cost of goods sold)		

After Wallace posts this entry, Manufacturing Overhead has a zero balance. In preparing an income statement for the year, Wallace reports cost of goods sold **after adjusting it** for either under- or overapplied overhead.

Conceptually, some argue, under- or overapplied overhead at the end of the year should be allocated among ending work in process, finished goods, and cost of goods sold. The discussion of this possible allocation approach is left to more advanced courses.

DECISION TOOLKIT

DECISION CHECKPOINTS	INFO NEEDED FOR DECISION	TOOL TO USE FOR DECISION	HOW TO EVALUATE RESULTS
Has the company over- or underapplied overhead for the period?	Actual overhead costs and overhead applied	Manufacturing overhead account	If the account balance is a credit, overhead applied exceeded actual overhead costs. If the account balance is a debit, overhead applied was less than actual overhead costs.

before you go on...

APPLIED MANUFACTURING OVERHEAD

Action Plan

- Calculate the amount of overhead applied by multiplying the predetermined overhead rate by actual activity.
- If actual manufacturing overhead is greater than applied, manufacturing overhead is underapplied.
- If actual manufacturing overhead is less than applied, manufacturing overhead is overapplied.

Do it! For Karr Company, the predetermined overhead rate is 140% of direct labor cost. During the month, Karr incurred $90,000 of factory labor costs, of which $80,000 is direct labor and $10,000 is indirect labor. Actual overhead incurred was $119,000.

Compute the amount of manufacturing overhead applied during the month. Determine the amount of under- or overapplied manufacturing overhead.

Solution

Manufacturing overhead applied = (140% × $80,000) = $112,000
Underapplied manufacturing overhead = ($119,000 − $112,000) = $7,000

Related exercise material: **BE15-9, Do it! 15-4, E15-5, E15-12,** and **E15-13.**

USING THE *DECISION TOOLKIT*

Martinez Building Products Company is one of the largest manufacturers and marketers of unique, custom-made residential garage doors in the United States. It also is a major supplier of industrial and commercial doors, grills, and counter shutters for the new-construction, repair, and remodel markets. Martinez has developed plans for continued expansion of a network of service operations that sell, install, and service manufactured fireplaces, garage doors, and related products.

Martinez uses a job order cost system and applies overhead to production on the basis of direct labor cost. In computing a predetermined overhead rate for the year 2012, the company estimated manufacturing overhead to be $24 million and direct labor costs to be $20 million. In addition, it developed the following information.

Actual Costs Incurred During 2012

Direct materials used	$30,000,000
Direct labor cost incurred	21,000,000
Insurance, factory	500,000
Indirect labor	7,500,000
Factory maintenance	1,000,000
Rent on factory building	11,000,000
Depreciation on factory equipment	2,000,000

Instructions

Answer each of the following.

(a) Why is Martinez Building Products Company using a job order costing system?
(b) On what basis does Martinez allocate its manufacturing overhead? Compute the predetermined overhead rate for 2012.
(c) Compute the amount of the under- or overapplied overhead for 2012.
(d) Martinez had balances in the beginning and ending work in process and finished goods accounts as follows.

	1/1/12	12/31/12
Work in process	$ 5,000,000	$ 4,000,000
Finished goods	13,000,000	11,000,000

Determine the (1) cost of goods manufactured and (2) cost of goods sold for Martinez during 2012. Assume that any under- or overapplied overhead should be included in the cost of goods sold.
(e) During 2012, Job G408 was started and completed. Its cost sheet showed a total cost of $100,000, and the company prices its product at 50% above its cost. What is the price to the customer if the company follows this pricing strategy?

Solution

(a) The company is using a job order cost system because it custom-makes garage doors. Each job has its own distinguishing characteristics. For example, each garage door would be different, and therefore a different cost per garage door can be assigned.
(b) The company allocates its overhead on the basis of direct labor cost. The predetermined overhead rate is 120%, computed as follows.

$$\$24,000,000 \div 20,000,000 = 120\%$$

(c)

Actual manufacturing overhead	$22,000,000
Applied overhead cost ($21,000,000 × 120%)	25,200,000
Overapplied overhead	$ 3,200,000

(d)	(1)	Work in process, 1/1/12		$ 5,000,000
		Direct materials used	$30,000,000	
		Direct labor	21,000,000	
		Manufacturing overhead applied	25,200,000	
		Total manufacturing costs		76,200,000
		Total cost of work in process		81,200,000
		Less: Work in process, 12/31/12		4,000,000
		Cost of goods manufactured		$77,200,000
	(2)	Finished goods inventory, 1/1/12	$13,000,000	
		Cost of goods manufactured (see above)	77,200,000	
		Cost of goods available for sale	90,200,000	
		Finished goods inventory, 12/31/12	11,000,000	
		Cost of goods sold (unadjusted)	79,200,000	
		Less: Overapplied overhead	3,200,000	
		Cost of goods sold	$76,000,000	
(e)		G408 cost	$ 100,000	
		Markup percentage	× 50%	
		Profit	$ 50,000	

Price to customer: $150,000 ($100,000 + $50,000)

Summary of Study Objectives

1 Explain the characteristics and purposes of cost accounting. Cost accounting involves the procedures for measuring, recording, and reporting product costs. From the data accumulated, companies determine the total cost and the unit cost of each product. The two basic types of cost accounting systems are job order cost and process cost.

2 Describe the flow of costs in a job order costing system. In job order costing, companies first accumulate manufacturing costs in three accounts: Raw Materials Inventory, Factory Labor, and Manufacturing Overhead. They then assign the accumulated costs to Work in Process Inventory and eventually to Finished Goods Inventory and Cost of Goods Sold.

3 Explain the nature and importance of a job cost sheet. A job cost sheet is a form used to record the costs chargeable to a specific job and to determine the total and unit costs of the completed job. Job cost sheets constitute the subsidiary ledger for the Work in Process Inventory control account.

4 Indicate how the predetermined overhead rate is determined and used. The predetermined overhead rate is based on the relationship between estimated annual overhead costs and expected annual operating activity. This is expressed in terms of a common activity base, such as direct labor cost. Companies use this rate to assign overhead costs to work in process and to specific jobs.

5 Prepare entries for jobs completed and sold. When jobs are completed, companies debit the cost to Finished Goods Inventory and credit it to Work in Process Inventory. When a job is sold, the entries are: (a) Debit Cash or Accounts Receivable and credit Sales for the selling price; and (b) debit Cost of Goods Sold and credit Finished Goods Inventory for the cost of the goods.

6 Distinguish between under- and overapplied manufacturing overhead. Underapplied manufacturing overhead indicates that the overhead assigned to work in process is less than the overhead incurred. Overapplied overhead indicates that the overhead assigned to work in process is greater than the overhead incurred.

DECISION TOOLKIT A SUMMARY

DECISION CHECKPOINTS	INFO NEEDED FOR DECISION	TOOL TO USE FOR DECISION	HOW TO EVALUATE RESULTS
What is the cost of a job?	Cost of material, labor, and overhead assigned to a specific job	Job cost sheet	Compare costs to those of previous periods and to those of competitors to ensure that costs are in line. Compare costs to expected selling price or service fees charged to determine overall profitability.
Has the company over- or underapplied overhead for the period?	Actual overhead costs and overhead applied	Manufacturing overhead account	If the account balance is a credit, overhead applied exceeded actual overhead costs. If the account balance is a debit, overhead applied was less than actual overhead costs.

Glossary

Cost accounting (p. 798) An area of accounting that involves measuring, recording, and reporting product costs.

Cost accounting system (p. 798) Manufacturing-cost accounts that are fully integrated into the general ledger of a company.

Job cost sheet (p. 803) A form used to record the costs chargeable to a specific job and to determine the total and unit costs of the completed job.

Job order cost system (p. 798) A cost accounting system in which costs are assigned to each job or batch.

Materials requisition slip (p. 804) A document authorizing the issuance of raw materials from the storeroom to production.

Overapplied overhead (p. 815) A situation in which overhead assigned to work in process is greater than the overhead incurred.

Predetermined overhead rate (p. 807) A rate based on the relationship between estimated annual overhead costs and expected annual operating activity, expressed in terms of a common activity base.

Process cost system (p. 799) A cost accounting system used when a company manufactures a large volume of similar products.

Summary entry (p. 802) A journal entry that summarizes the totals from multiple transactions.

Time ticket (p. 805) A document that indicates the employee, the hours worked, the account and job to be charged, and the total labor cost.

Underapplied overhead (p. 815) A situation in which overhead assigned to work in process is less than the overhead incurred.

Comprehensive Do it!

Cardella Manufacturing applies overhead on the basis of direct labor costs. The company estimates annual overhead costs will be $760,000 and annual direct labor costs will be $950,000. During February, Cardella Manufacturing works on two jobs: A16 and B17. Summary data concerning these jobs are as follows.

Manufacturing Costs Incurred

Purchased $54,000 of raw materials on account.
Factory labor $76,000, plus $4,000 employer payroll taxes.
Manufacturing overhead exclusive of indirect materials and indirect labor $59,800.

Assignment of Costs

Direct materials:	Job A16 $27,000, Job B17 $21,000
Indirect materials:	$3,000
Direct labor:	Job A16 $52,000, Job B17 $26,000
Indirect labor:	$2,000

The company completed Job A16 and sold it on account for $150,000. Job B17 was only partially completed.

Instructions

(a) Compute the predetermined overhead rate.

(b) Journalize the February transactions in the sequence followed in the chapter.

(c) What was the amount of under- or overapplied manufacturing overhead?

Action Plan

- Predetermined overhead rate = Estimated annual overhead cost ÷ Expected annual operating activity.
- In accumulating costs, debit three accounts: Raw Materials Inventory, Factory Labor, and Manufacturing Overhead.
- When Work in Process Inventory is debited, credit one of the three accounts listed above.
- Debit Finished Goods Inventory for the cost of completed jobs. Debit Cost of Goods Sold for the cost of jobs sold.
- Overhead is underapplied when Manufacturing Overhead has a debit balance.

Solution to Comprehensive Do it!

(a)

Estimated annual overhead costs	÷	Expected annual operating activity	=	Predetermined overhead rate
$760,000	÷	$950,000	=	80%

(b)

1.

Feb. 28	Raw Materials Inventory	54,000	
	Accounts Payable		54,000
	(Purchase of raw materials on account)		

2.

28	Factory Labor	80,000	
	Factory Wages Payable		76,000
	Employer Payroll Taxes Payable		4,000
	(To record factory labor costs)		

3.

28	Manufacturing Overhead	59,800	
	Accounts Payable, Accumulated Depreciation, and Prepaid Insurance		59,800
	(To record overhead costs)		

4.

28	Work in Process Inventory	48,000	
	Manufacturing Overhead	3,000	
	Raw Materials Inventory		51,000
	(To assign raw materials to production)		

5.

28	Work in Process Inventory	78,000	
	Manufacturing Overhead	2,000	
	Factory Labor		80,000
	(To assign factory labor to production)		

6.

28	Work in Process Inventory	62,400	
	Manufacturing Overhead		62,400
	(To assign overhead to jobs— 80% × $78,000)		

7.

28	Finished Goods Inventory	120,600	
	Work in Process Inventory		120,600
	(To record completion of Job A16: direct materials $27,000, direct labor $52,000, and manufacturing overhead $41,600)		

8.

28	Accounts Receivable	150,000	
	Sales		150,000
	(To record sale of Job A16)		

28	Cost of Goods Sold	120,600	
	Finished Goods Inventory		120,600
	(To record cost of sale for Job A16)		

(c) Manufacturing Overhead has a debit balance of $2,400 as shown below.

Manufacturing Overhead

(3)	59,800	(6)	62,400
(4)	3,000		
(5)	2,000		
Bal.	2,400		

Thus, manufacturing overhead is underapplied for the month.

 Self-Test, Brief Exercises, Exercises, Problem Set A, and many more resources are available for practice in WileyPLUS

Self-Test Questions

Answers are on page 837.

(SO 1) **1.** Cost accounting involves the measuring, recording, and reporting of:
(a) product costs.
(b) future costs.
(c) manufacturing processes.
(d) managerial accounting decisions.

(SO 1) **2.** A company is more likely to use a job order costing system if:
(a) it manufactures a large volume of similar products.
(b) its production is continuous.
(c) it manufactures products with unique characteristics.
(d) it uses a periodic inventory system.

(SO 2) **3.** In accumulating raw materials costs, companies debit the cost of raw materials purchased in a perpetual system to:
(a) Raw Materials Purchases.
(b) Raw Materials Inventory.
(c) Purchases.
(d) Work in Process.

(SO 2) **4.** When incurred, factory labor costs are debited to:
(a) Work in Process.
(b) Factory Wages Expense.
(c) Factory Labor.
(d) Factory Wages Payable.

(SO 2) **5.** The flow of costs in job order costing:
(a) begins with work in process inventory and ends with finished goods inventory.
(b) begins as soon as a sale occurs.
(c) parallels the physical flow of materials as they are converted into finished goods.
(d) is necessary to prepare the cost of goods manufactured schedule.

(SO 3) **6.** Raw materials are assigned to a job when:
(a) the job is sold.
(b) the materials are purchased.
(c) the materials are received from the vendor.
(d) the materials are issued by the materials storeroom.

(SO 3) **7.** The source documents for assigning costs to job cost sheets are:

(a) invoices, time tickets, and the predetermined overhead rate.
(b) materials requisition slips, time tickets, and the actual overhead costs.
(c) materials requisition slips, payroll register, and the predetermined overhead rate.
(d) materials requisition slips, time tickets, and the predetermined overhead rate.

8. In recording the issuance of raw materials in a job (SO 3) order cost system, it would be *incorrect* to:
(a) debit Work in Process Inventory.
(b) debit Finished Goods Inventory.
(c) debit Manufacturing Overhead.
(d) credit Raw Materials Inventory.

9. The entry when direct factory labor is assigned to (SO 3) jobs is a debit to:
(a) Work in Process Inventory and a credit to Factory Labor.
(b) Manufacturing Overhead and a credit to Factory Labor.
(c) Factory Labor and a credit to Manufacturing Overhead.
(d) Factory Labor and a credit to Work in Process Inventory.

10. The formula for computing the predetermined man- (SO 4) ufacturing overhead rate is estimated annual overhead costs divided by an expected annual operating activity, expressed as:
(a) direct labor cost.
(b) direct labor hours.
(c) machine hours.
(d) Any of the above.

11. In Crawford Company, the predetermined overhead (SO 4) rate is 80% of direct labor cost. During the month, Crawford incurs $210,000 of factory labor costs, of which $180,000 is direct labor and $30,000 is indirect labor. Actual overhead incurred was $200,000. The amount of overhead debited to Work in Process Inventory should be:
(a) $200,000.   (c) $168,000.
(b) $144,000.   (d) $160,000.

(SO 5) **12.** Mynex Company completes Job No. 26 at a cost of $4,500 and later sells it for $7,000 cash. A correct entry is:
  (a) Debit Finished Goods Inventory $7,000 and credit Work in Process Inventory $7,000.
  (b) Debit Cost of Goods Sold $7,000 and credit Finished Goods Inventory $7,000.
  (c) Debit Finished Goods Inventory $4,500 and credit Work in Process Inventory $4,500.
  (d) Debit Accounts Receivable $7,000 and credit Sales $7,000.

(SO 5) **13.** At the end of an accounting period, a company using a job order costing system prepares the cost of goods manufactured:
  (a) from the job cost sheet.
  (b) from the Work in Process Inventory account.
  (c) by adding direct materials used, direct labor incurred, and manufacturing overhead incurred.
  (d) from the Cost of Goods Sold account.

(SO 6) **14.** At end of the year, a company has a $1,200 debit balance in Manufacturing Overhead. The company:
  (a) makes an adjusting entry by debiting Manufacturing Overhead Applied for $1,200 and crediting Manufacturing Overhead for $1,200.
  (b) makes an adjusting entry by debiting Manufacturing Overhead Expense for $1,200 and crediting Manufacturing Overhead for $1,200.
  (c) makes an adjusting entry by debiting Cost of Goods Sold for $1,200 and crediting Manufacturing Overhead for $1,200.
  (d) makes no adjusting entry because differences between actual overhead and the amount applied are a normal part of job order costing and will average out over the next year.

15. Manufacturing overhead is underapplied if: (SO 6)
  (a) actual overhead is less than applied.
  (b) actual overhead is greater than applied.
  (c) the predetermined rate equals the actual rate.
  (d) actual overhead equals applied overhead.

Go to the book's companion website, **www.wiley.com/college/kimmel**, for additional Self-Test Questions.

Questions

1. (a) Mary Barett is not sure about the difference between cost accounting and a cost accounting system. Explain the difference to Mary. (b) What is an important feature of a cost accounting system?

2. (a) Distinguish between the two types of cost accounting systems. (b) May a company use both types of cost accounting systems?

3. What type of industry is likely to use a job order cost system? Give some examples.

4. What type of industry is likely to use a process cost system? Give some examples.

5. Your roommate asks your help in understanding the major steps in the flow of costs in a job order cost system. Identify the steps for your roommate.

6. There are three inventory control accounts in a job order system. Identify the control accounts and their subsidiary ledgers.

7. What source documents are used in accumulating direct labor costs?

8. "Entries to Manufacturing Overhead normally are only made daily." Do you agree? Explain.

9. Stan Kaiser is confused about the source documents used in assigning materials and labor costs. Identify the documents and give the entry for each document.

10. What is the purpose of a job cost sheet?

11. Indicate the source documents that are used in charging costs to specific jobs.

12. Explain the purpose and use of a "materials requisition slip" as used in a job order cost system.

13. Sam Bowden believes actual manufacturing overhead should be charged to jobs. Do you agree? Why or why not?

14. What elements are involved in computing a predetermined overhead rate?

15. How can the agreement of Work in Process Inventory and job cost sheets be verified?

16. Jane Neff believes that the cost of goods manufactured schedule in job order cost accounting is the same as shown in Chapter 14. Is Jane correct? Explain.

17. Matt Litkee is confused about under- and overapplied manufacturing overhead. Define the terms for Matt, and indicate the balance in the manufacturing overhead account applicable to each term.

18. "At the end of the year, under- or overapplied overhead is closed to Income Summary." Is this correct? If not, indicate the customary treatment of this amount.

Brief Exercises

BE15-1   Knox Tool & Die begins operations on January 1. Because all work is done to customer specifications, the company decides to use a job order costing system. Prepare a flowchart of a typical job order system with arrows showing the flow of costs. Identify the eight transactions.

Prepare a flowchart of a job order cost accounting system, and identify transactions.
(SO 2), C

BE15-2 During January, its first month of operations, Knox Tool & Die accumulated the following manufacturing costs: raw materials $4,000 on account, factory labor $6,000 of which $5,200 relates to factory wages payable and $800 relates to payroll taxes payable, and utilities payable $2,000. Prepare separate journal entries for each type of manufacturing cost.

Prepare entries in accumulating manufacturing costs.
(SO 2), AP

BE15-3 In January, Knox Tool & Die requisitions raw materials for production as follows: Job 1 $900, Job 2 $1,400, Job 3 $700, and general factory use $600. Prepare a summary journal entry to record raw materials used.

Prepare entry for the assignment of raw materials costs.
(SO 3), AP

BE15-4 Factory labor data for Knox Tool & Die is given in BE15-2. During January, time tickets show that the factory labor of $6,000 was used as follows: Job 1 $2,200, Job 2 $1,600, Job 3 $1,400, and general factory use $800. Prepare a summary journal entry to record factory labor used.

Prepare entry for the assignment of factory labor costs.
(SO 3), AP

BE15-5 Data pertaining to job cost sheets for Knox Tool & Die are given in BE15-3 and BE15-4. Prepare the job cost sheets for each of the three jobs. (*Note*: You may omit the column for Manufacturing Overhead.)

Prepare job cost sheets.
(SO 3), AP

BE15-6 Marquis Company estimates that annual manufacturing overhead costs will be $900,000. Estimated annual operating activity bases are: direct labor cost $500,000, direct labor hours 50,000, and machine hours 100,000. Compute the predetermined overhead rate for each activity base.

Compute predetermined overhead rates.
(SO 4), AP

BE15-7 During the first quarter, Roland Company incurs the following direct labor costs: January $40,000, February $30,000, and March $50,000. For each month, prepare the entry to assign overhead to production using a predetermined rate of 80% of direct labor cost.

Assign manufacturing overhead to production.
(SO 4), AP

BE15-8 In March, Stinson Company completes Jobs 10 and 11. Job 10 cost $20,000 and Job 11 $30,000. On March 31, Job 10 is sold to the customer for $35,000 in cash. Journalize the entries for the completion of the two jobs and the sale of Job 10.

Prepare entries for completion and sale of completed jobs.
(SO 5), AP

BE15-9 At December 31, balances in Manufacturing Overhead are: Shimeca Company—debit $1,200, Garcia Company—credit $900. Prepare the adjusting entry for each company at December 31, assuming the adjustment is made to cost of goods sold.

Prepare adjusting entries for under- and overapplied overhead.
(SO 6), C

Do it! Review

Do it! 15-1 During the current month, Tomlin Company incurs the following manufacturing costs:

Prepare journal entries for manufacturing costs.
(SO 2), AP

(a) Purchased raw materials of $16,000 on account.
(b) Incurred factory labor of $40,000. Of that amount, $31,000 relates to wages payable and $9,000 relates to payroll taxes payable.
(c) Factory utilities of $3,100 are payable, prepaid factory property taxes of $2,400 have expired, and depreciation on the factory building is $9,500.

Prepare journal entries for each type of manufacturing cost. (Use a summary entry to record manufacturing overhead.)

Do it! 15-2 Milner Company is working on two job orders. The job cost sheets show the following.

Assign costs to work in process.
(SO 3, 4), AP

	Job 201	Job 202
Direct materials	$7,200	$9,000
Direct labor	4,000	8,000
Manufacturing overhead	5,200	9,800

Prepare the three summary entries to record the assignment of costs to Work in Process from the data on the job cost sheets.

Do it! 15-3 During the current month, Reyes Corporation completed Job 310 and Job 312. Job 310 cost $60,000 and Job 312 cost $50,000. Job 312 was sold on account for $90,000. Journalize the entries for the completion of the two jobs and the sale of Job 312.

Prepare entries for completion and sale of jobs.
(SO 5), AP

Do it! 15-4 For Eckstein Company, the predetermined overhead rate is 130% of direct labor cost. During the month, Eckstein incurred $100,000 of factory labor costs, of which $85,000 is direct labor and $15,000 is indirect labor. Actual overhead incurred was $115,000. Compute the amount of manufacturing overhead applied during the month. Determine the amount of under- or overapplied manufacturing overhead.

Apply manufacturing overhead and determine under- or overapplication.
(SO 6), AN

Exercises

Prepare entries for factory labor.

(SO 2, 3), AP

E15-1   The gross earnings of the factory workers for Vargas Company during the month of January are $66,000. The employer's payroll taxes for the factory payroll are $8,000. The fringe benefits to be paid by the employer on this payroll are $6,000. Of the total accumulated cost of factory labor, 85% is related to direct labor and 15% is attributable to indirect labor.

Instructions
(a) Prepare the entry to record the factory labor costs for the month of January.
(b) Prepare the entry to assign factory labor to production.

Prepare journal entries for manufacturing costs.

(SO 2, 3, 4, 5), AP

E15-2   Stine Manufacturing uses a job order costing system. On May 1, the company has a balance in Work in Process Inventory of $3,500 and two jobs in process: Job No. 429 $2,000, and Job No. 430 $1,500. During May, a summary of source documents reveals the following.

Job Number	Materials Requisition Slips		Labor Time Tickets	
429	$2,500		$1,900	
430	3,500		3,000	
431	4,400	$10,400	7,600	$12,500
General use		800		1,200
		$11,200		$13,700

Stine Manufacturing applies manufacturing overhead to jobs at an overhead rate of 60% of direct labor cost. Job No. 429 is completed during the month.

Instructions
(a) Prepare summary journal entries to record: (i) the requisition slips, (ii) the time tickets, (iii) the assignment of manufacturing overhead to jobs, and (iv) the completion of Job No. 429.
(b) Post the entries to Work in Process Inventory, and prove the agreement of the control account with the job cost sheets. (Use a T account.)

Analyze a job cost sheet and prepare entries for manufacturing costs.

(SO 2, 3, 4, 5), AP

E15-3   A job order cost sheet for Lowry Company is shown below.

Job No. 92			For 2,000 Units
Date	Direct Materials	Direct Labor	Manufacturing Overhead
Beg. bal. Jan. 1	5,000	6,000	5,100
8	6,000		
12		8,000	6,400
25	2,000		
27		4,000	3,200
	13,000	18,000	14,700

Cost of completed job:	
Direct materials	$13,000
Direct labor	18,000
Manufacturing overhead	14,700
Total cost	$45,700
Unit cost ($45,700 ÷ 2,000)	$22.85

Instructions
(a) ▣▭▭▭▷ On the basis of the foregoing data, answer the following questions.
  (1) What was the balance in Work in Process Inventory on January 1 if this was the only unfinished job?
  (2) If manufacturing overhead is applied on the basis of direct labor cost, what overhead rate was used in each year?
(b) Prepare summary entries at January 31 to record the current year's transactions pertaining to Job No. 92.

E15-4 Manufacturing cost data for Orlando Company, which uses a job order cost system, are presented below.

Analyze costs of manufacturing and determine missing amounts.
(SO 2, 5), AN

	Case A	Case B	Case C
Direct materials used	$ (a)	$ 83,000	$ 63,150
Direct labor	50,000	140,000	(h)
Manufacturing overhead applied	42,500	(d)	(i)
Total manufacturing costs	145,650	(e)	213,000
Work in process 1/1/12	(b)	15,500	18,000
Total cost of work in process	201,500	(f)	(j)
Work in process 12/31/12	(c)	11,800	(k)
Cost of goods manufactured	192,300	(g)	222,000

Instructions

Indicate the missing amount for each letter. Assume that in all cases manufacturing overhead is applied on the basis of direct labor cost and the rate is the same.

E15-5 Duggan Company applies manufacturing overhead to jobs on the basis of machine hours used. Overhead costs are expected to total $325,000 for the year, and machine usage is estimated at 125,000 hours.

For the year, $342,000 of overhead costs are incurred and 130,000 hours are used.

Compute the manufacturing overhead rate and under- or overapplied overhead.
(SO 4, 5), AN

Instructions

(a) Compute the manufacturing overhead rate for the year.
(b) What is the amount of under- or overapplied overhead at December 31?
(c) Prepare the adjusting entry to assign the under- or overapplied overhead for the year to cost of goods sold.

E15-6 A job cost sheet of Sandoval Company is given below.

Analyze job cost sheet and prepare entry for completed job.
(SO 2, 3, 4, 5), AP

Job Cost Sheet

JOB NO.   469   Quantity   2,500
ITEM   White Lion Cages   Date Requested   7/2
FOR   Todd Company   Date Completed   7/31

Date	Direct Materials	Direct Labor	Manufacturing Overhead
7/10	700		
12	900		
15		440	550
22		380	475
24	1,600		
27	1,500		
31		540	675

Cost of completed job:
   Direct materials   ——
   Direct labor   ——
   Manufacturing overhead   ——
Total cost   ══
Unit cost   ══

Instructions

(a) ▢▣▣▣▣▶ Answer the following questions.
  (1) What are the source documents for direct materials, direct labor, and manufacturing overhead costs assigned to this job?
  (2) What is the predetermined manufacturing overhead rate?
  (3) What are the total cost and the unit cost of the completed job? (Round unit cost to nearest cent.)
(b) Prepare the entry to record the completion of the job.

Prepare entries for
manufacturing costs.
(SO 2, 3, 4, 5), AP

E15-7 Torre Corporation incurred the following transactions.

1. Purchased raw materials on account $46,300.
2. Raw Materials of $36,000 were requisitioned to the factory. An analysis of the materials requisition slips indicated that $6,800 was classified as indirect materials.
3. Factory labor costs incurred were $55,900, of which $51,000 pertained to factory wages payable and $4,900 pertained to employer payroll taxes payable.
4. Time tickets indicated that $50,000 was direct labor and $5,900 was indirect labor.
5. Overhead costs incurred on account were $80,500.
6. Manufacturing overhead was applied at the rate of 150% of direct labor cost.
7. Goods costing $88,000 were completed and transferred to finished goods.
8. Finished goods costing $75,000 to manufacture were sold on account for $103,000.

Instructions
Journalize the transactions. (Omit explanations.)

Prepare entries for
manufacturing costs.
(SO 2, 3, 4, 5), AP

E15-8 Enos Printing Corp. uses a job order cost system. The following data summarize the operations related to the first quarter's production.

1. Materials purchased on account $192,000, and factory wages incurred $87,300.
2. Materials requisitioned and factory labor used by job:

Job Number	Materials	Factory Labor	
A20	$ 35,240	$18,000	53740
A21	42,920	22,000	64920
A22	36,100	15,000	
A23	39,270	25,000	
General factory use	4,470	7,300	64270
	$158,000	$87,300	

3. Manufacturing overhead costs incurred on account $49,500.
4. Depreciation on equipment $14,550.
5. Manufacturing overhead rate is 90% of direct labor cost.
6. Jobs completed during the quarter: A20, A21, and A23.

Instructions
Prepare entries to record the operations summarized above. (Prepare a schedule showing the individual cost elements and total cost for each job in item 6.)

Prepare a cost of goods
manufactured schedule and
partial financial statements.
(SO 2, 5), AP

E15-9 At May 31, 2012, the accounts of Mantle Manufacturing Company show the following.

1. May 1 inventories—finished goods $12,600, work in process $14,700, and raw materials $8,200.
2. May 31 inventories—finished goods $9,500, work in process $17,900, and raw materials $7,100.
3. Debit postings to work in process were: direct materials $62,400, direct labor $50,000, and manufacturing overhead applied $40,000.
4. Sales totaled $210,000.

Instructions
(a) Prepare a condensed cost of goods manufactured schedule.
(b) Prepare an income statement for May through gross profit.
(c) Indicate the balance sheet presentation of the manufacturing inventories at May 31, 2012.

Compute work in process
and finished goods from job
cost sheets.
(SO 3, 5), AP

E15-10 Tierney Company begins operations on April 1. Information from job cost sheets shows the following.

Job Number	Manufacturing Costs Assigned			Month Completed
	April	May	June	
10	$5,200	$4,400		May
11	4,100	3,900	$2,000	June
12	1,200			April
13		4,700	4,500	June
14		5,900	3,600	Not complete

Job 12 was completed in April. Job 10 was completed in May. Jobs 11 and 13 were completed in June. Each job was sold for 25% above its cost in the month following completion.

Instructions
(a) What is the balance in Work in Process Inventory at the end of each month?
(b) What is the balance in Finished Goods Inventory at the end of each month?
(c) What is the gross profit for May, June, and July?

E15-11 Shown below are the job cost related accounts for the law firm of Jack, Bob, and Will and their manufacturing equivalents:

Prepare entries for costs of services provided.

(SO 2, 4, 5), AP

Law Firm Accounts	Manufacturing Firm Accounts
Supplies	Raw Materials
Salaries and Wages Payable	Factory Wages Payable
Operating Overhead	Manufacturing Overhead
Service Contracts in Process	Work in Process
Cost of Completed Service Contracts	Cost of Goods Sold

Cost data for the month of March follow.

1. Purchased supplies on account $1,500.
2. Issued supplies $1,200 (60% direct and 40% indirect).
3. Time cards for the month indicated labor costs of $60,000 (80% direct and 20% indirect).
4. Operating overhead costs incurred for cash totaled $40,000.
5. Operating overhead is applied at a rate of 90% of direct attorney cost.
6. Work completed totaled $75,000.

Instructions
(a) Journalize the transactions for March. Omit explanations.
(b) Determine the balance of the Work in Process account. Use a T account.

E15-12 Don Lieberman and Associates, a CPA firm, uses job order costing to capture the costs of its audit jobs. There were no audit jobs in process at the beginning of November. Listed below are data concerning the three audit jobs conducted during November.

Determine cost of jobs and ending balance in work in process and overhead accounts.

(SO 3, 4, 6), AP

	Lynn	Brian	Mike
Direct materials	$600	$400	$200
Auditor labor costs	$5,400	$6,600	$3,375
Auditor hours	72	88	45

Overhead costs are applied to jobs on the basis of auditor hours, and the predetermined overhead rate is $50 per auditor hour. The Lynn job is the only incomplete job at the end of November. Actual overhead for the month was $11,000.

Instructions
(a) Determine the cost of each job.
(b) Indicate the balance of the Work in Process account at the end of November.
(c) Calculate the ending balance of the Manufacturing Overhead account for November.

E15-13 Pure Decorating uses a job order costing system to collect the costs of its interior decorating business. Each client's consultation is treated as a separate job. Overhead is applied to each job based on the number of decorator hours incurred. Listed below are data for the current year.

Determine predetermined overhead rate, apply overhead and determine whether balance under- or overapplied.

(SO 4, 6), AP

Estimated overhead	$920,000
Actual overhead	$942,800
Estimated decorator hours	40,000
Actual decorator hours	40,500

The company uses Operating Overhead in place of Manufacturing Overhead.

Instructions
(a) Compute the predetermined overhead rate.
(b) Prepare the entry to apply the overhead for the year.
(c) Determine whether the overhead was under- or overapplied and by how much.

Exercises: Set B and Challenge Exercises

Visit the book's companion website, at **www.wiley.com/college/kimmel**, and choose the Student Companion site to access Exercise Set B and Challenge Exercises.

Problems: Set A

Prepare entries in a job order cost system and job cost sheets.

(SO 2, 3, 4, 5, 6), AP

P15-1A Deglman Manufacturing uses a job order cost system and applies overhead to production on the basis of direct labor costs. On January 1, 2012, Job No. 50 was the only job in process. The costs incurred prior to January 1 on this job were as follows: direct materials $20,000, direct labor $12,000, and manufacturing overhead $16,000. As of January 1, Job No. 49 had been completed at a cost of $90,000 and was part of finished goods inventory. There was a $15,000 balance in the Raw Materials Inventory account.

During the month of January, Deglman Manufacturing began production on Jobs 51 and 52, and completed Jobs 50 and 51. Jobs 49 and 50 were also sold on account during the month for $122,000 and $158,000, respectively. The following additional events occurred during the month.

1. Purchased additional raw materials of $90,000 on account.
2. Incurred factory labor costs of $70,000. Of this amount $16,000 related to employer payroll taxes.
3. Incurred manufacturing overhead costs as follows: indirect materials $17,000; indirect labor $20,000; depreciation expense on equipment $19,000; and various other manufacturing overhead costs on account $16,000.
4. Assigned direct materials and direct labor to jobs as follows.

Job No.	Direct Materials	Direct Labor
50	$10,000	$ 5,000
51	39,000	25,000
52	30,000	20,000

Instructions
(a) Calculate the predetermined overhead rate for 2012, assuming Deglman Manufacturing estimates total manufacturing overhead costs of $980,000, direct labor costs of $700,000, and direct labor hours of 20,000 for the year.
(b) Open job cost sheets for Jobs 50, 51, and 52. Enter the January 1 balances on the job cost sheet for Job No. 50.
(c) Prepare the journal entries to record the purchase of raw materials, the factory labor costs incurred, and the manufacturing overhead costs incurred during the month of January.
(d) Prepare the journal entries to record the assignment of direct materials, direct labor, and manufacturing overhead costs to production. In assigning manufacturing overhead costs, use the overhead rate calculated in (a). Post all costs to the job cost sheets as necessary.

(e) Job 50, $70,000
    Job 51, $99,000

(e) Total the job cost sheets for any job(s) completed during the month. Prepare the journal entry (or entries) to record the completion of any job(s) during the month.
(f) Prepare the journal entry (or entries) to record the sale of any job(s) during the month.
(g) What is the balance in the Finished Goods Inventory account at the end of the month? What does this balance consist of?
(h) What is the amount of over- or underapplied overhead?

Prepare entries in a job order cost system and partial income statement.

(SO 2, 3, 4, 5, 6), AN

P15-2A For the year ended December 31, 2012, the job cost sheets of Cinta Company contained the following data.

Job Number	Explanation	Direct Materials	Direct Labor	Manufacturing Overhead	Total Costs
7640	Balance 1/1	$25,000	$24,000	$28,800	$ 77,800
	Current year's costs	30,000	36,000	43,200	109,200
7641	Balance 1/1	11,000	18,000	21,600	50,600
	Current year's costs	43,000	48,000	57,600	148,600
7642	Current year's costs	58,000	55,000	66,000	179,000

Other data:

1. Raw materials inventory totaled $15,000 on January 1. During the year, $140,000 of raw materials were purchased on account.
2. Finished goods on January 1 consisted of Job No. 7638 for $87,000 and Job No. 7639 for $92,000.
3. Job No. 7640 and Job No. 7641 were completed during the year.
4. Job Nos. 7638, 7639, and 7641 were sold on account for $530,000.
5. Manufacturing overhead incurred on account totaled $120,000.
6. Other manufacturing overhead consisted of indirect materials $14,000, indirect labor $18,000, and depreciation on factory machinery $8,000.

Instructions
(a) Prove the agreement of Work in Process Inventory with job cost sheets pertaining to unfinished work. (*Hint:* Use a single T account for Work in Process Inventory.) Calculate each of the following, then post each to the T account: (1) beginning balance, (2) direct materials, (3) direct labor, (4) manufacturing overhead, and (5) completed jobs.
(b) Prepare the adjusting entry for manufacturing overhead, assuming the balance is allocated entirely to Cost of Goods Sold.
(c) Determine the gross profit to be reported for 2012.

(a) $179,000; Job 7642: $179,000

(b) Amount = $6,800

(c) $158,000

P15-3A Stellar Inc. is a construction company specializing in custom patios. The patios are constructed of concrete, brick, fiberglass, and lumber, depending upon customer preference. On June 1, 2012, the general ledger for Stellar Inc. contains the following data.

Prepare entries in a job order cost system and cost of goods manufactured schedule.
(SO 2, 3, 4, 5), AP

Raw Materials Inventory	$4,200	Manufacturing Overhead Applied	$32,640
Work in Process Inventory	$5,540	Manufacturing Overhead Incurred	$31,650

Subsidiary data for Work in Process Inventory on June 1 are as follows.

Job Cost Sheets

	Customer Job		
Cost Element	**Gannon**	**Rosenthal**	**Linton**
Direct materials	$ 600	$ 800	$ 900
Direct labor	320	540	580
Manufacturing overhead	400	675	725
	$1,320	$2,015	$2,205

During June, raw materials purchased on account were $4,900, and all wages were paid. Additional overhead costs consisted of depreciation on equipment $700 and miscellaneous costs of $400 incurred on account.

A summary of materials requisition slips and time tickets for June shows the following.

Customer Job	**Materials Requisition Slips**	**Time Tickets**
Gannon	$ 800	$ 450
Koss	2,000	800
Rosenthal	500	360
Linton	1,300	1,200
Gannon	300	390
	4,900	3,200
General use	1,500	1,200
	$6,400	$4,400

Overhead was charged to jobs at the same rate of $1.25 per dollar of direct labor cost. The patios for customers Gannon, Rosenthal, and Linton were completed during June and sold for a total of $18,900. Each customer paid in full.

Instructions
(a) Journalize the June transactions: (i) for purchase of raw materials, factory labor costs incurred, and manufacturing overhead costs incurred; (ii) assignment of direct materials, labor, and overhead to production; and (iii) completion of jobs and sale of goods.
(b) Post the entries to Work in Process Inventory.
(c) Reconcile the balance in Work in Process Inventory with the costs of unfinished jobs.
(d) Prepare a cost of goods manufactured schedule for June.

(d) Cost of goods manufactured $13,840

P15-4A Agassi Manufacturing Company uses a job order cost system in each of its three manufacturing departments. Manufacturing overhead is applied to jobs on the basis of direct labor cost in Department D, direct labor hours in Department E, and machine hours in Department K.

In establishing the predetermined overhead rates for 2012, the following estimates were made for the year.

	Department		
	D	**E**	**K**
Manufacturing overhead	$1,200,000	$1,500,000	$900,000
Direct labor costs	$1,500,000	$1,250,000	$450,000
Direct labor hours	100,000	125,000	40,000
Machine hours	400,000	500,000	120,000

During January, the job cost sheets showed the following costs and production data.

	Department		
	D	**E**	**K**
Direct materials used	$140,000	$126,000	$78,000
Direct labor costs	$120,000	$110,000	$37,500
Manufacturing overhead incurred	$ 99,000	$124,000	$79,000
Direct labor hours	8,000	11,000	3,500
Machine hours	34,000	45,000	10,400

Instructions

(a) Compute the predetermined overhead rate for each department.
(b) Compute the total manufacturing costs assigned to jobs in January in each department.
(c) Compute the under- or overapplied overhead for each department at January 31.

P15-5A Rodman Corporation's fiscal year ends on November 30. The following accounts are found in its job order cost accounting system for the first month of the new fiscal year.

Raw Materials Inventory

Dec. 1	Beginning balance	(a)	Dec. 31	Requisitions	16,850
31	Purchases	19,225			
Dec. 31	Ending balance	7,975			

Work in Process Inventory

Dec. 1	Beginning balance	(b)	Dec. 31	Jobs completed	(f)
31	Direct materials	(c)			
31	Direct labor	8,800			
31	Overhead	(d)			
Dec. 31	Ending balance	(e)			

Finished Goods Inventory

Dec. 1	Beginning balance	(g)	Dec. 31	Cost of goods sold	(i)
31	Completed jobs	(h)			
Dec. 31	Ending balance	(j)			

Factory Labor

Dec. 31	Factory wages	12,025	Dec. 31	Wages assigned	(k)

Manufacturing Overhead

Dec. 31	Indirect materials	1,900	Dec. 31	Overhead applied	(m)
31	Indirect labor	(l)			
31	Other overhead	1,245			

Other data:

1. On December 1, two jobs were in process: Job No. 154 and Job No. 155. These jobs had combined direct materials costs of $9,750 and direct labor costs of $15,000. Overhead was applied at a rate that was 75% of direct labor cost.

2. During December, Job Nos. 156, 157, and 158 were started. On December 31, Job No. 158 was unfinished. This job had charges for direct materials $3,800 and direct labor $4,800, plus manufacturing overhead. All jobs, except for Job No. 158, were completed in December.
3. On December 1, Job No. 153 was in the finished goods warehouse. It had a total cost of $5,000. On December 31, Job No. 157 was the only job finished that was not sold. It had a cost of $4,000.
4. Manufacturing overhead was $230 overapplied in December.

Instructions

List the letters (a) through (m) and indicate the amount pertaining to each letter.

(c) $14,950
(f) $54,150
(l) $55,150

Problems: Set B

P15-1B   Pedriani Manufacturing uses a job order cost system and applies overhead to production on the basis of direct labor hours. On January 1, 2012, Job No. 25 was the only job in process. The costs incurred prior to January 1 on this job were as follows: direct materials $10,000; direct labor $6,000; and manufacturing overhead $9,000. Job No. 23 had been completed at a cost of $42,000 and was part of finished goods inventory. There was a $5,000 balance in the Raw Materials Inventory account.

Prepare entries in a job order cost system and job cost sheets.
(SO 2, 3, 4, 5, 6), AP

During the month of January, the company began production on Jobs 26 and 27, and completed Jobs 25 and 26. Jobs 23 and 25 were sold on account during the month for $63,000 and $74,000, respectively. The following additional events occurred during the month.

1. Purchased additional raw materials of $45,000 on account.
2. Incurred factory labor costs of $33,500. Of this amount, $7,500 related to employer payroll taxes.
3. Incurred manufacturing overhead costs as follows: indirect materials $10,000; indirect labor $9,500; depreciation expense on equipment $12,000; and various other manufacturing overhead costs on account $11,000.
4. Assigned direct materials and direct labor to jobs as follows.

Job No.	Direct Materials	Direct Labor
25	$ 5,000	$ 3,000
26	17,000	12,000
27	13,000	9,000

5. The company uses direct labor hours as the activity base to assign overhead. Direct labor hours incurred on each job were as follows: Job No. 25, 200; Job No. 26, 800; and Job No. 27, 600.

Instructions

(a) Calculate the predetermined overhead rate for the year 2012, assuming Pedriani Manufacturing estimates total manufacturing overhead costs of $440,000, direct labor costs of $300,000, and direct labor hours of 20,000 for the year.
(b) Open job cost sheets for Jobs 25, 26, and 27. Enter the January 1 balances on the job cost sheet for Job No. 25.
(c) Prepare the journal entries to record the purchase of raw materials, the factory labor costs incurred, and the manufacturing overhead costs incurred during the month of January.
(d) Prepare the journal entries to record the assignment of direct materials, direct labor, and manufacturing overhead costs to production. In assigning manufacturing overhead costs, use the overhead rate calculated in (a). Post all costs to the job cost sheets as necessary.
(e) Total the job cost sheets for any job(s) completed during the month. Prepare the journal entry (or entries) to record the completion of any job(s) during the month.
(f) Prepare the journal entry (or entries) to record the sale of any job(s) during the month.
(g) What is the balance in the Work in Process Inventory account at the end of the month? What does this balance consist of?
(h) What is the amount of over- or underapplied overhead?

(e) Job 25, $37,400
Job 26, $48,900

Prepare entries in a job order cost system and partial income statement.

(SO 2, 3, 4, 5, 6), AN

P15-2B For the year ended December 31, 2012, the job cost sheets of Dosey Company contained the following data.

Job Number	Explanation	Direct Materials	Direct Labor	Manufacturing Overhead	Total Costs
7650	Balance 1/1	$18,000	$20,000	$25,000	$ 63,000
	Current year's costs	32,000	36,000	45,000	113,000
7651	Balance 1/1	12,000	16,000	20,000	48,000
	Current year's costs	30,000	40,000	50,000	120,000
7652	Current year's costs	35,000	68,000	85,000	188,000

Other data:

1. Raw materials inventory totaled $20,000 on January 1. During the year, $100,000 of raw materials were purchased on account.
2. Finished goods on January 1 consisted of Job No. 7648 for $93,000 and Job No. 7649 for $62,000.
3. Job No. 7650 and Job No. 7651 were completed during the year.
4. Job Nos. 7648, 7649, and 7650 were sold on account for $490,000.
5. Manufacturing overhead incurred on account totaled $135,000.
6. Other manufacturing overhead consisted of indirect materials $12,000, indirect labor $16,000 and depreciation on factory machinery $19,500.

Instructions

(a) Prove the agreement of Work in Process Inventory with job cost sheets pertaining to unfinished work. (*Hint:* Use a single T account for Work in Process Inventory.) Calculate each of the following, then post each to the T account: (1) beginning balance, (2) direct materials, (3) direct labor, (4) manufacturing overhead, and (5) completed jobs.

(b) Prepare the adjusting entry for manufacturing overhead, assuming the balance is allocated entirely to cost of goods sold.

(c) Determine the gross profit to be reported for 2012.

(a) (1) $111,000
(4) $180,000
Unfinished job 7652, $188,000

(b) Amount = $2,500

(c) $156,500

Prepare entries in a job order cost system and cost of goods manufactured schedule.

(SO 2, 3, 4, 5), AP

P15-3B Robert Perez is a contractor specializing in custom-built jacuzzis. On May 1, 2012, his ledger contains the following data.

Raw Materials Inventory	$30,000
Work in Process Inventory	12,200
Manufacturing Overhead	2,500 (dr.)

The Manufacturing Overhead account has debit totals of $12,500 and credit totals of $10,000. Subsidiary data for Work in Process Inventory on May 1 include:

Job Cost Sheets

Job by Customer	Direct Materials	Direct Labor	Manufacturing Overhead
Stiner	$2,500	$2,000	$1,400
Alton	2,000	1,200	840
Herman	900	800	560
	$5,400	$4,000	$2,800

During May, the following costs were incurred: raw materials purchased on account $4,000, labor paid $7,000, and manufacturing overhead paid $1,400.

A summary of materials requisition slips and time tickets for the month of May reveals the following.

Job by Customer	Materials Requisition Slips	Time Tickets
Stiner	$ 500	$ 400
Alton	600	1,000
Herman	2,300	1,300
Smith	1,900	2,300
	5,300	5,000
General use	1,500	2,000
	$6,800	$7,000

Overhead was charged to jobs on the basis of $0.70 per dollar of direct labor cost. The jacuzzis for customers Stiner, Alton, and Herman were completed during May. The three jacuzzis were sold for a total of $36,000.

Instructions

(a) Prepare journal entries for the May transactions: (i) for purchase of raw materials, factory labor costs incurred, and manufacturing overhead costs incurred; (ii) assignment of raw materials, labor, and overhead to production; and (iii) completion of jobs and sale of goods.

(b) Post the entries to Work in Process Inventory.

(c) Reconcile the balance in Work in Process Inventory with the costs of unfinished jobs.

(d) Prepare a cost of goods manufactured schedule for May.

(d) Cost of goods manufactured
$20,190

P15-4B Net Play Manufacturing uses a job order cost system in each of its three manufacturing departments. Manufacturing overhead is applied to jobs on the basis of direct labor cost in Department A, direct labor hours in Department B, and machine hours in Department C.

In establishing the predetermined overhead rates for 2012, the following estimates were made for the year.

Compute predetermined overhead rates, apply overhead, and calculate under- or overapplied overhead.

(SO 4, 6), AP

	Department		
	A	**B**	**C**
Manufacturing overhead	$720,000	$640,000	$900,000
Direct labor cost	$600,000	$100,000	$600,000
Direct labor hours	50,000	40,000	40,000
Machine hours	100,000	120,000	150,000

During January, the job cost sheets showed the following costs and production data.

	Department		
	A	**B**	**C**
Direct materials used	$92,000	$86,000	$64,000
Direct labor cost	$48,000	$35,000	$50,400
Manufacturing overhead incurred	$60,000	$60,000	$72,100
Direct labor hours	4,000	3,500	4,200
Machine hours	8,000	10,500	12,600

Instructions

(a) Compute the predetermined overhead rate for each department.

(b) Compute the total manufacturing costs assigned to jobs in January in each department.

(c) Compute the under- or overapplied overhead for each department at January 31.

(a) 120%, $16, $6
(b) $197,600, $177,000, $190,000
(c) $2,400 $4,000, $(3,500)

P15-5B Bell Company's fiscal year ends on June 30. The following accounts are found in its job order cost accounting system for the first month of the new fiscal year.

Analyze manufacturing accounts and determine missing amounts.

(SO 2, 3, 4, 5, 6), AN

Raw Materials Inventory

July	1	Beginning balance	19,000	July 31	Requisitions	(a)
	31	Purchases	90,400			
July 31		Ending balance	(b)			

Work in Process Inventory

July	1	Beginning balance	(c)	July 31	Jobs completed	(f)
	31	Direct materials	80,000			
	31	Direct labor	(d)			
	31	Overhead	(e)			
July 31		Ending balance	(g)			

Finished Goods Inventory

July	1	Beginning balance	(h)	July 31	Cost of goods sold	(j)
	31	Completed jobs	(i)			
July 31		Ending balance	(k)			

Factory Labor

July 31	Factory wages	(l)	July 31	Wages assigned	(m)

Manufacturing Overhead

July 31	Indirect materials	8,900	July 31	Overhead applied	117,000
31	Indirect labor	16,000			
31	Other overhead	(n)			

Other data:

1. On July 1, two jobs were in process: Job No. 4085 and Job No. 4086, with costs of $19,000 and $8,200, respectively.
2. During July, Job Nos. 4087, 4088, and 4089 were started. On July 31, only Job No. 4089 was unfinished. This job had charges for direct materials $2,000 and direct labor $1,500, plus manufacturing overhead. Manufacturing overhead was applied at the rate of 130% of direct labor cost.
3. On July 1, Job No. 4084, costing $145,000, was in the finished goods warehouse. On July 31, Job No. 4088, costing $138,000, was in finished goods.
4. Overhead was $3,000 underapplied in July.

(d) $ 90,000
(f) $308,750
(i) $106,000

Instructions
List the letters (a) through (n) and indicate the amount pertaining to each letter. Show computations.

Problems: Set C

Visit the book's companion website, at **www.wiley.com/college/kimmel**, and choose the Student Companion site to access Problem Set C.

Waterways Continuing Problem

(*Note:* This is a continuation of the Waterways Problem from Chapter 14.)

WCP15 Waterways has two major public-park projects to provide with comprehensive irrigation in one of its service locations this month. Job J57 and Job K52 involve 15 acres of landscaped terrain which will require special-order sprinkler heads to meet the specifications of the project. This problem asks you to help Waterways use a job order cost system to account for production of these parts.

> Go to the book's companion website, at **www.wiley.com/college/kimmel**, to find the completion of this problem.

broadening your perspective

DECISION MAKING ACROSS THE ORGANIZATION

BYP15-1 Khan Products Company uses a job order cost system. For a number of months, there has been an ongoing rift between the sales department and the production department concerning a special-order product, TC-1. TC-1 is a seasonal product that is manufactured in batches of 1,000 units. TC-1 is sold at cost plus a markup of 40% of cost.

The sales department is unhappy because fluctuating unit production costs significantly affect selling prices. Sales personnel complain that this has caused excessive customer complaints and the loss of considerable orders for TC-1.

The production department maintains that each job order must be fully costed on the basis of the costs incurred during the period in which the goods are produced. Production personnel maintain that the only real solution to the problem is for the sales department to increase sales in the slack periods.

Andrea Parley, president of the company, asks you as the company accountant to collect quarterly data for the past year on TC-1. From the cost accounting system, you accumulate the following production quantity and cost data.

Costs	Quarter			
	1	2	3	4
Direct materials	$100,000	$220,000	$ 80,000	$200,000
Direct labor	60,000	132,000	48,000	120,000
Manufacturing overhead	105,000	153,000	97,000	125,000
Total	$265,000	$505,000	$225,000	$445,000
Production in batches	5	11	4	10
Unit cost (per batch)	$ 53,000	$ 45,909	$ 56,250	$ 44,500

Instructions

With the class divided into groups, answer the following questions.

(a) What manufacturing cost element is responsible for the fluctuating unit costs? Why?

(b) What is your recommended solution to the problem of fluctuating unit cost?

(c) Restate the quarterly data on the basis of your recommended solution.

MANAGERIAL ANALYSIS

BYP15-2 In the course of routine checking of all journal entries prior to preparing year-end reports, Betty Eller discovered several strange entries. She recalled that the president's son Joe had come in to help out during an especially busy time and that he had recorded some journal entries. She was relieved that there were only a few of his entries, and even more relieved that he had included rather lengthy explanations. The entries Joe made were:

1.

Work in Process Inventory	25,000	
Cash		25,000

(This is for materials put into process. I don't find the record that we paid for these, so I'm crediting Cash, because I know we'll have to pay for them sooner or later.)

2.

Manufacturing Overhead	12,000	
Cash		12,000

(This is for bonuses paid to salespeople. I know they're part of overhead, and I can't find an account called "Non-factory Overhead" or "Other Overhead" so I'm putting it in Manufacturing Overhead. I have the check stubs, so I know we paid these.)

3.

Wages Expense	120,000	
Cash		120,000

(This is for the factory workers' wages. I have a note that payroll taxes are $18,000. I still think that's part of wages expense, and that we'll have to pay it all in cash sooner or later, so I credited Cash for the wages and the taxes.)

4.

Work in Process Inventory	3,000	
Raw Materials Inventory		3,000

(This is for the glue used in the factory. I know we used this to make the products, even though we didn't use very much on any one of the products. I got it out of inventory, so I credited an inventory account.)

Instructions

(a) How should Joe have recorded each of the four events?

(b) If the entry was not corrected, which financial statements (income statement or balance sheet) would be affected? What balances would be overstated or understated?

REAL-WORLD FOCUS

BYP15-3 Founded in 1970, Parlex Corporation is a world leader in the design and manufacture of flexible interconnect products. Utilizing proprietary and patented technologies, Parlex produces custom flexible interconnects including flexible circuits, polymer thick film, laminated cables, and value-added assemblies for sophisticated electronics used in automotive, telecommunications, computer, diversified electronics, and aerospace applications. In addition to manufacturing sites in Methuen, Massachusetts; Salem, New Hampshire; Cranston, Rhode Island; San Jose, California; Shanghai, China; Isle of Wight, UK; and Empalme, Mexico, Parlex has logistic support centers and strategic alliances throughout North America, Asia, and Europe.

The following information was provided in the company's annual report.

PARLEX COMPANY
Notes to the Financial Statements

The Company's products are manufactured on a job order basis to customers' specifications. Customers submit requests for quotations on each job, and the Company prepares bids based on its own cost estimates. The Company attempts to reflect the impact of changing costs when establishing prices. However, during the past several years, the market conditions for flexible circuits and the resulting price sensitivity haven't always allowed this to transpire. Although still not satisfactory, the Company was able to reduce the cost of products sold as a percentage of sales to 85% this year versus 87% that was experienced in the two immediately preceding years. Management continues to focus on improving operational efficiency and further reducing costs.

Instructions
(a) Parlex management discusses the job order cost system employed by their company. What are several advantages of using the job order approach to costing?
(b) Contrast the products produced in a job order environment, like Parlex, to those produced when process cost systems are used.

MANAGERIAL ACCOUNTING ON THE WEB

BYP15-4 The Institute of Management Accountants sponsors a certification for management accountants, allowing them to obtain the title of Certified Management Accountant.

Address: **www.imanet.org**, or go to **www.wiley.com/college/kimmel**

Steps
 1. Go to the site shown above.
 2. Choose **CMA Certification**, and then, **Earning & Maintaining Your Credential**.

Instructions
(a) What is the experience qualification requirement?
(b) How many hours of continuing education are required, and what types of courses qualify?

COMMUNICATION ACTIVITY

BYP15-5 You are the management accountant for Williams Manufacturing. Your company does custom carpentry work and uses a job order costing system. Williams sends detailed job cost sheets to its customers, along with an invoice. The job cost sheets show the date materials were used, the dollar cost of materials, and the hours and cost of labor. A predetermined overhead application rate is used, and the total overhead applied is also listed.

Nancy Kopay is a customer who recently had custom cabinets installed. Along with her check in payment for the work done, she included a letter. She thanked the company for including the detailed cost information but questioned why overhead was estimated. She stated that she would be interested in knowing exactly what costs were included in overhead, and she thought that other customers would, too.

Instructions

Prepare a letter to Ms. Kopay (address: 123 Cedar Lane, Altoona, KS 66651) and tell her why you did not send her information on exact costs of overhead included in her job. Respond to her suggestion that you provide this information.

ETHICS CASE

BYP15-6 LRF Printing provides printing services to many different corporate clients. Although LRF bids most jobs, some jobs, particularly new ones, are negotiated on a "cost-plus" basis. Cost-plus means that the buyer is willing to pay the actual cost plus a return (profit) on these costs to LRF.

Alice Reiley, controller for LRF, has recently returned from a meeting where LRF's president stated that he wanted her to find a way to charge more costs to any project that was on a cost-plus basis. The president noted that the company needed more profits to meet its stated goals this period. By charging more costs to the cost-plus projects and therefore fewer costs to the jobs that were bid, the company should be able to increase its profit for the current year.

Alice knew why the president wanted to take this action. Rumors were that he was looking for a new position and if the company reported strong profits, the president's opportunities would be enhanced. Alice also recognized that she could probably increase the cost of certain jobs by changing the basis used to allocate manufacturing overhead.

Instructions
(a) Who are the stakeholders in this situation?
(b) What are the ethical issues in this situation?
(c) What would you do if you were Alice Reiley?

"ALL ABOUT YOU" ACTIVITY

BYP15-7 Many of you will work for a small business. Some of you will even own your own business. In order to operate a small business, you will need a good understanding of managerial accounting, as well as many other skills. Much information is available to assist people who are interested in starting a new business. A great place to start is the website provided by the Small Business Administration, which is an agency of the federal government whose purpose is to support small business.

Instructions

Go to **www.sba.gov** and in the Small Business Planner, Plan Your Business link, review the material under "Get Ready." Answer the following questions.
(a) What are some of the characteristics required of a small business owner?
(b) What are the top 10 reasons given for business failure?

Answers to Insight and Accounting Across the Organization Questions

p. 800 Jobs Won, Money Lost Q: What type of costs do you think the company had been underestimating? **A:** It is most likely that the company failed to estimate and track overhead. In a highly diversified company, overhead associated with the diesel locomotive jobs may have been "lost" in the total overhead pool for the entire company.

p. 811 Sales Are Nice, but Service Revenue Pays the Bills Q: Explain why GE would use job order costing to keep track of the cost of repairing a malfunctioning engine for a major airline. **A:** GE operates in a competitive environment. Other companies offer competing bids to win service contracts on GE's airplane engines. GE needs to know what it costs to repair engines, so that it can present competitive bids while still generating a reasonable profit.

Answers to Self-Test Questions

1. a **2.** c **3.** b **4.** c **5.** c **6.** d **7.** d **8.** b **9.** a **10.** d **11.** b ($180,000 × 80%) **12.** c **13.** b
14. c **15.** b

Remember to go back to the navigator box on the chapter opening page and check off your completed work.

chapter 16

PROCESS COSTING

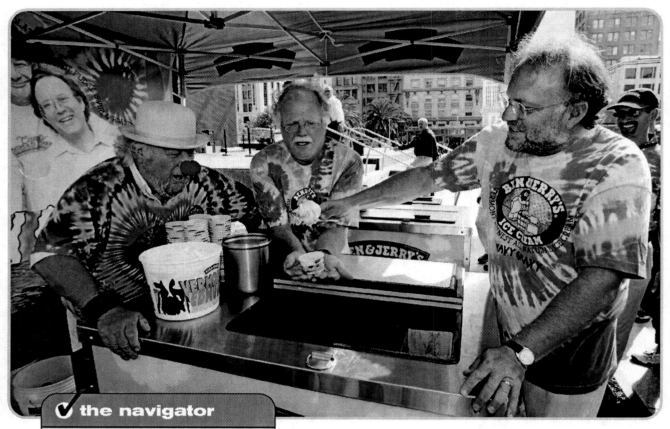

✔ the navigator

- Scan **Study Objectives** ○
- Read **Feature Story** ○
- Scan **Preview** ○
- Read Text and Answer **Do it!**
  p. 843 ○ p. 846 ○ p. 849 ○ p. 854 ○
- Work Using the **Decision Toolkit** ○
- Review **Summary of Study Objectives** ○
- Work Comprehensive **Do it!** p. 866 ○
- Answer **Self-Test Questions** ○
- Complete **Assignments** ○
- Go to **WileyPLUS** for practice and tutorials ○

study objectives

After studying this chapter, you should be able to:

1 Understand who uses process cost systems.

2 Explain the similarities and differences between job order cost and process cost systems.

3 Explain the flow of costs in a process cost system.

4 Make the journal entries to assign manufacturing costs in a process cost system.

5 Compute equivalent units.

6 Explain the four steps necessary to prepare a production cost report.

7 Prepare a production cost report.

Ben & Jerry's Homemade, Inc. (*www.benjerry.com*) is one of the "hottest" and "coolest" U.S. companies. Based in Waterbury, Vermont, the ice cream company that started out of a garage in 1978 is now a public company.

Making ice cream is a process—a movement of product from a mixing department to a prepping department to a pint department. The mixing department is where the ice cream is created. In the prep area, the production process adds extras such as cherries and walnuts to make plain ice cream into "Cherry Garcia," Ben & Jerry's most popular flavor, or fudge-covered waffle cone pieces and a swirl of caramel for "Stephen Colbert's Americone Dream." The pint department is where the ice cream is actually put into containers. As the product is processed from one department to the next, the appropriate materials, labor, and overhead are added to it.

BEN & JERRY'S TRACKS ITS MIX-UPS

"The incoming ingredients from the shipping and receiving departments are stored in certain locations, either in a freezer or dry warehouse," says Beecher Eurich, staff accountant. "As ingredients get added, so do the costs associated with them." How much ice cream is produced? Running plants around the clock, the company produces 18 million gallons a year.

With the company's process costing system, Eurich can tell you how much a certain batch of ice cream costs to make—its materials, labor, and overhead in each of the production departments. She generates reports for the production department heads, but makes sure not to overdo it. "You can get bogged down in numbers," says Eurich. "If you're generating a report that no one can use, then that's a waste of time."

It's more likely, though, that Ben & Jerry's production people want to know how efficient they are. Why? Many own stock in the company.

✔ the
navigator

INSIDE CHAPTER 16 . . .

The cost accounting system used by companies such as *Ben & Jerry's* is **process cost accounting**. In contrast to job order cost accounting, which focuses on the individual job, process cost accounting focuses on the *processes* involved in mass-producing products that are identical or very similar in nature. The primary objective of the chapter is to explain and illustrate process costing.

The content and organization of this chapter are as follows.

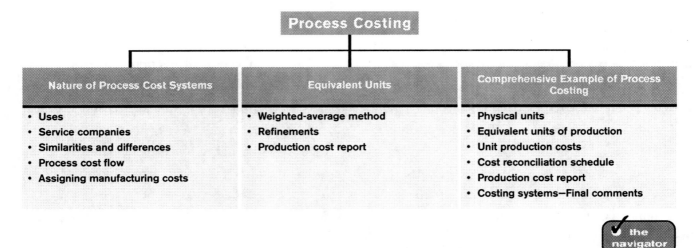

Process Costing		
Nature of Process Cost Systems	**Equivalent Units**	**Comprehensive Example of Process Costing**
• Uses	• Weighted-average method	• Physical units
• Service companies	• Refinements	• Equivalent units of production
• Similarities and differences	• Production cost report	• Unit production costs
• Process cost flow		• Cost reconciliation schedule
• Assigning manufacturing costs		• Production cost report
		• Costing systems—Final comments

The Nature of Process Cost Systems

USES OF PROCESS COST SYSTEMS

study objective 1

Understand who uses process cost systems.

Companies use process cost systems to apply costs to similar products that are mass-produced in a continuous fashion. Ben & Jerry's uses a process cost system: Production of the ice cream, once it begins, continues until the ice cream emerges, and the processing is the same for the entire run—with precisely the same amount of materials, labor, and overhead. Each finished pint of ice cream is indistinguishable from another.

A company such as USX uses process costing in the manufacturing of steel. Kellogg and General Mills use process costing for cereal production; ExxonMobil uses process costing for its oil refining. Sherwin Williams uses process costing for its paint products. At a bottling company like Coca-Cola, the manufacturing process begins with the blending of ingredients. Next, automated machinery moves the bottles into position and fills them. The production process then caps, packages, and forwards the bottles to the finished goods warehouse. Illustration 16-1 shows this process.

Illustration 16-1
Manufacturing processes

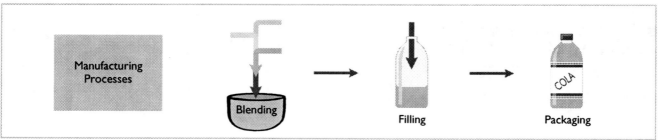

For Coca-Cola, as well as the other companies just mentioned, once production begins, it continues until the finished product emerges, and each unit of finished product is like every other unit.

In comparison, a job order cost system assigns costs to a *specific job*. Examples are the construction of a customized home, the making of a motion picture, or the manufacturing of a specialized machine. Illustration 16-2 provides examples of companies that primarily use either a process cost system or a job order cost system.

Illustration 16-2   Process cost and job order cost companies and products

Process Cost System Company	Product	Job Order Cost System Company	Product
Coca-Cola, PepsiCo	Soft drinks	Young & Rubicam, J. Walter Thompson	Advertising
ExxonMobil, Royal Dutch Shell	Oil	Walt Disney, Warner Brothers	Motion pictures
Intel, Advanced Micro Devices	Computer chips	Center Ice Consultants, Ice Pro	Ice rinks
Dow Chemical, DuPont	Chemicals	Kaiser, Mayo Clinic	Patient health care

PROCESS COSTING FOR SERVICE COMPANIES

Frequently, when we think of service companies, we think of specific, nonroutine tasks, such as rebuilding an automobile engine, providing consulting services on a business acquisition, or working on a major lawsuit. However, many service companies specialize in performing repetitive, routine aspects of a particular business. For example, auto-care vendors such as Jiffy Lube focus on the routine aspects of car care. H&R Block focuses on the routine aspects of basic tax practice, and many large law firms focus on routine legal services, such as uncomplicated divorces. Service companies that provide specific, nonroutine services will probably benefit from using a job order cost system. Those that perform routine, repetitive services will probably be better off with a process cost system.

SIMILARITIES AND DIFFERENCES BETWEEN JOB ORDER COST AND PROCESS COST SYSTEMS

In a job order cost system, companies assign costs to each job. In a process cost system, companies track costs through a series of connected manufacturing processes or departments, rather than by individual jobs. Thus, companies use process cost systems when they produce a large volume of uniform or relatively homogeneous products. Illustration 16-3 (page 842) shows the basic flow of costs in these two systems.

The following analysis highlights the basic similarities and differences between these two systems.

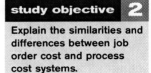

study objective 2

Explain the similarities and differences between job order cost and process cost systems.

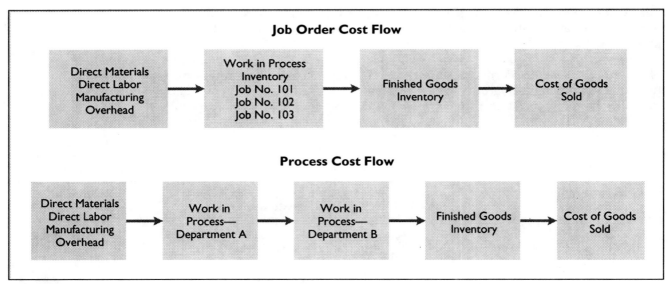

Illustration 16-3 Job order cost and process cost flow

Similarities

Job order cost and process cost systems are similar in three ways:

1. **The manufacturing cost elements.** Both costing systems track three manufacturing cost elements—direct materials, direct labor, and manufacturing overhead.

2. **The accumulation of the costs of materials, labor, and overhead.** Both costing systems debit raw materials to Raw Materials Inventory; factory labor to Factory Labor; and manufacturing overhead costs to Manufacturing Overhead.

3. **The flow of costs.** As noted above, both systems accumulate all manufacturing costs by debits to Raw Materials Inventory, Factory Labor, and Manufacturing Overhead. Both systems then assign these costs to the same accounts—Work in Process, Finished Goods Inventory, and Cost of Goods Sold. **The methods of assigning costs, however, differ significantly.** These differences are explained and illustrated later in the chapter.

Differences

The differences between a job order cost and a process cost system are as follows.

1. **The number of work in process accounts used.** A job order cost system uses only one work in process account. A process cost system uses multiple work in process accounts.

2. **Documents used to track costs.** A job order cost system charges costs to individual jobs and summarizes them in a job cost sheet. A process cost system summarizes costs in a production cost report for each department.

3. **The point at which costs are totaled.** A job order cost system totals costs when the job is completed. A process cost system totals costs at the end of a period of time.

4. **Unit cost computations.** In a job order cost system, the unit cost is the total cost per job divided by the units produced. In a process cost system, the unit cost is total manufacturing costs for the period divided by the units produced during the period.

Illustration 16-4 summarizes the major differences between a job order cost and a process cost system.

Features	Job Order Cost System	Process Cost System
Work in process accounts	• One work in process account	• Multiple work in process accounts
Documents used	• Job cost sheets	• Production cost reports
Determination of total manufacturing costs	• Each job	• Each period
Unit-cost computations	• Cost of each job ÷ Units produced for the job	• Total manufacturing costs ÷ Units produced during the period

Illustration 16-4
Job order versus process cost systems

before you go on...

Do it!

Indicate whether each of the following statements is true or false.

1. A law firm is likely to use process costing for major lawsuits.
2. A manufacturer of paintballs is likely to use process costing.
3. Both job order and process costing determine total costs at the end of a period of time.
4. Process costing does not keep track of manufacturing overhead.

Solution

1. false.   2. true.   3. false.   4. false.

Related exercise material: **Do it!** 16-1 and E16-1.

COMPARE JOB ORDER AND PROCESS COST SYSTEMS

Action Plan

• Use job order costing in situations where unit costs are high, unit volume is low, and products are unique.

• Use process costing when there is a large volume of relatively homogeneous products.

PROCESS COST FLOW

Illustration 16-5 shows the flow of costs in the process cost system for Tyler Company. Tyler Company manufactures automatic can openers that it sells to retail outlets. Manufacturing consists of two processes: machining and assembly. The Machining Department shapes, hones, and drills the raw materials. The Assembly Department assembles and packages the parts.

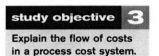

study objective 3
Explain the flow of costs in a process cost system.

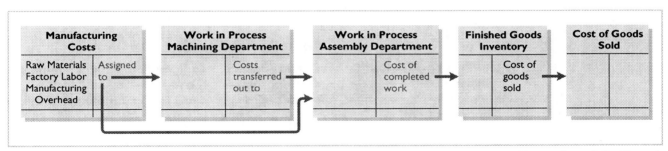

Manufacturing Costs		Work in Process Machining Department		Work in Process Assembly Department		Finished Goods Inventory		Cost of Goods Sold	
Raw Materials Factory Labor Manufacturing Overhead	Assigned to		Costs transferred out to		Cost of completed work		Cost of goods sold		

Illustration 16-5 Flow of costs in process cost system

As the flow of costs indicates, the company can add materials, labor, and manufacturing overhead in both the Machining and Assembly departments. When it finishes its work, the Machining Department transfers the partially completed units to the Assembly Department. The Assembly Department finishes the goods and then transfers them to the finished goods inventory. Upon sale, Tyler removes the goods from the finished goods inventory. Within each department, a similar set of activities is performed on each unit processed.

ASSIGNING MANUFACTURING COSTS– JOURNAL ENTRIES

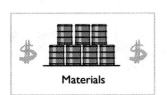

study objective 4

Make the journal entries to assign manufacturing costs in a process cost system.

As indicated, the accumulation of the costs of materials, labor, and manufacturing overhead is the same in a process cost system as in a job order cost system. That is, both systems follow these procedures:

- Companies debit all raw materials to Raw Materials Inventory at the time of purchase.
- They debit all factory labor to Factory Labor as the labor costs are incurred.
- They debit overhead costs to Manufacturing Overhead as these costs are incurred.

However, the assignment of the three manufacturing cost elements to Work in Process in a process cost system is different from a job order cost system. Here we'll look at how companies assign these manufacturing cost elements in a process cost system.

Materials Costs

All raw materials issued for production are a materials cost to the producing department. A process cost system may use materials requisition slips, but **it generally requires fewer requisitions than in a job order cost system, because the materials are used for processes rather than for specific jobs** and therefore typically are for larger quantities.

At the beginning of the first process, a company usually adds most of the materials needed for production. However, other materials may be added at various points. For example, in the manufacture of Hershey candy bars, the chocolate and other ingredients are added at the beginning of the first process, and the wrappers and cartons are added at the end of the packaging process. Tyler Company adds materials at the beginning of each process. Tyler makes the following entry to record the materials used:

Work in Process—Machining	XXXX	
Work in Process—Assembly	XXXX	
Raw Materials Inventory		XXXX
(To record materials used)		

Ice cream maker Ben & Jerry's adds materials in three departments: milk and flavoring in the mixing department, extras such as cherries and walnuts in the prepping department, and cardboard containers in the pinting (packaging) department.

Factory Labor Costs

In a process cost system, as in a job order cost system, companies may use time tickets to determine the cost of labor assignable to production departments. Since they assign labor costs to a process rather than a job, they can obtain, from the payroll register or departmental payroll summaries, the labor cost chargeable to a process.

Labor costs for the Machining Department will include the wages of employees who shape, hone, and drill the raw materials. The entry to assign these costs for Tyler Company is:

Work in Process—Machining	XXXX	
Work in Process—Assembly	XXXX	
Factory Labor		XXXX
(To assign factory labor to production)		

Manufacturing Overhead Costs

The objective in assigning overhead in a process cost system is to allocate the overhead costs to the production departments on an objective and equitable basis. That basis is the activity that "drives" or causes the costs. A primary driver of overhead costs in continuous manufacturing operations is **machine time used**, not direct labor. Thus, companies **widely use machine hours** in allocating manufacturing overhead costs using predetermined overhead rates. Tyler's entry to allocate overhead to the two processes is:

Manufacturing Overhead

Work in Process—Machining	XXXX	
Work in Process—Assembly	XXXX	
Manufacturing Overhead		XXXX
(To assign overhead to production)		

Management Insight
Choosing a Cost Driver

In one of its automated cost centers, Caterpillar feeds work into the cost center, where robotic machines process it and transfer the finished job to the next cost center without human intervention. One person tends all of the machines and spends more time maintaining machines than operating them. In such cases, overhead rates based on direct labor hours may be misleading. Surprisingly, some companies continue to assign manufacturing overhead on the basis of direct labor despite the fact that there is no cause-and-effect relationship between labor and overhead.

 What is the result if a company uses the wrong "cost driver" to assign manufacturing overhead? (See page 887.)

Transfer to Next Department

At the end of the month, Tyler needs an entry to record the cost of the goods transferred out of the Machining Department. In this case, the transfer is to the Assembly Department, and Tyler makes the following entry.

Work in Process—Assembly	XXXXX	
Work in Process—Machining		XXXXX
(To record transfer of units to the Assembly		
Department)		

Transfer to Finished Goods

When the Assembly Department completes the units, it transfers them to the finished goods warehouse. The entry for this transfer is as follows.

Finished Goods Inventory	XXXXX	
Work in Process—Assembly		XXXXX
(To record transfer of units to finished goods)		

Transfer to Cost of Goods Sold

When Tyler sells the finished goods, it records the cost of goods sold as follows.

Cost of Goods Sold	XXXXX	
Finished Goods Inventory		XXXXX
(To record cost of units sold)		

before you go on...

MANUFACTURING COSTS IN PROCESS COSTING

Do it! Ruth Company manufactures ZEBO through two processes: blending and bottling. In June, raw materials used were Blending $18,000 and Bottling $4,000. Factory labor costs were Blending $12,000 and Bottling $5,000. Manufacturing overhead costs were Blending $6,000 and Bottling $2,500. The company transfers units completed at a cost of $19,000 in the Blending Department to the Bottling Department. The Bottling Department transfers units completed at a cost of $11,000 to Finished Goods. Journalize the assignment of these costs to the two processes and the transfer of units as appropriate.

Action Plan

- In process cost accounting, keep separate work in process accounts for each process.
- When the costs are assigned to production, debit the separate work in process accounts.
- Transfer cost of completed units to the next process or to Finished Goods.

Solution

The entries are:

Work in Process—Blending	18,000	
Work in Process—Bottling	4,000	
Raw Materials Inventory		22,000
(To record materials used)		
Work in Process—Blending	12,000	
Work in Process—Bottling	5,000	
Factory Labor		17,000
(To assign factory labor to production)		
Work in Process—Blending	6,000	
Work in Process—Bottling	2,500	
Manufacturing Overhead		8,500
(To assign overhead to production)		
Work in Process—Bottling	19,000	
Work in Process—Blending		19,000
(To record transfer of units to the Bottling Department)		
Finished Goods Inventory	11,000	
Work in Process—Bottling		11,000
(To record transfer of units to finished goods)		

Related exercise material: **BE16-1, BE16-2, BE16-3, Do it! 16-2, E16-2,** and **E16-4.**

Equivalent Units

Suppose you have a work-study job in the office of your college's president, and she asks you to compute the cost of instruction per full-time equivalent student at your college. The college's vice president for finance provides the following information.

study objective 5
Compute equivalent units.

Costs:	
Total cost of instruction	$9,000,000
Student population:	
Full-time students	900
Part-time students	1,000

Illustration 16-6
Information for full-time student example

Part-time students take 60% of the classes of a full-time student during the year. To compute the number of full-time equivalent students per year, you would make the following computation.

Full-time Students	+	**Equivalent Units of Part-time Students**	=	**Full-time Equivalent Students**
900	+	(60% × 1,000)	=	1,500

Illustration 16-7
Full-time equivalent unit computation

The cost of instruction per full-time equivalent student is therefore the total cost of instruction ($9,000,000) divided by the number of full-time equivalent students (1,500), which is $6,000 ($9,000,000 ÷ 1,500).

A process cost system uses the same idea, called equivalent units of production. Equivalent units of production measure the work done during the period, expressed in fully completed units. Companies use this measure to determine the cost per unit of completed product.

WEIGHTED-AVERAGE METHOD

The formula to compute equivalent units of production is as follows.

Units Completed and Transferred Out	+	**Equivalent Units of Ending Work in Process**	=	**Equivalent Units of Production**

Illustration 16-8
Equivalent units of production formula

To better understand this concept of equivalent units, consider the following two separate examples.

Example 1: In a specific period the entire output of Sullivan Company's Blending Department consists of ending work in process of 4,000 units which are 60% complete as to materials, labor, and overhead. The equivalent units of production for the Blending Department are therefore 2,400 units (4,000 × 60%).

Example 2: The output of Kori Company's Packaging Department during the period consists of 10,000 units completed and transferred out, and 5,000 units in ending work in process which are 70% completed. The equivalent units of production are therefore 13,500 [10,000 + (5,000 × 70%)].

This method of computing equivalent units is referred to as the weighted-average method. It considers the degree of completion (weighting) of the units completed and transferred out and the ending work in process.

REFINEMENTS ON THE WEIGHTED-AVERAGE METHOD

Kellogg Company has produced Eggo® Waffles since 1970. Three departments produce these waffles: Mixing, Baking, and Freezing/Packaging. The Mixing Department combines dry ingredients, including flour, salt, and baking powder, with liquid ingredients, including eggs and vegetable oil, to make waffle batter. Illustration 16-9 provides information related to the Mixing Department at the end of June.

Illustration 16-9
Information for Mixing
Department

MIXING DEPARTMENT

		Percentage Complete	
	Physical Units	Materials	Conversion Costs
Work in process, June 1	100,000	100%	70%
Started into production	800,000		
Total units	900,000		
Units transferred out	700,000		
Work in process, June 30	200,000	100%	60%
Total units	900,000		

Helpful Hint When are separate unit cost computations needed for materials and conversion costs? Answer: Whenever the two types of costs do not occur in the process at the same time.

Illustration 16-9 indicates that the beginning work in process is 100% complete as to materials cost and 70% complete as to conversion costs. Conversion costs **are the sum of labor costs and overhead costs.** In other words, Kellogg adds both the dry and liquid ingredients (materials) at the beginning of the waffle-making process, and the conversion costs (labor and overhead) related to the mixing of these ingredients are incurred uniformly and are 70% complete. The ending work in process is 100% complete as to materials cost and 60% complete as to conversion costs.

We then use the Mixing Department information to determine equivalent units. **In computing equivalent units, the beginning work in process is not part of the equivalent-units-of-production formula.** The units transferred out to the Baking Department are fully complete as to both materials and conversion costs. The ending work in process is fully complete as to materials, but only 60% complete as to conversion costs. We therefore need to make **two equivalent unit computations**: one for materials, and the other for conversion costs. Illustration 16-10 shows these computations.

Illustration 16-10
Computation of equivalent units—Mixing Department

Ethics Note An unethical manager might use incorrect completion percentages when determining equivalent units. This results in either raising or lowering costs. Since completion percentages are somewhat subjective, this form of income manipulation can be difficult to detect.

MIXING DEPARTMENT

	Equivalent Units	
	Materials	Conversion Costs
Units transferred out	700,000	700,000
Work in process, June 30		
200,000 × 100%	200,000	
200,000 × 60%		120,000
Total equivalent units	900,000	820,000

We can refine the earlier formula used to compute equivalent units of production (Illustration 16-8, page 847) to show the computations for materials and for conversion costs, as follows.

Units Completed and Transferred Out– Materials	+	Equivalent Units of Ending Work in Process–Materials	=	Equivalent Units of Production– Materials
Units Completed and Transferred Out– Conversion Costs	**+**	**Equivalent Units of Ending Work in Process–Conversion Costs**	**=**	**Equivalent Units of Production– Conversion Costs**

Illustration 16-11
Refined equivalent units of production formula

Management Insight

Keeping Score for the Xbox

When you are as big and as profitable as Microsoft, you get to a point where continued rapid growth is very difficult. For example, many believe it is unlikely that Microsoft will see much growth in software sales. As a result, the company is looking for new markets, such as the video game market with its Xbox player.

Profitability in the video-game hardware market has been elusive. Microsoft has struggled to control the costs of both manufacturing and distribution. One analyst predicted that Microsoft's "snowballing" costs in the next period could exceed budget by $2.4 billion. Microsoft's Chief Financial Officer blamed the high costs on unexpectedly high volumes, saying, "We pushed market volumes very high in the Xbox business. As a result of that we incurred some costs in the supply chain." Given these issues, and despite its incredible success as a software company, some observers question whether Microsoft will be able to make the changes that are required to become a successful hardware manufacturer.

Source: Rober A. Guth, "Microsoft Net Rises 16%, but Costs Damp Results," *Wall Street Journal* (April 28, 2006).

In what ways has cost accounting probably become more critical for Microsoft in recent years? (See page 887.)

before you go on...

Do it!

The fabricating department has the following production and cost data for the current month.

Beginning Work in Process	Units Transferred Out	Ending Work in Process
–0–	15,000	10,000

Materials are entered at the beginning of the process. The ending work in process units are 30% complete as to conversion costs. Compute the equivalent units of production for (a) materials and (b) conversion costs.

EQUIVALENT UNITS

Action Plan
- To measure the work done during the period, expressed in fully completed units, compute equivalent units of production.
- Use the appropriate formula: Units completed and transferred out + Equivalent units of ending work in process = Equivalent units of production.

Solution

(a) Since materials are entered at the beginning of the process, the equivalent units of ending work in process are 10,000. Thus, 15,000 units + 10,000 units = 25,000 equivalent units of production for materials.

(b) Since ending work in process is only 30% complete as to conversion costs, the equivalent units of ending work in process are 3,000 (30% × 10,000 units). Thus, 15,000 units + 3,000 units = 18,000 equivalent units of production for conversion costs.

Related exercise material: **BE16-5, BE16-10,** **Do it!** 16-3, E16-5, E16-6, E16-8, E16-9, E16-10, E16-11, E16-13, E16-14, and E16-15.

PRODUCTION COST REPORT

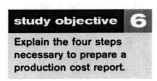

As mentioned earlier, companies prepare a production cost report for each department. A production cost report is the key document that management uses to understand the activities in a department; it shows the production quantity and cost data related to that department. For example, in producing Eggo® Waffles, Kellogg Company uses three production cost reports: Mixing, Baking, and Freezing/Packaging. Illustration 16-12 shows the flow of costs to make an Eggo® Waffle and the related production cost reports for each department.

Illustration 16-12
Flow of costs in making
Eggo® Waffles

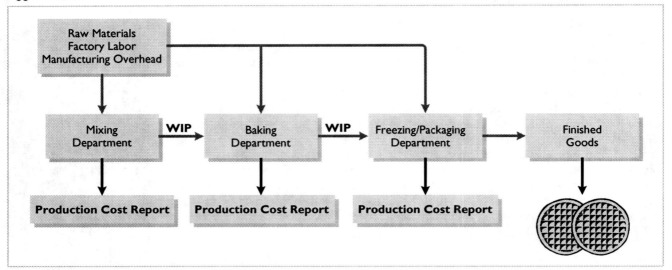

In order to complete a production cost report, the company must perform four steps, which, as a whole, make up the process costing system.

1. Compute the physical unit flow.
2. Compute the equivalent units of production.
3. Compute unit production costs.
4. Prepare a cost reconciliation schedule.

The next section explores these steps in an extended example.

Comprehensive Example of Process Costing

Illustration 16-13 shows assumed data for the Mixing Department at Kellogg Company for the month of June. We will use this information to complete a production cost report for the Mixing Department.

COMPUTE THE PHYSICAL UNIT FLOW (STEP 1)

Physical units are the actual units to be accounted for during a period, irrespective of any work performed. To keep track of these units, add the units started (or transferred) into production during the period to the units in process at the beginning of the period. This amount is referred to as the total units to be accounted for.

Illustration 16-13
Unit and cost data—Mixing
Department

MIXING DEPARTMENT

Units

Work in process, June 1	100,000
Direct materials: 100% complete	
Conversion costs: 70% complete	
Units started into production during June	800,000
Units completed and transferred out to Baking Department	700,000
Work in process, June 30	200,000
Direct materials: 100% complete	
Conversion costs: 60% complete	

Costs

Work in process, June 1	
Direct materials: 100% complete	$ 50,000
Conversion costs: 70% complete	35,000
Cost of work in process, June 1	$ 85,000
Costs incurred during production in June	
Direct materials	$400,000
Conversion costs	170,000
Costs incurred in June	$570,000

The total units then are accounted for by the output of the period. The output consists of units transferred out during the period and any units in process at the end of the period. This amount is referred to as the total units accounted for. Illustration 16-14 shows the flow of physical units for Kellogg's Mixing Department for the month of June.

Illustration 16-14
Physical unit flow—Mixing
Department

MIXING DEPARTMENT

	Physical Units
Units to be accounted for	
Work in process, June 1	100,000
Started (transferred) into production	800,000
Total units	900,000
Units accounted for	
Completed and transferred out	700,000
Work in process, June 30	200,000
Total units	900,000

The records indicate that the Mixing Department must account for 900,000 units. Of this sum, 700,000 units were transferred to the Baking Department and 200,000 units were still in process.

COMPUTE EQUIVALENT UNITS OF PRODUCTION (STEP 2)

Once the physical flow of the units is established, Kellogg must measure the Mixing Department's productivity in terms of equivalent units of production. The Mixing Department adds materials at the beginning of the process, and it incurs conversion costs uniformly during the process. Thus, we need two computations of equivalent units: one for materials and one for conversion costs. The equivalent unit computation is as follows.

Helpful Hint Materials are not always added at the beginning of the process. For example, materials are sometimes added uniformly during the process.

Illustration 16-15
Computation of equivalent units–Mixing Department

Helpful Hint Remember that we ignore the beginning work in process in this computation.

	Equivalent Units	
	Materials	**Conversion Costs**
Units transferred out	700,000	700,000
Work in process, June 30		
200,000 × 100%	200,000	
200,000 × 60%		120,000
Total equivalent units	900,000	820,000

COMPUTE UNIT PRODUCTION COSTS (STEP 3)

Armed with the knowledge of the equivalent units of production, we can now compute the unit production costs. Unit production costs are costs expressed in terms of equivalent units of production. When equivalent units of production are different for materials and conversion costs, we compute three unit costs: (1) materials, (2) conversion, and (3) total manufacturing.

The computation of total materials cost related to Eggo® Waffles is as follows.

Illustration 16-16
Total materials cost computation

Work in process, June 1	
Direct materials cost	$ 50,000
Costs added to production during June	
Direct materials cost	400,000
Total materials cost	$450,000

The computation of unit materials cost is as follows.

Illustration 16-17
Unit materials cost computation

Total Materials Cost	÷	**Equivalent Units of Materials**	=	**Unit Materials Cost**
$450,000	÷	900,000	=	$0.50

Illustration 16-18 shows the computation of total conversion costs.

Illustration 16-18
Total conversion costs computation

Work in process, June 1	
Conversion costs	$ 35,000
Costs added to production during June	
Conversion costs	170,000
Total conversion costs	$205,000

The computation of unit conversion cost is as follows.

Illustration 16-19
Unit conversion cost computation

Total Conversion Costs	÷	**Equivalent Units of Conversion Costs**	=	**Unit Conversion Cost**
$205,000	÷	820,000	=	$0.25

Total manufacturing cost per unit is therefore computed as shown in Illustration 16-20.

Unit Materials Cost	+	Unit Conversion Cost	=	Total Manufacturing Cost per Unit
$0.50	+	$0.25	=	$0.75

Illustration 16-20
Total manufacturing cost per unit

PREPARE A COST RECONCILIATION SCHEDULE (STEP 4)

We are now ready to determine the cost of goods transferred out of the Mixing Department to the Baking Department and the costs in ending work in process. Kellogg charged total costs of $655,000 to the Mixing Department in June, calculated as follows.

Costs to be accounted for	
Work in process, June 1	$ 85,000
Started into production	570,000
Total costs	$655,000

Illustration 16-21
Costs charged to Mixing Department

The company then prepares a cost reconciliation schedule to assign these costs to (a) units transferred out to the Baking Department and (b) ending work in process.

MIXING DEPARTMENT
Cost Reconciliation Schedule

Costs accounted for		
Transferred out (700,000 × $0.75)		$ 525,000
Work in process, June 30		
Materials (200,000 × $0.50)	$100,000	
Conversion costs (120,000 × $0.25)	30,000	130,000
Total costs		$655,000

Illustration 16-22
Cost reconciliation schedule–Mixing Department

Kellogg uses the total manufacturing cost per unit, $0.75, in costing the **units completed** and transferred to the Baking Department. In contrast, the unit cost of materials and the unit cost of conversion are needed in costing **units in process**. The cost reconciliation schedule shows that the total costs accounted for (Illustration 16-22) equal the total costs to be accounted for (Illustration 16-21).

PREPARING THE PRODUCTION COST REPORT

At this point, Kellogg is ready to prepare the production cost report for the Mixing Department. As indicated earlier, this report is an internal document for management that shows production quantity and cost data for a production department.

There are four steps in preparing a production cost report. They are:

1. Compute the physical unit flow.
2. Compute the equivalent units of production.
3. Compute unit production costs.
4. Prepare a cost reconciliation schedule.

Illustration 16-23 (page 854) shows the production cost report for the Mixing Department. The report identifies the four steps.

study objective 7

Prepare a production cost report.

Illustration 16-23
Production cost report

Mixing Department.xls

File   Edit   View   Insert   Format   Tools   Data   Window   Help

	A	B	C	D	E	F
			Mixing Department			
			Production Cost Report			
			For the Month Ended June 30, 2012			
				Equivalent Units		
			Physical Units	Materials	Conversion Costs	
6	QUANTITIES		Step 1	Step 2		
7	Units to be accounted for					
8	Work in process, June 1		100,000			
9	Started into production		800,000			
10	Total units		900,000			
11	Units accounted for					
12	Transferred out		700,000	700,000	700,000	
13	Work in process, June 30		200,000	200,000	120,000	(200,000 × 60%)
14	Total units		900,000	900,000	820,000	
15	COSTS Unit costs Step 3			Materials	Conversion Costs	Total
16	Costs in June	(a)		$450,000	$205,000	$655,000
17	Equivalent units	(b)		900,000	820,000	
18	Unit costs [(a) ÷ (b)]			$0.50	$0.25	$0.75
19	Costs to be accounted for					
20	Work in process, June 1					$85,000
21	Started into production					570,000
22	Total costs					$655,000
23	Cost Reconciliation Schedule Step 4					
24	Costs accounted for					
25	Transferred out (700,000 × $0.75)					$525,000
26	Work in process, June 30					
27	Materials (200,000 × $0.50)				$100,000	
28	Conversion costs (120,000 × $0.25)				30,000	130,000
29	Total costs					$655,000

Production cost reports provide a basis for evaluating the productivity of a department. In addition, managers can use the cost data to assess whether unit costs and total costs are reasonable. By comparing the quantity and cost data with predetermined goals, top management can also judge whether current performance is meeting planned objectives.

DECISION TOOLKIT

DECISION CHECKPOINTS	INFO NEEDED FOR DECISION	TOOL TO USE FOR DECISION	HOW TO EVALUATE RESULTS
What is the cost of a product?	Cost of materials, labor, and overhead assigned to processes used to make the product	Production cost report	Compare costs to previous periods, to competitors, and to expected selling price to evaluate overall profitability.

before you go on...

COST RECONCILIATION SCHEDULE

Do it! In March, Rodayo Manufacturing had the following unit production costs: materials $6 and conversion costs $9. On March 1, it had zero work in process. During March, Rodayo transferred out 12,000 units. As of March 31, 800 units that were 25 percent complete as to conversion costs and 100 percent complete as to materials were in ending work in process. Assign the costs to the units transferred out and in process.

Solution

The assignment of costs is as follows.

Costs accounted for		
Transferred out (12,000 × $15)		$180,000
Work in process, March 31		
Materials (800 × $6)	$4,800	
Conversion costs (200ª × $9)	1,800	6,600
Total costs		$186,600
ª800 × 25%		

Action Plan

- Assign the total manufacturing cost of $15 per unit to the 12,000 units transferred out.
- Assign the materials cost and conversion costs based on equivalent units of production to units in ending work in process.

Related exercise material: **BE16-4, BE16-6, BE16-7, BE16-8, BE16-9, BE16-10, Do it! 16-4, E16-5, E16-6, E16-8, E16-9, E16-10, E16-11, E16-14, and E16-15.**

COSTING SYSTEMS–FINAL COMMENTS

Companies often use a combination of a process cost and a job order cost system. Called operations costing, this hybrid system is similar to process costing in its assumption that standardized methods are used to manufacture the product. At the same time, the product may have some customized, individual features that require the use of a job order cost system.

Consider, for example, the automobile manufacturer Ford Motor Company. Each vehicle at a given plant goes through the same assembly line, but Ford uses different materials (such as seat coverings, paint, and tinted glass) for different vehicles. Similarly, Kellogg's Pop-Tarts® toaster pastries go through numerous standardized processes—mixing, filling, baking, frosting, and packaging. The pastry dough, though, comes in different flavors—plain, chocolate, and graham—and fillings include Smucker's® real fruit, chocolate fudge, vanilla creme, brown sugar cinnamon, and s'mores.

A cost-benefit tradeoff occurs as a company decides which costing system to use. A job order cost system, for example, provides detailed information related to the cost of the product. Because each job has its own distinguishing characteristics, the system can provide an accurate cost per job. This information is useful in controlling costs and pricing products. However, the cost of implementing a job order cost system is often expensive because of the accounting costs involved.

On the other hand, for a company like Intel, which makes computer chips, is there a benefit in knowing whether the cost of the one hundredth chip produced is different from the one thousandth chip produced? Probably not. An average cost of the product will suffice for control and pricing purposes.

In summary, when deciding to use one of these systems, or a combination system, a company must weigh the costs of implementing the system against the benefits from the additional information provided.

DECISION TOOLKIT

DECISION CHECKPOINTS	INFO NEEDED FOR DECISION	TOOL TO USE FOR DECISION	HOW TO EVALUATE RESULTS
What costing method should be used?	Type of product or service produced	Cost of accounting system; benefits of additional information	The benefits of providing the additional information should exceed the costs of the accounting system needed to develop the information.

USING THE DECISION TOOLKIT

Essence Company manufactures a high-end after-shave lotion, called Eternity, in 10-ounce plastic bottles. Because the market for after-shave lotion is highly competitive, the company is very concerned about keeping its costs under control. Eternity is manufactured through three processes: mixing, filling, and corking. Materials are added at the beginning of the process, and labor and overhead are incurred uniformly throughout each process. The company uses a weighted-average method to cost its product. A partially completed production cost report for the month of May for the Mixing Department is shown below.

ESSENCE COMPANY
Mixing Department
Production Cost Report
For the Month Ended May 31, 2012

		Equivalent Units	
Quantities	**Physical Units**	**Materials**	**Conversion Costs**
Units to be accounted for	Step 1	Step 2	
Work in process, May 1	1,000		
Started into production	2,000		
Total units	3,000		
Units accounted for			
Transferred out	2,200	?	?
Work in process, May 31	800	?	?
Total units	3,000	?	?

Costs		**Materials**	**Conversion Costs**	**Total**
Unit costs Step 3				
Costs in May	(a)	?	?	?
Equivalent units	(b)	?	?	
Unit costs [(a) ÷ (b)]		?	?	?
Costs to be accounted for				
Work in process, May 1				$ 56,300
Started into production				119,320
Total costs				$175,620

Cost Reconciliation Schedule Step 4

Costs accounted for			
Transferred out			?
Work in process, May 31			
Materials		?	
Conversion costs		?	?
Total costs			?

Additional information:
Work in process, May 1, 1000 units

Materials cost, 1,000 units (100% complete)	$49,100	
Conversion costs, 1,000 units (70% complete)	7,200	$ 56,300
Materials cost for May, 2,000 units		$100,000

Work in process, May 31, 800 units, 100% complete as to materials and 50% complete as to conversion costs.

Instructions

(a) Prepare a production cost report for the Mixing Department for the month of May.

(b) Prepare the journal entry to record the transfer of goods from the Mixing Department to the Filling Department.

(c) Explain why Essence Company is using a process cost system to account for its costs.

Solution

(a) A completed production cost report for the Mixing Department is shown below. Computations to support the amounts reported follow the report.

ESSENCE COMPANY
Mixing Department
Production Cost Report
For the Month Ended May 31, 2012

		Equivalent Units	
	Physical		Conversion
Quantities	**Units**	**Materials**	**Costs**
Units to be accounted for	Step 1		Step 2
Work in process, May 1	1,000		
Started into production	2,000		
Total units	3,000		
Units accounted for			
Transferred out	2,200	2,200	2,200
Work in process, May 31	800	800	400 (800 × 50%)
Total units	3,000	3,000	2,600

Costs			Conversion	
Unit costs Step 3		**Materials**	**Costs**	**Total**
Costs in May*	(a)	$149,100	$26,520	$175,620
Equivalent units	(b)	3,000	2,600	
Unit costs [(a) ÷ (b)]		$49.70	$10.20	$59.90
Costs to be accounted for				
Work in process, May 1				$ 56,300
Started into production				119,320
Total costs				$175,620

*Additional computations to support production cost report data:
Materials cost—$49,100 + $100,000
Conversion costs—$7,200 + $19,320 ($119,320 − $100,000)

Cost Reconciliation Schedule Step 4

Costs accounted for			
Transferred out (2,200 × $59.90)			$131,780
Work in process, May 31			
Materials (800 × $49.70)		$39,760	
Conversion costs (400 × $10.20)		4,080	43,840
Total costs			$175,620

(b)

Work in Process—Filling	131,780	
Work in Process—Mixing		131,780

Action Plan

- Compute the physical unit flow—that is, the total units to be accounted for.
- Compute the equivalent units of production.
- Compute the unit production costs, expressed in terms of equivalent units of production.
- Prepare a cost reconciliation schedule, which shows that the total costs accounted for equal the total costs to be accounted for.

(c) Companies use process cost systems to apply costs to similar products that are mass-produced in a continuous fashion. Essence Company uses a process cost system because production of the after-shave lotion, once it begins, continues until the after-shave lotion emerges. The processing is the same for the entire run—with precisely the same amount of materials, labor, and overhead. Each bottle of Eternity after-shave lotion is indistinguishable from another.

Summary of Study Objectives

1 **Understand who uses process cost systems.** Companies that mass-produce similar products in a continuous fashion use process cost systems. Once production begins, it continues until the finished product emerges. Each unit of finished product is indistinguishable from every other unit.

2 **Explain the similarities and differences between job order cost and process cost systems.** Job order cost systems are similar to process cost systems in three ways: (1) Both systems track the same cost elements—direct materials, direct labor, and manufacturing overhead. (2) Both accumulate costs in the same accounts—Raw Materials Inventory, Factory Labor, and Manufacturing Overhead. (3) Both assign accumulated costs to the same accounts—Work in Process, Finished Goods Inventory, and Cost of Goods Sold. However, the method of assigning costs differs significantly.

There are four main differences between the two cost systems: (1) A process cost system uses separate accounts for each department or manufacturing process, rather than only one work in process account used in a job order cost system. (2) A process cost system summarizes costs in a production cost report for each department. A job order cost system charges costs to individual jobs and summarizes them in a job cost sheet. (3) Costs are totaled at the end of a time period in a process cost system, but at the completion of a job in a job order cost system. (4) A process cost system calculates unit cost as: Total manufacturing costs for the period ÷ Units produced during the period. A job order cost system calculates unit cost as: Total cost per job ÷ Units produced.

3 **Explain the flow of costs in a process cost system.** A process cost system assigns manufacturing costs for raw materials, labor, and overhead to work in process accounts for various departments or manufacturing processes. It transfers the costs of partially completed units from one department to another as those units move through the manufacturing process. The system transfers the costs of completed work to Finished Goods Inventory. Finally, when inventory is sold, the system transfers the costs to Cost of Goods Sold.

4 **Make the journal entries to assign manufacturing costs in a process cost system.** Entries to assign the costs of raw materials, labor, and overhead consist of a credit to Raw Materials Inventory, Factory Labor, and Manufacturing Overhead, and a debit to Work in Process for each department. Entries to record the cost of goods transferred to another department are a credit to Work in Process for the department whose work is finished and a debit to the department to which the goods are transferred. The entry to record units completed and transferred to the warehouse is a credit to Work in Process for the department whose work is finished and a debit to Finished Goods Inventory. The entry to record the sale of goods is a credit to Finished Goods Inventory and a debit to Cost of Goods Sold.

5 **Compute equivalent units.** Equivalent units of production measure work done during a period, expressed in fully completed units. Companies use this measure to determine the cost per unit of completed product. Equivalent units are the sum of units completed and transferred out plus equivalent units of ending work in process.

6 **Explain the four steps necessary to prepare a production cost report.** The four steps to complete a production cost report are: (1) Compute the physical unit flow—that is, the total units to be accounted for. (2) Compute the equivalent units of production. (3) Compute the unit production costs, expressed in terms of equivalent units of production. (4) Prepare a cost reconciliation schedule, which shows that the total costs accounted for equal the total costs to be accounted for.

7 **Prepare a production cost report.** The production cost report contains both quantity and cost data for a production department. There are four sections in the report: (1) number of physical units, (2) equivalent units determination, (3) unit costs, and (4) cost reconciliation schedule.

DECISION TOOLKIT   A SUMMARY

DECISION CHECKPOINTS	INFO NEEDED FOR DECISION	TOOL TO USE FOR DECISION	HOW TO EVALUATE RESULTS
What is the cost of a product?	Costs of materials, labor, and overhead assigned to processes used to make the product	Production cost report	Compare costs to previous periods, to competitors, and to expected selling price to evaluate overall profitability.
Which costing method should be used?	Type of product or service produced	Cost of accounting system; benefits of additional information	The benefits of providing the additional information should exceed the costs of the accounting system needed to develop the information.

appendix 16A

FIFO Method

In this chapter, we demonstrated the weighted-average method of computing equivalent units. Some companies use a different method, referred to as the **first-in, first-out (FIFO) method**, to compute equivalent units. The purpose of this appendix is to illustrate how companies use the FIFO method to prepare a production cost report.

EQUIVALENT UNITS UNDER FIFO

Under the FIFO method, companies compute equivalent units on a first-in, first-out basis. Some companies favor the FIFO method because the FIFO cost assumption usually corresponds to the actual physical flow of the goods. Under the FIFO method, companies therefore assume that the beginning work in process is completed before new work is started.

study objective 8

Compute equivalent units using the FIFO method.

Using the FIFO method, equivalent units are the sum of the work performed to:

1. Finish the units of beginning work in process inventory.
2. Complete the units started into production during the period (referred to as the **units started and completed**).
3. Start, but only partially complete, the units in ending work in process inventory.

Normally, in a process costing system, some units will always be in process at both the beginning and end of the period.

Illustration

Illustration 16A-1 (page 860) shows the physical flow of units for the Assembly Department of Shutters Inc. In addition, it indicates the degree of completion of the work in process accounts in regard to conversion costs.

Illustration 16A-1
Physical unit flow–
Assembly Department

ASSEMBLY DEPARTMENT

	Physical Units
Units to be accounted for	
Work in process, June 1 (40% complete)	500
Started (transferred) into production	8,000
Total units	8,500
Units accounted for	
Completed and transferred out	8,100
Work in process, June 30 (75% complete)	400
Total units	8,500

In Illustration 16A-1, the units completed and transferred out (8,100) plus the units in ending work in process (400) equal the total units to be accounted for (8,500). Using FIFO, we then compute equivalent units as follows.

1. The 500 units of beginning work in process were 40 percent complete. Thus, 300 equivalent units (60% × 500 units) were required to complete the beginning inventory.

2. The units started and completed during the current month are the units transferred out minus the units in beginning work in process. For the Assembly Department, units started and completed are 7,600 (8,100 − 500).

3. The 400 units of ending work in process were 75 percent complete. Thus, equivalent units were 300 (400 × 75%).

Equivalent units for the Assembly Department are 8,200, computed as follows.

Illustration 16A-2
Computation of equivalent
units–FIFO method

ASSEMBLY DEPARTMENT

Production Data	Physical Units	Work Added This Period	Equivalent Units
Work in process, June 1	500	60%	300
Started and completed	7,600	100%	7,600
Work in process, June 30	400	75%	300
Total	8,500		8,200

COMPREHENSIVE EXAMPLE

To provide a complete illustration of the FIFO method, we will use the data for the Mixing Department at Kellogg Company for the month of June, as shown in Illustration 16A-3 (page 861).

Compute the Physical Unit Flow (Step 1)

Illustration 16A-4 (page 861) shows the physical flow of units for Kellogg for the month of June for the Mixing Department.

Under the FIFO method, companies often expand the physical units schedule, as shown in Illustration 16A-5 (page 861) to explain the transferred-out section. As a result, this section reports the beginning work in process and the units started and completed. These two items further explain the completed and transferred-out section.

MIXING DEPARTMENT

Units

Work in process, June 1	100,000
Direct materials: 100% complete	
Conversion costs: 70% complete	
Units started into production during June	800,000
Units completed and transferred out to Baking Department	700,000
Work in process, June 30	200,000
Direct materials: 100% complete	
Conversion costs: 60% complete	

Costs

Work in process, June 1	
Direct materials: 100% complete	$ 50,000
Conversion costs: 70% complete	35,000
Cost of work in process, June 1	$ 85,000
Costs incurred during production in June	
Direct materials	$400,000
Conversion costs	170,000
Costs incurred in June	$570,000

Illustration 16A-3
Unit and cost data—Mixing Department

MIXING DEPARTMENT

	Physical Units
Units to be accounted for	
Work in process, June 1	100,000
Started (transferred) into production	800,000
Total units	900,000
Units accounted for	
Completed and transferred out	700,000
Work in process, June 30	200,000
Total units	900,000

Illustration 16A-4
Physical unit flow—Mixing Department

MIXING DEPARTMENT

	Physical Units
Units to be accounted for	
Work in process, June 1	100,000
Started (transferred) into production	800,000
Total units	900,000
Units accounted for	
Completed and transferred out	
Work in process, June 1	100,000
Started and completed	600,000
	700,000
Work in process, June 30	200,000
Total units	900,000

Illustration 16A-5
Physical unit flow (FIFO)—Mixing Department

The records indicate that the Mixing Department must account for 900,000 units. Of this sum, 700,000 units were transferred to the Baking Department and 200,000 units were still in process.

Compute Equivalent Units of Production (Step 2)

Helpful Hint Materials are not always added at the beginning of the process. For example, companies sometimes add materials uniformly during the process.

As with the method presented in the chapter, once they determine the physical flow of the units, companies need to determine equivalent units of production. The Mixing Department adds materials at the beginning of the process, and it incurs conversion costs uniformly during the process. Thus, Kellogg must make two computations of equivalent units: one for materials and one for conversion costs.

EQUIVALENT UNITS FOR MATERIALS Since Kellogg adds materials at the beginning of the process, no additional materials costs are required to complete the beginning work in process. In addition, 100 percent of the materials costs has been incurred on the ending work in process. Thus, the computation of equivalent units for materials is as follows.

Illustration 16A-6
Computation of equivalent units—materials

MIXING DEPARTMENT—MATERIALS			
Production Data	Physical Units	Materials Added This Period	Equivalent Units
Work in process, June 1	100,000	–0–	–0–
Started and finished	600,000	100%	600,000
Work in process, June 30	200,000	100%	200,000
Total	900,000		800,000

EQUIVALENT UNITS FOR CONVERSION COSTS The 100,000 units of beginning work in process were 70 percent complete in terms of conversion costs. Thus, the Mixing Department required 30,000 equivalent units (30% × 100,000 units) of conversion costs to complete the beginning inventory. In addition, the 200,000 units of ending work in process were 60 percent complete in terms of conversion costs. Thus, the equivalent units for conversion costs is 750,000, computed as follows.

Illustration 16A-7
Computation of equivalent units—conversion costs

MIXING DEPARTMENT—CONVERSION COSTS			
Production Data	Physical Units	Work Added This Period	Equivalent Units
Work in process, June 1	100,000	30%	30,000
Started and finished	600,000	100%	600,000
Work in process, June 30	200,000	60%	120,000
Total	900,000		750,000

Compute Unit Production Costs (Step 3)

Armed with the knowledge of the equivalent units of production, Kellogg can now compute the unit production costs. Unit production costs are costs expressed in terms of equivalent units of production. When equivalent units of production are different for materials and conversion costs, companies compute three unit costs: (1) materials, (2) conversion, and (3) total manufacturing.

Under the FIFO method, the unit costs of production are based entirely on the production costs incurred during the month. Thus, the costs in the beginning work in process are not relevant, because they were incurred on work done in the preceding month. As Illustration 16A-3 (page 861) indicated, the costs incurred during production in June were:

Direct materials	$400,000
Conversion costs	170,000
Total costs	$570,000

Illustration 16A-8
Costs incurred during production in June

Illustration 16A-9 shows the computation of unit materials cost, unit conversion costs, and total unit cost related to Eggo® Waffles.

Illustration 16A-9
Unit cost formulas and computations–Mixing Department

(1)	Total Materials Cost	÷	Equivalent Units of Materials	=	Unit Materials Cost
	$400,000	÷	800,000	=	$0.50
(2)	Total Conversion Costs	÷	Equivalent Units of Conversion Costs	=	Unit Conversion Cost
	$170,000	÷	750,000	=	$0.227 (rounded)*
(3)	Unit Materials Cost	+	Unit Conversion Cost	=	Total Manufacturing Cost per Unit
	$0.50	+	$0.227	=	$0.727

*For homework problems, round unit costs to three decimal places.

As shown, the unit costs are $0.50 for materials, $0.227 for conversion costs, and $0.727 for total manufacturing costs.

Prepare a Cost Reconciliation Schedule (Step 4)

Kellogg is now ready to determine the cost of goods transferred out of the Mixing Department to the Baking Department and the costs in ending work in process. The total costs charged to the Mixing Department in June are $655,000, calculated as follows.

Illustration 16A-10
Costs charged to Mixing Department

Costs to be accounted for	
Work in process, June 1	$ 85,000
Started into production	570,000
Total costs	$655,000

Kellogg next prepares a cost reconciliation to assign these costs to (1) units transferred out to the Baking Department and (2) ending work in process. Under the FIFO method, the first goods to be completed during the period are the units in beginning work in process. Thus, the cost of the beginning work in process is always assigned to the goods transferred to the next department (or finished goods, if processing is complete). Under the FIFO method, ending work in process also will be assigned only the production costs incurred in the current period. Illustration 16A-11 shows a cost reconciliation schedule for the Mixing Department.

Illustration 16A-11
Cost reconciliation report

MIXING DEPARTMENT
Cost Reconciliation Schedule

Costs accounted for		
Transferred out		
Work in process, June 1		$ 85,000
Costs to complete beginning work in process		
Conversion costs (30,000 × $0.227)		6,810
Total costs		91,810
Units started and completed (600,000 × $0.727)		435,950*
Total costs transferred out		527,760
Work in process, June 30		
Materials (200,000 × $0.50)	$100,000	
Conversion costs (120,000 × $0.227)	27,240	127,240
Total costs		$655,000

*Any rounding errors should be adjusted in the "Units started and completed" calculation.

As you can see, the total costs accounted for ($655,000 from Illustration 16A-11) equal the total costs to be accounted for ($655,000 from Illustration 16A-10).

Preparing the Production Cost Report

At this point, Kellogg is ready to prepare the production cost report for the Mixing Department. This report is an internal document for management that shows production quantity and cost data for a production department.

As discussed on page 850, there are four steps in preparing a production cost report:

1. Compute the physical unit flow.
2. Compute the equivalent units of production.
3. Compute unit production costs.
4. Prepare a cost reconciliation schedule.

Illustration 16A-12 (page 865) shows the production cost report for the Mixing Department, with the four steps identified in the report.

As indicated in the chapter, production cost reports provide a basis for evaluating the productivity of a department. In addition, managers can use the cost data to assess whether unit costs and total costs are reasonable. By comparing the quantity and cost data with predetermined goals, top management can also judge whether current performance is meeting planned objectives.

FIFO AND WEIGHTED-AVERAGE

The weighted-average method of computing equivalent units has **one major advantage:** It is simple to understand and apply. In cases where prices do not fluctuate significantly from period to period, the weighted-average method will be very similar to the FIFO method. In addition, companies that have been using just-in-time procedures effectively for inventory control purposes will have minimal inventory balances, and therefore differences between the weighted-average and the FIFO methods will not be material.

Conceptually, the FIFO method is superior to the weighted-average method because it measures **current performance** using only costs incurred in the current

Mixing Department.xls

File   Edit   View   Insert   Format   Tools   Data   Window   Help

	A	B	C	D	E	F	G
1			**Mixing Department**				
2			**Production Cost Report**				
3			**For the Month Ended June 30, 2012**				
4					Equivalent Units		
5			Physical Units	Materials	Conversion Costs		
6	**QUANTITIES**		Step 1	Step 2			
7	Units to be accounted for						
8	Work in process (WIP), June 1		100,000				
9	Started into production		800,000				
10	Total units		900,000				
11							
12	Units accounted for						
13	Completed and transferred out						
14	Work in process, June 1		100,000	0	30,000		
15	Started and completed		600,000	600,000	600,000		
16	Work in process, June 30		200,000	200,000	120,000		
17	Total units		900,000	800,000	750,000		
18							
19	**COSTS**						
20	Unit costs Step 3			Materials	Conversion Costs	Total	
21	Costs in June (excluding beginning WIP)	(a)		$400,000	$170,000	$570,000	
22	Equivalent units	(b)		800,000	750,000		
23	Unit costs [(a) ÷ (b)]			$0.50	$0.227	$0.727	
24							
25	Costs to be accounted for						
26	Work in process, June 1					$85,000	
27	Started into production					570,000	
28	Total costs					$655,000	
29							
30	**Cost Reconciliation Schedule** Step 4						
31	Costs accounted for						
32	Transferred out						
33	Work in process, June 1					$85,000	
34	Costs to complete beginning work in process						
35	Conversion costs (30,000 × $0.227)					6,810	
36	Total costs					91,810	
37	Units started and completed (600,000 × $0.727)**					435,950	**Any rounding errors
38	Total costs transferred out					527,760	should be adjusted in
39	Work in process, June 30						the "Units started and
40	Materials (200,000 × $0.50)				$100,000		completed"
41	Conversions costs (120,000 × $0.227)				27,240	127,240	
42	Total costs					$655,000	
43							

Illustration 16A-12
Production cost report–
FIFO method

period. Managers are, therefore, not held responsible for costs from prior periods over which they may not have had control. In addition, the FIFO method **provides current cost information**, which the company can use to establish **more accurate pricing strategies** for goods manufactured and sold in the current period.

Helpful Hint What are the two self-checks in the report? Answer: (1) Total physical units accounted for must equal the total units to be accounted for. (2) Total costs accounted for must equal the total costs to be accounted for.

Summary of Study Objective for Appendix 16A

8 **Compute equivalent units using the FIFO method.** Equivalent units under the FIFO method are the sum of the work performed to: (1) Finish the units of beginning work in process inventory, if any; (2) complete the units started into production during the period; and (3) start, but only partially complete, the units in ending work in process inventory.

✔ the navigator

Glossary

Conversion costs *(p. 848)* The sum of labor costs and overhead costs.

Cost reconciliation schedule *(p. 853)* A schedule that shows that the total costs accounted for equal the total costs to be accounted for.

Equivalent units of production *(p. 847)* A measure of the work done during the period, expressed in fully completed units.

Operations costing *(p. 855)* A combination of a process cost and a job order cost system, in which products are manufactured primarily by standardized methods, with some customization.

Physical units *(p. 850)* Actual units to be accounted for during a period, irrespective of any work performed.

Process cost system *(p. 840)* An accounting system used to apply costs to similar products that are mass-produced in a continuous fashion.

Production cost report *(p. 850)* An internal report for management that shows both production quantity and cost data for a production department.

Total units (costs) accounted for *(pp. 851, 853)* The sum of the units (costs) transferred out during the period plus the units (costs) in process at the end of the period.

Total units (costs) to be accounted for *(pp. 850, 853)* The sum of the units (costs) started (or transferred) into production during the period plus the units (costs) in process at the beginning of the period.

Unit production costs *(p. 852)* Costs expressed in terms of equivalent units of production.

Weighted-average method *(p. 847)* Method of computing equivalent units of production which considers the degree of completion (weighting) of the units completed and transferred out and the ending work in process.

Comprehensive *Do it!*

Karlene Industries produces plastic ice cube trays in two processes: heating and stamping. All materials are added at the beginning of the Heating Department process. Karlene uses the weighted-average method to compute equivalent units.

On November 1, the Heating Department had in process 1,000 trays that were 70% complete. During November, it started into production 12,000 trays. On November 30, 2012, 2,000 trays that were 60% complete were in process.

The following cost information for the Heating Department was also available.

Work in process, November 1:			Costs incurred in November:	
Materials		$ 640	Material	$3,000
Conversion costs		360	Labor	2,300
Cost of work in process, Nov. 1		$1,000	Overhead	4,050

Instructions

(a) Prepare a production cost report for the Heating Department for the month of November 2012, using the weighted-average method.

(b) Journalize the transfer of costs to the Stamping Department.

Solution to Comprehensive Do it!

(a)

KARLENE INDUSTRIES
Heating Department
Production Cost Report
For the Month Ended November 30, 2012

		Equivalent Units	
	Physical Units	Materials	Conversion Costs
Quantities	Step 1	Step 2	
Units to be accounted for			
Work in process, November 1	1,000		
Started into production	12,000		
Total units	13,000		
Units accounted for			
Transferred out	11,000	11,000	11,000
Work in process, November 30	2,000	2,000	1,200
Total units	13,000	13,000	12,200

Costs			Conversion	
Unit costs Step 3		Materials	Costs	Total
Costs in November	(a)	$ 3,640*	$ 6,710**	$10,350
Equivalent units	(b)	13,000	12,200	
Unit costs [(a) ÷ (b)]		$0.28	$0.55	$0.83
Costs to be accounted for				
Work in process, November 1				$ 1,000
Started into production				9,350
Total costs				$10,350

*$640 + $3,000
**$360 + $2,300 + $4,050

Cost Reconciliation Schedule   Step 4

Costs accounted for		
Transferred out (11,000 × $0.83)		$ 9,130
Work in process, November 30		
Materials (2,000 × $0.28)	$560	
Conversion costs (1,200 × $0.55)	660	1,220
Total costs		$10,350

(b) Work in Process—Stamping	9,130	
Work in Process—Heating		9,130
(To record transfer of units to the Stamping Department)		

Action Plan
- Compute the physical unit flow—that is, the total units to be accounted for.
- Compute the equivalent units of production.
- Compute the unit production costs, expressed in terms of equivalent units of production.
- Prepare a cost reconciliation schedule, which shows that the total costs accounted for equal the total costs to be accounted for.

 Self-Test, Brief Exercises, Exercises, Problem Set A, and many more resources are available for practice in WileyPLUS

Note: All asterisked Questions, Exercises, and Problems relate to material in the appendix to the chapter.

Self-Test Questions

Answers are on page 887.

(SO 1)   **1.** Which of the following items is *not* characteristic of a process cost system?
  (a) Once production begins, it continues until the finished product emerges.

  (b) The products produced are heterogeneous in nature.
  (c) The focus is on continually producing homogeneous products.

(d) When the finished product emerges, all units have precisely the same amount of materials, labor, and overhead.

(SO 2) **2.** Indicate which of the following statements is *not* correct.
   (a) Both a job order and a process cost system track the same three manufacturing cost elements—direct materials, direct labor, and manufacturing overhead.
   (b) A job order cost system uses only one work in process account, whereas a process cost system uses multiple work in process accounts.
   (c) Manufacturing costs are accumulated the same way in a job order and in a process cost system.
   (d) Manufacturing costs are assigned the same way in a job order and in a process cost system.

(SO 3) **3.** In a process cost system, the flow of costs is:
   (a) work in process, cost of goods sold, finished goods.
   (b) finished goods, work in process, cost of goods sold.
   (c) finished goods, cost of goods sold, work in process.
   (d) work in process, finished goods, cost of goods sold.

(SO 4) **4.** In making journal entries to assign raw materials costs, a company using process costing:
   (a) debits Finished Goods Inventory.
   (b) often debits two or more work in process accounts.
   (c) generally credits two or more work in process accounts.
   (d) credits Finished Goods Inventory.

(SO 4) **5.** In a process cost system, manufacturing overhead:
   (a) is assigned to finished goods at the end of each accounting period.
   (b) is assigned to a work in process account for each job as the job is completed.
   (c) is assigned to a work in process account for each production department on the basis of a predetermined overhead rate.
   (d) is assigned to a work in process account for each production department as overhead costs are incurred.

(SO 5) **6.** Conversion costs are the sum of:
   (a) fixed and variable overhead costs.
   (b) labor costs and overhead costs.
   (c) direct material costs and overhead costs.
   (d) direct labor and indirect labor costs.

(SO 5) **7.** The Mixing Department's output during the period consists of 20,000 units completed and transferred out, and 5,000 units in ending work in process 60% complete as to materials and conversion costs. Beginning inventory is 1,000 units, 40% complete as to materials and conversion costs. The equivalent units of production are:
   (a) 22,600. (c) 24,000.
   (b) 23,000. (d) 25,000.

(SO 6) **8.** In RYZ Company, there are zero units in beginning work in process, 7,000 units started into production, and 500 units in ending work in process 20% completed. The physical units to be accounted for are:
   (a) 7,000. (c) 7,500.
   (b) 7,360. (d) 7,340.

(SO 6) **9.** Mora Company has 2,000 units in beginning work in process, 20% complete as to conversion costs, 23,000 units transferred out to finished goods, and 3,000 units in ending work in process $33\frac{1}{3}\%$ complete as to conversion costs.

   The beginning and ending inventory is fully complete as to materials costs. Equivalent units for materials and conversion costs are, respectively:
   (a) 22,000, 24,000.
   (b) 24,000, 26,000.
   (c) 26,000, 24,000.
   (d) 26,000, 26,000.

(SO 6) **10.** Fortner Company has no beginning work in process; 9,000 units are transferred out and 3,000 units in ending work in process are one-third finished as to conversion costs and fully complete as to materials cost. If total materials cost is $60,000, the unit materials cost is:
   (a) $5.00.
   (b) $5.45 rounded.
   (c) $6.00.
   (d) No correct answer is given.

(SO 6) **11.** Largo Company has unit costs of $10 for materials and $30 for conversion costs. If there are 2,500 units in ending work in process, 40% complete as to conversion costs, and fully complete as to materials cost, the total cost assignable to the ending work in process inventory is:
   (a) $45,000.
   (b) $55,000.
   (c) $75,000.
   (d) $100,000.

(SO 7) **12.** A production cost report:
   (a) is an external report.
   (b) shows both the production quantity and cost data related to a department.
   (c) shows equivalent units of production but not physical units.
   (d) contains six sections.

(SO 7) **13.** In a production cost report, units to be accounted for are calculated as:
   (a) Units started into production + Units in ending work in process.
   (b) Units started into production − Units in beginning work in process.
   (c) Units transferred out + Units in beginning work in process.
   (d) Units started into production + Units in beginning work in process.

(SO 8) *14. Hollins Company uses the FIFO method to compute equivalent units. It has 2,000 units in beginning work in process, 20% complete as to conversion costs, 25,000 units started and completed, and 3,000 units in ending work in process, 30% complete as to conversion costs. All units are 100% complete as to materials. Equivalent units for materials and conversion costs are, respectively:
(a) 28,000 and 26,600.
(b) 28,000 and 27,500.
(c) 27,000 and 26,200.
(d) 27,000 and 29,600.

(SO 8) *15. KLM Company uses the FIFO method to compute equivalent units. It has no beginning work in process; 9,000 units are started and completed and 3,000 units in ending work in process are one-third completed. All material is added at the beginning of the process. If total materials cost is $60,000, the unit materials cost is:
(a) $5.00.
(b) $6.00.

(c) $6.67 (rounded).
(d) No correct answer given.

*16. Toney Company uses the FIFO method to compute (SO 3) equivalent units. It has unit costs of $10 for materials and $30 for conversion costs. If there are 2,500 units in ending work in process, 100% complete as to materials and 40% complete as to conversion costs, the total cost assignable to the ending work in process inventory is:
(a) $45,000.
(b) $55,000.
(c) $75,000.
(d) $100,000.

Go to the book's companion website, **www.wiley.com/college/kimmel**, for additional Self-Test Questions.

Questions

1. Identify which costing system—job order or process cost—the following companies would primarily use: (a) Quaker Oats, (b) Ford Motor Company, (c) Kinko's Print Shop, and (d) Warner Bros. Motion Pictures.

2. Contrast the primary focus of job order cost accounting and of process cost accounting.

3. What are the similarities between a job order and a process cost system?

4. Your roommate is confused about the features of process cost accounting. Identify and explain the distinctive features for your roommate.

5. Sam Bowyer believes there are no significant differences in the flow of costs between job order cost accounting and process cost accounting. Is Bowyer correct? Explain.

6. (a) What source documents are used in assigning (1) materials and (2) labor to production in a process cost system?
   (b) What criterion and basis are commonly used in allocating overhead to processes?

7. At Ely Company, overhead is assigned to production departments at the rate of $5 per machine hour. In July, machine hours were 3,000 in the Machining Department and 2,400 in the Assembly Department. Prepare the entry to assign overhead to production.

8. Mark Haley is uncertain about the steps used to prepare a production cost report. State the procedures that are required in the sequence in which they are performed.

9. John Harbeck is confused about computing physical units. Explain to John how physical units to be accounted for and physical units accounted for are determined.

10. What is meant by the term "equivalent units of production"?

11. How are equivalent units of production computed?

12. Coats Company had zero units of beginning work in process. During the period, 9,000 units were completed, and there were 600 units of ending work in process. What were the units started into production?

13. Sanchez Co. has zero units of beginning work in process. During the period, 12,000 units were completed, and there were 500 units of ending work in process one-fifth complete as to conversion cost and 100% complete as to materials cost. What were the equivalent units of production for (a) materials and (b) conversion costs?

14. Hindi Co. started 3,000 units for the period. Its beginning inventory is 500 units one-fourth complete as to conversion costs and 100% complete as to materials costs. Its ending inventory is 300 units one-fifth complete as to conversion costs and 100% complete as to materials costs. How many units were transferred out this period?

15. Clauss Company transfers out 14,000 units and has 2,000 units of ending work in process that are 25% complete. Materials are entered at the beginning of the process and there is no beginning work in process.

Assuming unit materials costs of $3 and unit conversion costs of $5, what are the costs to be assigned to units (a) transferred out and (b) in ending work in process?

16. (a) Ann Quinn believes the production cost report is an external report for stockholders. Is Ann correct? Explain.
    (b) Identify the sections in a production cost report.

17. What purposes are served by a production cost report?

18. At Trent Company, there are 800 units of ending work in process that are 100% complete as to materials and 40% complete as to conversion costs. If the unit cost of materials is $3 and the costs assigned to the 800 units is $6,000, what is the per unit conversion cost?

19. What is the difference between operations costing and a process costing system?

20. How does a company decide whether to use a job order or a process cost system?

*21. Soria Co. started and completed 2,000 units for the period. Its beginning inventory is 800 units 25% complete and its ending inventory is 400 units 20% complete. Soria uses the FIFO method to compute equivalent units. How many units were transferred out this period?

*22. Reyes Company transfers out 12,000 units and has 2,000 units of ending work in process that are 25% complete. Materials are entered at the beginning of the process and there is no beginning work in process. Reyes uses the FIFO method to compute equivalent units. Assuming unit materials costs of $3 and unit conversion costs of $7, what are the costs to be assigned to units (a) transferred out and (b) in ending work in process?

Brief Exercises

Journalize entries for accumulating costs.
(SO 4), AP

BE16-1 Weber Manufacturing purchases $45,000 of raw materials on account, and it incurs $60,000 of factory labor costs. Journalize the two transactions on March 31 assuming the labor costs are not paid until April.

Journalize the assignment of materials and labor costs.
(SO 4), AP

BE16-2 Data for Weber Manufacturing are given in BE16-1. Supporting records show that (a) the Assembly Department used $24,000 of raw materials and $35,000 of the factory labor, and (b) the Finishing Department used the remainder. Journalize the assignment of the costs to the processing departments on March 31.

Journalize the assignment of overhead costs.
(SO 4), AP

BE16-3 Factory labor data for Weber Manufacturing are given in BE16-2. Manufacturing overhead is assigned to departments on the basis of 200% of labor costs. Journalize the assignment of overhead to the Assembly and Finishing Departments.

Compute physical units of production.
(SO 6), AP

BE16-4 Goode Manufacturing Company has the following production data for selected months.

			Ending Work in Process	
Month	Beginning Work in Process	Units Transferred Out	Units	% Complete as to Conversion Cost
January	–0–	35,000	10,000	40%
March	–0–	40,000	8,000	75
July	–0–	45,000	16,000	25

Compute the physical units for each month.

Compute equivalent units of production.
(SO 5), AP

BE16-5 Using the data in BE16-4, compute equivalent units of production for materials and conversion costs, assuming materials are entered at the beginning of the process.

Compute unit costs of production.
(SO 6), AP

BE16-6 In Lopez Company, total material costs are $36,000, and total conversion costs are $54,000. Equivalent units of production are materials 10,000 and conversion costs 12,000. Compute the unit costs for materials, conversion costs, and total manufacturing costs.

Assign costs to units transferred out and in process.
(SO 6), AP

BE16-7 Trek Company has the following production data for April: units transferred out 40,000, and ending work in process 5,000 units that are 100% complete for materials and 40% complete for conversion costs. If unit materials cost is $4 and unit conversion cost is $7, determine the costs to be assigned to the units transferred out and the units in ending work in process.

BE16-8 Production costs chargeable to the Finishing Department in June in Cascio Company are materials $16,000, labor $29,500, overhead $18,000. Equivalent units of production are materials 20,000 and conversion costs 19,000. Compute the unit costs for materials and conversion costs.

Compute unit costs.
(SO 6), AP

BE16-9 Data for Cascio Company are given in BE16-8. Production records indicate that 18,000 units were transferred out, and 2,000 units in ending work in process were 50% complete as to conversion cost and 100% complete as to materials. Prepare a cost reconciliation schedule.

Prepare cost reconciliation schedule.
(SO 6), AP

BE16-10 The Smelting Department of Mathews Manufacturing Company has the following production and cost data for November.

Production: Beginning work in process 2,000 units that are 100% complete as to materials and 20% complete as to conversion costs; units transferred out 8,000 units; and ending work in process 7,000 units that are 100% complete as to materials and 40% complete as to conversion costs.

Compute the equivalent units of production for (a) materials and (b) conversion costs for the month of November.

Compute equivalent units of production.
(SO 5), AP

***BE16-11** Sanderson Company has the following production data for March: no beginning work in process, units started and completed 30,000, and ending work in process 5,000 units that are 100% complete for materials and 40% complete for conversion costs. Sanderson uses the FIFO method to compute equivalent units. If unit materials cost is $6 and unit conversion cost is $12, determine the costs to be assigned to the units transferred out and the units in ending work in process. The total costs to be assigned are $594,000.

Assign costs to units transferred out and in process.
(SO 8), AP

***BE16-12** Using the data in BE16-11, prepare the cost section of the production cost report for Sanderson Company.

Prepare a partial production cost report.
(SO 7, 8), AP

***BE16-13** Production costs chargeable to the Finishing Department in May at Kim Company are materials $8,000, labor $20,000, overhead $18,000, and transferred-in costs $67,000. Equivalent units of production are materials 20,000 and conversion costs 19,000. Kim uses the FIFO method to compute equivalent units. Compute the unit costs for materials and conversion costs. Transferred-in costs are considered materials costs.

Compute unit costs.
(SO 8), AP

Do it! Review

Do it! 16-1 Indicate whether each of the following statements is true or false.

1. Many hospitals use job order costing for small, routine medical procedures.
2. A manufacturer of computer flash drives would use a job order cost system.
3. A process cost system uses multiple work in process accounts.
4. A process cost system keeps track of costs on job cost sheets.

Compare job order and process cost systems.
(SO 1, 2), C

Do it! 16-2 Kopa Company manufactures CH-21 through two processes: Mixing and Packaging. In July, the following costs were incurred.

Assign and journalize manufacturing costs.
(SO 4), AP

	Mixing	**Packaging**
Raw materials used	$10,000	$28,000
Factory labor costs	8,000	36,000
Manufacturing overhead costs	12,000	54,000

Units completed at a cost of $21,000 in the Mixing Department are transferred to the Packaging Department. Units completed at a cost of $106,000 in the Packaging Department are transferred to Finished Goods. Journalize the assignment of these costs to the two processes and the transfer of units as appropriate.

Do it! 16-3 The assembly department has the following production and cost data for the current month.

Compute equivalent units.
(SO 5), AP

Beginning Work in Process	Units Transferred Out	Ending Work in Process
–0–	20,000	12,000

Materials are entered at the beginning of the process. The ending work in process units are 70% complete as to conversion costs. Compute the equivalent units of production for (a) materials and (b) conversion costs.

Prepare cost reconciliation schedule.

(SO 6, 7), AP

Do it! 16-4 In March, Kelly Manufacturing had the following unit production costs: materials $10 and conversion costs $8. On March 1, it had zero work in process. During March, Kelly transferred out 22,000 units. As of March 31, 4,000 units that were 40% complete as to conversion costs and 100% complete as to materials were in ending work in process.

(a) Compute the total units to be accounted for.
(b) Compute the equivalent units of production.
(c) Prepare a cost reconciliation schedule, including the costs of materials transferred out and the costs of materials in process.

Exercises

Understand process cost accounting.

(SO 1, 2), C

E16-1 Robert Mallory has prepared the following list of statements about process cost accounting.

1. Process cost systems are used to apply costs to similar products that are mass-produced in a continuous fashion.
2. A process cost system is used when each finished unit is indistinguishable from another.
3. Companies that produce soft drinks, motion pictures, and computer chips would all use process cost accounting.
4. In a process cost system, costs are tracked by individual jobs.
5. Job order costing and process costing track different manufacturing cost elements.
6. Both job order costing and process costing account for direct materials, direct labor, and manufacturing overhead.
7. Costs flow through the accounts in the same basic way for both job order costing and process costing.
8. In a process cost system, only one work in process account is used.
9. In a process cost system, costs are summarized in a job cost sheet.
10. In a process cost system, the unit cost is total manufacturing costs for the period divided by the units produced during the period.

Instructions
Identify each statement as true or false. If false, indicate how to correct the statement.

Journalize transactions.

(SO 4), AP

E16-2 Harrelson Company manufactures pizza sauce through two production departments: Cooking and Canning. In each process, materials and conversion costs are incurred evenly throughout the process. For the month of April, the work in process accounts show the following debits.

	Cooking	**Canning**
Beginning work in process	$ –0–	$ 4,000
Materials	21,000	9,000
Labor	8,500	7,000
Overhead	31,500	25,800
Costs transferred in		53,000

Instructions
Journalize the April transactions.

Answer questions on costs and production.

(SO 3, 5, 6), AP

E16-3 The ledger of Custer Company has the following work in process account.

Work in Process—Painting

5/1	Balance	3,590	5/31	Transferred out	?
5/31	Materials	5,160			
5/31	Labor	2,740			
5/31	Overhead	1,380			
5/31	Balance	?			

Production records show that there were 400 units in the beginning inventory, 30% complete, 1,400 units started, and 1,500 units transferred out. The beginning work in process had materials cost of $2,040 and conversion costs of $1,550. The units in ending inventory were 40% complete. Materials are entered at the beginning of the painting process.

Instructions
(a) How many units are in process at May 31?
(b) What is the unit materials cost for May?
(c) What is the unit conversion cost for May?
(d) What is the total cost of units transferred out in May?
(e) What is the cost of the May 31 inventory?

E16-4 Schrager Manufacturing Company has two production departments: Cutting and Assembly. July 1 inventories are Raw Materials $4,200, Work in Process—Cutting $2,900, Work in Process—Assembly $10,600, and Finished Goods $31,000. During July, the following transactions occurred.

Journalize transactions for two processes.
(SO 4), AP

1. Purchased $62,500 of raw materials on account.
2. Incurred $60,000 of factory labor. (Credit Wages Payable.)
3. Incurred $70,000 of manufacturing overhead; $40,000 was paid and the remainder is unpaid.
4. Requisitioned materials for Cutting $15,700 and Assembly $8,900.
5. Used factory labor for Cutting $33,000 and Assembly $27,000.
6. Applied overhead at the rate of $18 per machine hour. Machine hours were Cutting 1,680 and Assembly 1,720.
7. Transferred goods costing $67,600 from the Cutting Department to the Assembly Department.
8. Transferred goods costing $134,900 from Assembly to Finished Goods.
9. Sold goods costing $150,000 for $200,000 on account.

Instructions
Journalize the transactions. (Omit explanations.)

E16-5 In Wayne Company, materials are entered at the beginning of each process. Work in process inventories, with the percentage of work done on conversion costs, and production data for its Sterilizing Department in selected months during 2012 are as follows.

Compute physical units and equivalent units of production.
(SO 5, 6), AP

Month	Beginning Work in Process Units	Beginning Work in Process Conversion Cost%	Units Transferred Out	Ending Work in Process Units	Ending Work in Process Conversion Cost%
January	–0–	—	9,000	2,000	60
March	–0–	—	12,000	3,000	30
May	–0–	—	16,000	7,000	80
July	–0–	—	10,000	1,500	40

Instructions
(a) Compute the physical units for January and May.
(b) Compute the equivalent units of production for (1) materials and (2) conversion costs for each month.

E16-6 The Cutting Department of Cassel Manufacturing has the following production and cost data for July.

Determine equivalent units, unit costs, and assignment of costs.
(SO 5, 8), AP

Production	Costs	
1. Transferred out 12,000 units.	Beginning work in process	$ –0–
2. Started 3,000 units that are 60%	Materials	45,000
complete as to conversion	Labor	16,200
costs and 100% complete as	Manufacturing overhead	18,300
to materials at July 31.		

Materials are entered at the beginning of the process. Conversion costs are incurred uniformly during the process.

Instructions

(a) Determine the equivalent units of production for (1) materials and (2) conversion costs.

(b) Compute unit costs and prepare a cost reconciliation schedule.

Prepare a production cost report.

(SO 5, 6, 7), AP

E16-7 The Sanding Department of Richards Furniture Company has the following production and manufacturing cost data for March 2012, the first month of operation.

Production: 9,000 units finished and transferred out; 3,000 units started that are 100% complete as to materials and 20% complete as to conversion costs.

Manufacturing costs: Materials $33,000; labor $24,000; overhead $36,000.

Instructions

Prepare a production cost report.

Determine equivalent units, unit costs, and assignment of costs.

(SO 5, 6), AP

E16-8 The Blending Department of Luongo Company has the following cost and production data for the month of April.

Costs:
Work in process, April 1
Direct materials: 100% complete	$100,000
Conversion costs: 20% complete	70,000
Cost of work in process, April 1	$170,000

Costs incurred during production in April
Direct materials	$ 800,000
Conversion costs	365,000
Costs incurred in April	$1,165,000

Units transferred out totaled 17,000. Ending work in process was 1,000 units that are 100% complete as to materials and 40% complete as to conversion costs.

Instructions

(a) Compute the equivalent units of production for (1) materials and (2) conversion costs for the month of April.

(b) Compute the unit costs for the month.

(c) Determine the costs to be assigned to the units transferred out and in ending work in process.

Determine equivalent units, unit costs, and assignment of costs.

(SO 5, 6), AP

E16-9 Kostrivas Company has gathered the following information.

Units in beginning work in process	−0−
Units started into production	40,000
Units in ending work in process	6,000
Percent complete in ending work in process:	
Conversion costs	40%
Materials	100%
Costs incurred:	
Direct materials	$72,000
Direct labor	$81,000
Overhead	$101,000

Instructions

(a) Compute equivalent units of production for materials and for conversion costs.

(b) Determine the unit costs of production.

(c) Show the assignment of costs to units transferred out and in process.

E16-10 Overton Company has gathered the following information.

Determine equivalent units, unit costs, and assignment of costs.

(SO 5, 6), AP

Units in beginning work in process	20,000
Units started into production	164,000
Units in ending work in process	24,000
Percent complete in ending work in process:	
Conversion costs	60%
Materials	100%
Costs incurred:	
Direct materials	$101,200
Direct labor	$164,800
Overhead	$184,000

Instructions
(a) Compute equivalent units of production for materials and for conversion costs.
(b) Determine the unit costs of production.
(c) Show the assignment of costs to units transferred out and in process.

E16-11 The Polishing Department of Harbin Manufacturing Company has the following production and manufacturing cost data for September. Materials are entered at the beginning of the process.

Compute equivalent units, unit costs, and costs assigned.

(SO 5, 6), AP

Production: Beginning inventory 1,600 units that are 100% complete as to materials and 30% complete as to conversion costs; units started during the period are 38,400; ending inventory of 5,000 units 10% complete as to conversion costs.

Manufacturing costs: Beginning inventory costs, comprised of $20,000 of materials and $43,180 of conversion costs; materials costs added in Polishing during the month, $177,200; labor and overhead applied in Polishing during the month, $125,680 and $257,140, respectively.

Instructions
(a) Compute the equivalent units of production for materials and conversion costs for the month of September.
(b) Compute the unit costs for materials and conversion costs for the month.
(c) Determine the costs to be assigned to the units transferred out and in process.

E16-12 David Skaros has recently been promoted to production manager, and so he has just started to receive various managerial reports. One of the reports he has received is the production cost report that you prepared. It showed that his department had 2,000 equivalent units in ending inventory. His department has had a history of not keeping enough inventory on hand to meet demand. He has come to you, very angry, and wants to know why you credited him with only 2,000 units when he knows he had at least twice that many on hand.

Explain the production cost report.

(SO 7), S

Instructions
▭▭▭▭▷ Explain to him why his production cost report showed only 2,000 equivalent units in ending inventory. Write an informal memo. Be kind and explain very clearly why he is mistaken.

E16-13 The Welding Department of Thorpe Manufacturing Company has the following production and manufacturing cost data for February 2012. All materials are added at the beginning of the process.

Prepare a production cost report.

(SO 5, 6, 7), AP

Manufacturing Costs			**Production Data**	
Beginning work in process			Beginning work in process	15,000 units
Materials	$18,000			1/10 complete
Conversion costs	14,175	$ 32,175	Units transferred out	49,000
Materials		180,000	Units started	45,000
Labor		52,380	Ending work in process	11,000 units
Overhead		61,445		1/5 complete

Instructions
Prepare a production cost report for the Welding Department for the month of February.

Compute physical units and equivalent units of production.

(SO 5, 0), AP

E16-14 Remington Shipping, Inc. is contemplating the use of process costing to track the costs of its operations. The operation consists of three segments (departments): receiving, shipping, and delivery. Containers are received at Remington's docks and sorted according to the ship they will be carried on. The containers are loaded onto a ship, which carries them to the appropriate port of destination. The containers are then off-loaded and delivered to the receiving company.

Remington Shipping wants to begin using process costing in the shipping department. Direct materials represent the fuel costs to run the ship, and "Containers in transit" represents work in process. Listed below is information about the shipping department's first month's activity.

Containers in transit, April 1	0
Containers loaded	1,200
Containers in transit, April 30	350, 40% of direct materials and 20% of conversion costs

Instructions
(a) Determine the physical flow of containers for the month.
(b) Calculate the equivalent units for direct materials and conversion costs.

Determine equivalent units, unit costs, and assignment of costs.

(SO 5, 0), AP

E16-15 Royale Mortgage Company uses a process costing system to accumulate costs in its loan application department. When an application is completed, it is forwarded to the loan department for final processing. The following processing and cost data pertain to September.

1. Applications in process on September 1, 100	Beginning WIP:	
	Direct materials	$ 1,000
2. Applications started in September, 900	Conversion costs	3,960
	September costs:	
3. Completed applications during September, 800	Direct materials	$ 4,500
	Direct labor	12,000
4. Applications still in process at September 30 were 100% complete as to materials (forms) and 60% complete as to conversion costs.	Overhead	9,340

Materials are the forms used in the application process, and these costs are incurred at the beginning of the process. Conversion costs are incurred uniformly during the process.

Instructions
(a) Determine the equivalent units of service (production) for materials and conversion costs.
(b) Compute the unit costs and prepare a cost reconciliation schedule.

Compute equivalent units, unit costs, and costs assigned.

(SO 6, 0), AP

*E16-16 Using the data in E16-15, assume Royale Mortgage Company uses the FIFO method. Also assume that the applications in process on September 1 were 100% complete as to materials (forms) and 40% complete as to conversion costs.

Instructions
(a) Determine the equivalent units of service (production) for materials and conversion costs.
(b) Compute the unit costs and prepare a cost reconciliation schedule.

Determine equivalent units, unit costs, and assignment of costs.

(SO 6, 0), AP

*E16-17 The Cutting Department of Keigi Manufacturing has the following production and cost data for August.

Production	**Costs**	
1. Started and completed 8,000 units.	Beginning work in process	$ –0–
2. Started 2,000 units that are 40% completed at August 31.	Materials	45,000
	Labor	14,700
	Manufacturing overhead	16,100

Materials are entered at the beginning of the process. Conversion costs are incurred uniformly during the process. Keigi Manufacturing uses the FIFO method to compute equivalent units.

Instructions
(a) Determine the equivalent units of production for (1) materials and (2) conversion costs.
(b) Compute unit costs and show the assignment of manufacturing costs to units transferred out and in work in process.

*E16-18 The Smelting Department of Polzin Manufacturing Company has the following production and cost data for September.

Compute equivalent units, unit costs, and costs assigned.
(SO 6, 9), AP

Production: Beginning work in process 2,000 units that are 100% complete as to materials and 20% complete as to conversion costs; units started and finished 9,000 units; and ending work in process 1,000 units that are 100% complete as to materials and 40% complete as to conversion costs.

Manufacturing costs: Work in process, September 1, $15,200; materials added $60,000; labor and overhead $132,000.

Polzin uses the FIFO method to compute equivalent units.

Instructions
(a) Compute the equivalent units of production for (1) materials and (2) conversion costs for the month of September.
(b) Compute the unit costs for the month.
(c) Determine the costs to be assigned to the units transferred out and in process.

*E16-19 The ledger of Hannon Company has the following work in process account.

Answer questions on costs and production.
(SO 6, 9), AP

Work in Process—Painting

3/1	Balance	3,680	3/31	Transferred out	?
3/31	Materials	6,600			
3/31	Labor	2,500			
3/31	Overhead	1,150			
3/31	Balance	?			

Production records show that there were 800 units in the beginning inventory, 30% complete, 1,200 units started, and 1,500 units transferred out. The units in ending inventory were 40% complete. Materials are entered at the beginning of the painting process. Hannon uses the FIFO method to compute equivalent units.

Instructions
Answer the following questions.
(a) How many units are in process at March 31?
(b) What is the unit materials cost for March?
(c) What is the unit conversion cost for March?
(d) What is the total cost of units started in February and completed in March?
(e) What is the total cost of units started and finished in March?
(f) What is the cost of the March 31 inventory?

*E16-20 The Welding Department of Majestic Manufacturing Company has the following production and manufacturing cost data for February 2012. All materials are added at the beginning of the process. Majestic uses the FIFO method to compute equivalent units.

Prepare a production cost report for a second process.
(SO 9), AP

Manufacturing Costs		Production Data	
Beginning work in process	$ 32,175	Beginning work in process	15,000 units,
Costs transferred in	135,000		10% complete
Materials	57,000	Units transferred out	50,000
Labor	35,100	Units transferred in	64,000
Overhead	68,400	Ending work in process	25,000,
			20% complete

Instructions
Prepare a production cost report for the Welding Department for the month of February. Transferred-in costs are considered materials costs.

Exercises: Set B and Challenge Exercises

Visit the book's companion website, at **www.wiley.com/college/kimmel**, and choose the Student Companion site to access Exercise Set B and Challenge Exercises.

Problems: Set A

Journalize transactions.
(SO 3, 4), AP

P16-1A   Conwell Company manufactures its product, Vitadrink, through two manufacturing processes: Mixing and Packaging. All materials are entered at the beginning of each process. On October 1, 2012, inventories consisted of Raw Materials $26,000, Work in Process—Mixing $0, Work in Process—Packaging $250,000, and Finished Goods $289,000. The beginning inventory for Packaging consisted of 10,000 units that were 50% complete as to conversion costs and fully complete as to materials. During October, 50,000 units were started into production in the Mixing Department and the following transactions were completed.

1. Purchased $300,000 of raw materials on account.
2. Issued raw materials for production: Mixing $210,000 and Packaging $45,000.
3. Incurred labor costs of $258,900.
4. Used factory labor: Mixing $182,500 and Packaging $76,400.
5. Incurred $810,000 of manufacturing overhead on account.
6. Applied manufacturing overhead on the basis of $24 per machine hour. Machine hours were 28,000 in Mixing and 6,000 in Packaging.
7. Transferred 45,000 units from Mixing to Packaging at a cost of $979,000.
8. Transferred 53,000 units from Packaging to Finished Goods at a cost of $1,315,000.
9. Sold goods costing $1,604,000 for $2,500,000 on account.

Instructions

Journalize the October transactions.

Complete four steps
necessary to prepare a
production cost report.
(SO 5, 6, 7), AP

P16-2A   Rosenthal Company manufactures bowling balls through two processes: Molding and Packaging. In the Molding Department, the urethane, rubber, plastics, and other materials are molded into bowling balls. In the Packaging Department, the balls are placed in cartons and sent to the finished goods warehouse. All materials are entered at the beginning of each process. Labor and manufacturing overhead are incurred uniformly throughout each process. Production and cost data for the Molding Department during June 2012 are presented below.

Production Data	June
Beginning work in process units	–0–
Units started into production	22,000
Ending work in process units	2,000
Percent complete—ending inventory	40%

Cost Data	
Materials	$198,000
Labor	53,600
Overhead	112,800
Total	$364,400

(c) Materials $9.00
CC $8.00
(d) Transferred
*   out $340,000*
*   WIP $ 24,400*

Instructions

(a) Prepare a schedule showing physical units of production.
(b) Determine the equivalent units of production for materials and conversion costs.
(c) Compute the unit costs of production.
(d) Determine the costs to be assigned to the units transferred and in process for June.
(e) Prepare a production cost report for the Molding Department for the month of June.

Complete four steps
necessary to prepare a
production cost report.
(SO 5, 6, 7), AP

P16-3A   Seagren Industries Inc. manufactures in separate processes furniture for homes. In each process, materials are entered at the beginning, and conversion costs are incurred uniformly. Production and cost data for the first process in making two products in two different manufacturing plants are as follows.

	Cutting Department	
	Plant 1	**Plant 2**
Production Data—July	**T12-Tables**	**C10-Chairs**
Work in process units, July 1	–0–	–0–
Units started into production	19,000	16,000
Work in process units, July 31	3,000	500
Work in process percent complete	60	80
Cost Data—July		
Work in process, July 1	$ –0–	$ –0–
Materials	380,000	288,000
Labor	234,200	110,000
Overhead	104,000	96,700
Total	$718,200	$494,700

Instructions

(a) For each plant:
  (1) Compute the physical units of production.
  (2) Compute equivalent units of production for materials and for conversion costs.
  (3) Determine the unit costs of production.
  (4) Show the assignment of costs to units transferred out and in process.
(b) Prepare the production cost report for Plant 1 for July 2012.

(a) (3) T12:
  Materials $20
  CC $19
(4) T12:
  Transferred
    out $624,000
  WIP $ 94,200

P16-4A Rivera Company has several processing departments. Costs charged to the Assembly Department for November 2012 totaled $2,280,000 as follows.

Assign costs and prepare production cost report.
(SO 5, 6, 7), AP

Work in process, November 1		
Materials	$79,000	
Conversion costs	48,150	$ 127,150
Materials added		1,589,000
Labor		225,920
Overhead		337,930

Production records show that 35,000 units were in beginning work in process 30% complete as to conversion costs, 660,000 units were started into production, and 25,000 units were in ending work in process 40% complete as to conversion costs. Materials are entered at the beginning of each process.

Instructions

(a) Determine the equivalent units of production and the unit production costs for the Assembly Department.
(b) Determine the assignment of costs to goods transferred out and in process.
(c) Prepare a production cost report for the Assembly Department.

(b) Transferred
  out $2,211,000
  WIP $ 69,000

P16-5A Morse Company manufactures basketballs. Materials are added at the beginning of the production process and conversion costs are incurred uniformly. Production and cost data for the month of July 2012 are as follows.

Determine equivalent units and unit costs and assign costs.
(SO 5, 6, 7), AP

Production Data—Basketballs	Units	Percent Complete
Work in process units, July 1	500	60%
Units started into production	1,250	
Work in process units, July 31	600	40%

Cost Data—Basketballs		
Work in process, July 1		
Materials	$750	
Conversion costs	600	$1,350
Direct materials		2,400
Direct labor		1,580
Manufacturing overhead		1,295

*Compute equivalent units
and complete production
cost report.*

(SO 5, 7), AP

Instructions

(a) Calculate the following.
  (1) The equivalent units of production for materials and conversion costs.
  (2) The unit costs of production for materials and conversion costs.
  (3) The assignment of costs to units transferred out and in process at the end of the accounting period.
(b) Prepare a production cost report for the month of July for the basketballs.

P16-6A Hamilton Processing Company uses a weighted-average process costing system and manufactures a single product—a premium rug shampoo and cleaner. The manufacturing activity for the month of October has just been completed. A partially completed production cost report for the month of October for the mixing and cooking department is shown below.

Instructions

(a) Prepare a schedule that shows how the equivalent units were computed so that you can complete the "Quantities: Units accounted for" equivalent units section shown in the production cost report, and compute October unit costs.
(b) Complete the "Cost Reconciliation Schedule" part of the production cost report below.

HAMILTON PROCESSING COMPANY
Mixing and Cooking Department
Production Cost Report
For the Month Ended October 31

Quantities	Physical Units	Equivalent Units Materials	Conversion Costs
Units to be accounted for			
Work in process, October 1 (all materials, 70% conversion costs)	20,000		
Started into production	150,000		
Total units	170,000		
Units accounted for			
Transferred out	120,000	?	?
Work in process, October 31 (60% materials, 40% conversion costs)	50,000	?	?
Total units accounted for	170,000	?	?

Costs

Unit costs

	Materials	Conversion Costs	Total
Costs in October	$240,000	$105,000	$345,000
Equivalent units	?	?	
Unit costs	$? +	$? =	$?

Costs to be accounted for			
Work in process, October 1			$ 30,000
Started into production			315,000
Total costs			$345,000

Cost Reconciliation Schedule

Costs accounted for		
Transferred out		$?
Work in process, October 31		
Materials	?	
Conversion costs	?	?
Total costs		?

*P16-7A Rondeli Company manufactures bicycles and tricycles. For both products, materials are added at the beginning of the production process, and conversion costs are incurred uniformly. Rondeli Company uses the FIFO method to compute equivalent units. Production and cost data for the month of March are as follows.

Determine equivalent units and unit costs and assign costs for processes; prepare production cost report.
(SO 3), AP

Production Data—Bicycles	Units	Percent Complete
Work in process units, March 1	200	80%
Units started into production	1,250	
Work in process units, March 31	300	40%

Cost Data—Bicycles	Units	Percent Complete
Work in process, March 1	$19,280	
Direct materials	50,000	
Direct labor	25,500	
Manufacturing overhead	30,000	

Production Data—Tricycles	Units	Percent Complete
Work in process units, March 1	100	75%
Units started into production	800	
Work in process units, March 31	60	25%

Cost Data—Tricycles	
Work in process, March 1	$ 6,125
Direct materials	30,400
Direct labor	15,100
Manufacturing overhead	20,000

Instructions
(a) Calculate the following for both the bicycles and the tricycles.
   (1) The equivalent units of production for materials and conversion costs.
   (2) The unit costs of production for materials and conversion costs.
   (3) The assignment of costs to units transferred out and in process at the end of the accounting period.
(b) Prepare a production cost report for the month of March for the bicycles only.

(a) Bicycles:
(1) Materials   1,250
(2) Materials $40
(3) Transferred
      out $106,760
      WIP $ 18,000

Problems: Set B

P16-1B Wilbury Company manufactures a nutrient, Everlife, through two manufacturing processes: Blending and Packaging. All materials are entered at the beginning of each process. On August 1, 2012, inventories consisted of Raw Materials $5,000, Work in Process—Blending $0, Work in Process—Packaging $3,945, and Finished Goods $7,500. The beginning inventory for Packaging consisted of 500 units, two-fifths complete as to conversion costs and fully complete as to materials. During August, 9,000 units were started into production in Blending, and the following transactions were completed.

Journalize transactions.
(SO 3, 4), AP

1. Purchased $25,000 of raw materials on account.
2. Issued raw materials for production: Blending $18,930 and Packaging $9,140.
3. Incurred labor costs of $25,770.
4. Used factory labor: Blending $15,320 and Packaging $10,450.
5. Incurred $36,500 of manufacturing overhead on account.

6. Applied manufacturing overhead at the rate of $28 per machine hour. Machine hours were Blending 900 and Packaging 300.
7. Transferred 8,200 units from Blending to Packaging at a cost of $44,940.
8. Transferred 8,600 units from Packaging to Finished Goods at a cost of $67,490.
9. Sold goods costing $62,000 for $90,000 on account.

Instructions
Journalize the August transactions.

Complete four steps necessary to prepare a production cost report.
(SO 5, 6, 7), AP

P16-2B Steiner Corporation manufactures water skis through two processes: Molding and Packaging. In the Molding Department, fiberglass is heated and shaped into the form of a ski. In the Packaging Department, the skis are placed in cartons and sent to the finished goods warehouse. Materials are entered at the beginning of both processes. Labor and manufacturing overhead are incurred uniformly throughout each process. Production and cost data for the Molding Department for January 2012 are presented below.

Production Data	January
Beginning work in process units	–0–
Units started into production	50,000
Ending work in process units	2,500
Percent complete—ending inventory	40%

Cost Data	
Materials	$510,000
Labor	92,500
Overhead	150,000
Total	$752,500

Instructions
(a) Compute the physical units of production.
(b) Determine the equivalent units of production for materials and conversion costs.
(c) Compute the unit costs of production.
(d) Determine the costs to be assigned to the units transferred out and in process.
(e) Prepare a production cost report for the Molding Department for the month of January.

(c) Materials $10.20
CC $5
(d) Transferred out $722,000
WIP $ 30,500

Complete four steps necessary to prepare a production cost report.
(SO 5, 6, 7), AP

P16-3B Borman Corporation manufactures in separate processes refrigerators and freezers for homes. In each process, materials are entered at the beginning and conversion costs are incurred uniformly. Production and cost data for the first process in making two products in two different manufacturing plants are as follows.

	Stamping Department	
	Plant A	**Plant B**
Production Data—June	R12 Refrigerators	F24 Freezers
Work in process units, June 1	–0–	–0–
Units started into production	20,000	20,000
Work in process units, June 30	4,000	2,500
Work in process percent complete	75	60

Cost Data—June		
Work in process, June 1	$ –0–	$ –0–
Materials	840,000	720,000
Labor	245,000	259,000
Overhead	420,000	292,000
Total	$1,505,000	$1,271,000

Instructions

(a) For each plant:
  (1) Compute the physical units of production.
  (2) Compute equivalent units of production for materials and for conversion costs.
  (3) Determine the unit costs of production.
  (4) Show the assignment of costs to units transferred out and in process.
(b) Prepare the production cost report for Plant A for June 2012.

(a) (3) R12:
Materials $42
CC $35
(4) R12:
Transferred out $1,232,000
WIP $ 273,000

P16-4B Luxman Company has several processing departments. Costs charged to the Assembly Department for October 2012 totaled $1,298,400 as follows.

Assign costs and prepare production cost report.
(SO 5, 6, 7), AP

Work in process, October 1		
Materials	$29,000	
Conversion costs	16,500	$ 45,500
Materials added		1,006,000
Labor		138,900
Overhead		108,000

Production records show that 25,000 units were in beginning work in process 40% complete as to conversion cost, 435,000 units were started into production, and 35,000 units were in ending work in process 40% complete as to conversion costs. Materials are entered at the beginning of each process.

Instructions

(a) Determine the equivalent units of production and the unit production costs for the Assembly Department.
(b) Determine the assignment of costs to goods transferred out and in process.
(c) Prepare a production cost report for the Assembly Department.

(b) Transferred out $1,211,250
WIP $ 87,150

P16-5B Swinn Company manufactures bicycles. Materials are added at the beginning of the production process, and conversion costs are incurred uniformly. Production and cost data for the month of May are as follows.

Determine equivalent units and unit costs and assign costs.
(SO 5, 6, 7), AP

Production Data—Bicycles	Units	Percent Complete
Work in process units, May 1	500	80%
Units started in production	2,000	
Work in process units, May 31	800	40%

Cost Data—Bicycles		
Work in process, May 1		
Materials	$15,000	
Conversion costs	18,000	$33,000
Direct materials		50,000
Direct labor		19,020
Manufacturing overhead		33,680

Instructions

(a) Calculate the following.
  (1) The equivalent units of production for materials and conversion.
  (2) The unit costs of production for materials and conversion costs.
  (3) The assignment of costs to units transferred out and in process at the end of the accounting period.
(b) Prepare a production cost report for the month of May for the bicycles.

(2) Materials $26
CC $35
(3) Transferred out $103,700
WIP $ 32,000

Compute equivalent units and complete production cost report.

(SO 5, 7), AP

P16-6B Venuchi Cleaner Company uses a weighted-average process costing system and manufactures a single product—an all-purpose liquid cleaner. The manufacturing activity for the month of March has just been completed. A partially completed production cost report for the month of March for the mixing and blending department is shown below.

VENUCHI CLEANER COMPANY
Mixing and Blending Department
Production Cost Report
For the Month Ended March 31

		Equivalent Units	
QUANTITIES	Physical Units	Materials	Conversion Costs
Units to be accounted for			
Work in process, March 1	10,000		
Started into production	76,000		
Total units	86,000		
Units accounted for			
Transferred out	66,000	?	?
Work in process, March 31 (60% materials, 20% conversion costs)	20,000	?	?
Total units	86,000	?	?

		Conversion	
COSTS			
Unit costs	Materials	Costs	Total
Costs in March	$156,000	$98,000	$254,000
Equivalent units	?	?	
Unit costs	$? +	$? =	$?
Costs to be accounted for			
Work in process, March 1			$ 8,700
Started into production			245,300
Total costs			$254,000

COST RECONCILIATION SCHEDULE

Costs accounted for		
Transferred out		$?
Work in process, March 31		
Materials	?	
Conversion costs	?	?
Total costs		?

Instructions

(a) Prepare a schedule that shows how the equivalent units were computed so that you can complete the "Quantities: Units accounted for" equivalent units section shown in the production cost report above, and compute March unit costs.

(b) Complete the "Cost Reconciliation Schedule" part of the production cost report above.

(a) Materials $2.00

(b) Transferred out $224,400
WIP $ 29,600

Determine equivalent units and unit costs and assign costs for processes; prepare production cost report.

(SO 8), AP

*P16-7B** Holiday Company manufactures basketballs and soccer balls. For both products, materials are added at the beginning of the production process and conversion costs are incurred uniformly. Holiday uses the FIFO method to compute equivalent units. Production and cost data for the month of August are shown on the next page.

Production Data—Basketballs	Units	Percent Complete	Production Data—Soccer Balls	Units	Percent Complete
Work in process units, August 1	500	60%	Work in process units, August 1	200	80%
Units started into production	2,000		Units started into production	2,000	
Work in process units, August 31	600	50%	Work in process units, August 31	150	70%

Cost Data—Basketballs		Cost Data—Soccer Balls	
Work in process, August 1	$1,125	Work in process, August 1	$ 450
Direct materials	1,600	Direct materials	2,800
Direct labor	1,280	Direct labor	1,000
Manufacturing overhead	1,000	Manufacturing overhead	1,394

Instructions
(a) Calculate the following for both the basketballs and the soccer balls.
  (1) The equivalent units of production for materials and conversion costs.
  (2) The unit costs of production for materials and conversion costs.
  (3) The assignment of costs to units transferred out and in process at the end of the accounting period.
(b) Prepare a production cost report for the month of August for the basketballs only.

(a) Basketballs:
(1) Materials   2,000
(2) Materials $.80
(3) Transferred out $4,165
      WIP $840

Problems: Set C

Visit the book's companion website, at **www.wiley.com/college/kimmel**, and choose the Student Companion site to access Problem Set C.

Waterways Continuing Problem

(*Note:* This is a continuation of the Waterways Problem from Chapters 14 and 15.)

WCP16 Because most of the parts for its irrigation systems are standard, Waterways handles the majority of its manufacturing as a process cost system. There are multiple process departments. Three of these departments are the Molding, Cutting, and Welding departments. All items eventually end up in the Packaging department which prepares items for sale in kits or individually. This problem asks you to help Waterways calculate equivalent units and prepare a production cost report.

> Go to the book's companion website, at **www.wiley.com/college/kimmel**, to see the completion of this problem.

broadening your perspective

DECISION MAKING ACROSS THE ORGANIZATION

BYP16-1 Florida Beach Company manufactures suntan lotion, called Surtan, in 11-ounce plastic bottles. Surtan is sold in a competitive market. As a result, management is very cost-conscious. Surtan is manufactured through two processes: mixing and filling. Materials are entered at the beginning of each process, and labor and manufacturing overhead occur uniformly throughout each process. Unit costs are based on the cost per gallon of Surtan using the weighted-average costing approach.

On June 30, 2012, Mary Ritzman, the chief accountant for the past 20 years, opted to take early retirement. Her replacement, Joe Benili, had extensive accounting experience with motels in the area but only limited contact with manufacturing accounting. During July, Joe correctly accumulated the following production quantity and cost data for the Mixing Department.

Production quantities: Work in process, July 1, 8,000 gallons 75% complete; started into production 100,000 gallons; work in process, July 31, 5,000 gallons 20% complete. Materials are added at the beginning of the process.

Production costs: Beginning work in process $88,000, comprised of $21,000 of materials costs and $67,000 of conversion costs; incurred in July: materials $573,000, conversion costs $765,000.

Joe then prepared a production cost report on the basis of physical units started into production. His report showed a production cost of $14.26 per gallon of Surtan. The management of Florida Beach was surprised at the high unit cost. The president comes to you, as Mary's top assistant, to review Joe's report and prepare a correct report if necessary.

Instructions

With the class divided into groups, answer the following questions.
(a) Show how Joe arrived at the unit cost of $14.26 per gallon of Surtan.
(b) What error(s) did Joe make in preparing his production cost report?
(c) Prepare a correct production cost report for July.

MANAGERIAL ANALYSIS

BYP16-2 Harris Furniture Company manufactures living room furniture through two departments: Framing and Upholstering. Materials are entered at the beginning of each process. For May, the following cost data are obtained from the two work in process accounts.

	Framing	Upholstering
Work in process, May 1	$ –0–	$?
Materials	450,000	?
Conversion costs	261,000	330,000
Costs transferred in	–0–	600,000
Costs transferred out	600,000	?
Work in process, May 31	100,000	?

Instructions

Answer the following questions.
(a) If 3,000 sofas were started into production on May 1 and 2,500 sofas were transferred to Upholstering, what was the unit cost of materials for May in the Framing Department?
(b) Using the data in (a) above, what was the per unit conversion cost of the sofas transferred to Upholstering?
(c) Continuing the assumptions in (a) above, what is the percentage of completion of the units in process at May 31 in the Framing Department?

REAL-WORLD FOCUS

BYP16-3 The May 10, 2004, edition of the *Wall Street Journal* includes an article by Evan Ramstad entitled "A Tight Squeeze" (page R9).

Instructions
Read the article and answer the following questions.
(a) What is Proview's profit margin on computer monitors? Why is the profit margin so thin on computer monitors?
(b) What are some of the steps that Proview International has taken to control costs?
(c) Why does the company continue to build tube-based monitors even as many consumers are moving away from them?
(d) Mr. Wang's final comment is, "Every aspect of the business is important, but the most important is cost." Why does he feel this way?

MANAGERIAL ACCOUNTING ON THE WEB

BYP16-4 Paintball is now played around the world. The process of making paintballs is actually quite similar to the process used to make certain medical pills. In fact, paintballs were previously often made at the same factories that made pharmaceuticals.

Address: **http://video.google.com/videoplay?docid=6864066340713942400**, or go to **www.wiley. com/college/kimmel**

Instructions
View that video at the site listed above and then answer the following questions.
(a) Describe in sequence the primary steps used to manufacture paintballs.
(b) Explain the costs incurred by the company that would fall into each of the following categories: materials, labor, and overhead. Of these categories, which do you think would be the greatest cost in making paintballs?
(c) Discuss whether a paintball manufacturer would use job order costing or process costing.

COMMUNICATION ACTIVITY

BYP16-5   Diane Barone was a good friend of yours in high school and is from your home town. While you chose to major in accounting when you both went away to college, she majored in marketing and management. You have recently been promoted to accounting manager for the Snack Foods Division of Melton Enterprises, and your friend was promoted to regional sales manager for the same division of Melton. Diane recently telephoned you. She explained that she was familiar with job cost sheets, which had been used by the Special Projects division where she had formerly worked. She was, however, very uncomfortable with the production cost reports prepared by your division. She emailed you a list of her particular questions:

1. Since Melton occasionally prepares snack foods for special orders in the Snack Foods Division, why don't we track costs of the orders separately?
2. What is an equivalent unit?
3. Why am I getting four production cost reports? Isn't there one Work in Process account?

Instructions
Prepare a memo to Diane. Answer her questions, and include any additional information you think would be helpful. You may write informally, but do use proper grammar and punctuation.

ETHICS CASE

BYP16-6   R. B. Dillman Company manufactures a high-tech component that passes through two production processing departments, Molding and Assembly. Department managers are partially compensated on the basis of units of products completed and transferred out relative to units of product put into production. This was intended as encouragement to be efficient and to minimize waste.

Jan Wooten is the department head in the Molding Department, and Tony Ferneti is her quality control inspector. During the month of June, Jan had three new employees who were not yet technically skilled. As a result, many of the units produced in June had minor molding defects. In order to maintain the department's normal high rate of completion, Jan told Tony to pass through inspection and on to the Assembly Department all units that had defects nondetectable to the human eye. "Company and industry tolerances on this product are too high anyway," says Jan. "Less than 2% of the units we produce are subjected in the market to the stress tolerance we've designed into them. The odds of those 2% being any of this month's units are even less. Anyway, we're saving the company money."

Instructions
(a) Who are the potential stakeholders involved in this situation?
(b) What alternatives does Tony have in this situation? What might the company do to prevent this situation from occurring?

Answers to Insight and Accounting Across the Organization Questions

p. 845 Choosing a Cost Driver Q: What is the result if a company uses the wrong "cost driver" to assign manufacturing overhead? **A:** Incorrect assignment of manufacturing overhead will result in some products receiving too much overhead and others receiving too little.

p. 849 Keeping Score for the Xbox Q: In what ways has cost accounting probably become more critical for Microsoft in recent years? **A:** In the past, Microsoft enjoyed very high profit margins on its software sales. As a consequence, it could afford to be less cost-conscious than most companies. In addition, in producing software, manufacturing costs represented a very small part of its total product cost. But the video-game hardware market is very competitive. As a result, to achieve its profitability goals, Microsoft will have to manufacture its product efficiently in order to meet its cost targets to ensure adequate margins. The information provided by process cost accounting will be critical to its efforts.

Answers to Self-Test Questions

1. b   **2.** d   **3.** d   **4.** b   **5.** c   **6.** b   **7.** b [20,000 + (5,000 × 60%)]   **8.** a (7,000 ÷ 0)   **9.** c (23,000 + 3,000), [23,000 + (3,000 × 33⅓%)]   **10.** a [$60,000 ÷ (9,000 + 3,000)]   **11.** b [($10 × 2,500) + ($30 × 2,500 × 40%)]   **12.** b   **13.** d   *****14.** b [25,000 + (3,000 × 100%)]; [(2,000 × 80%) + 25,000 + (3,000 × 30%)]   *****15.** a [$60,000 ÷ (9,000 + 3,000)]   *****16.** b [($10 × 2,500) + ($30 × 2,500 × 40%)]

 Remember to go back to the navigator box on the chapter opening page and check off your completed work.